INTERNATIONAL REGULATION OF MARINE FISHERIES

A Study of Regional Fisheries Organizations

by Albert W Koers

Fishing News (Books) Ltd
23 Rosemount Avenue, West Byfleet, Surrey, England
and 110 Fleet Street, London, EC4A 2JL

ISBN 0 85238 057 7

Printed in England by Eyre & Spottiswoode Ltd, Her Majesty's Printers,
at Thanet Press, Margate.

Contents

Chapter III THE STRUCTURE OF INTERNATIONAL FISHERIES ORGANIZATIONS *119*

Chapter IV THE FUNCTIONS AND POWERS
OF INTERNATIONAL FISHERIES
ORGANIZATIONS *171*

8

Acknowledgments

The completion of this book would have been unattainable without the generous assistance and encouragement of many institutions and persons. I acknowledge very gratefully my indebtedness to the following organizations for their financial and intellectual support: the Institute of International Law of the University of Utrecht; the Netherlands Organization for the Advancement of Pure Research; the Harvard Law School; the Law of the Sea Institute of the University of Rhode Island; and the Woodrow Wilson International Center for Scholars in Washington, DC. My appointment as a Fellow at the Woodrow Wilson Center made the final stages of this project intellectually a most stimulating experience. Many persons also gave me the privilege of their counsel and advice. I would like to record my thanks to the following in particular: Dr Lewis M Alexander, University of Rhode Island; Dr Dayton L Alverson, Northwest Fisheries Center, Seattle; Professor R R Baxter, Harvard Law School; Professor M Bos, University of Utrecht; Dr L J Bouchez, University of Utrecht; Dr J E Carroz, Food and Agriculture Organization; Dr Francis T Christy, Jr., Resources for the Future, Inc and Dr William C Herrington, Law of the Sea Institute. I am especially grateful to my friend E W Seabrook Hull, editor *Ocean Science News*, for his always encouraging interest in my work. Both Mrs Helen Clayton and Mr Wybo P. Heere gave most valuable editorial assistance. Finally, my thanks are due to the publishers and printers for their courteous and efficient cooperation.

Utrecht, 1 October 1972   AWK

List of Abbreviations

ACMRR	Advisory Committee on Marine Resources Research.
AJIL	American Journal of International Law.
CARPAS	Regional Fisheries Advisory Commission for the South West Atlantic.
CECAF	Fishery Committee for the Eastern Central Atlantic.
COFI	Committee on Fisheries.
FAO	Food and Agriculture Organization of the United Nations.
GFCM	General Fisheries Council for the Mediterranean.
IATTC	Inter-American Tropical Tuna Commission.
ICCAT	International Commission for the Conservation of Atlantic Tunas.
ICES	International Council for the Exploration of the Sea.
ICJ	International Court of Justice.
ICLQ	International and Comparative Law Quarterly.
ICNAF	International Commission for the Northwest Atlantic Fisheries.
ICSEAF	International Commission for the Southeast Atlantic Fisheries.
ILM	International Legal Materials.
INPFC	International North Pacific Fisheries Commission.
IOFC	Indian Ocean Fishery Commission.
IPFC	Indo-Pacific Fisheries Council.
IPHC	International Pacific Halibut Commission.

IPSFC	International Pacific Salmon Fisheries Commission.
IWC	International Whaling Commission.
LNTS	League of Nations Treaty Series.
NEAFC	North-East Atlantic Fisheries Commission.
NPFSC	North Pacific Fur Seal Commission.
NTIR	Nederlands Tijdschrift voor Internationaal Recht.
RdC	Recueil des Cours de l'Académie de Droit International.
RGDIP	Revue Générale de Droit International Public.
UNTS	United Nations Treaty Series.
WLR	Washington Law Review.

Introductory Remarks

1. THE FREEDOM OF FISHING
ON THE HIGH SEAS

The exploration and exploitation of the sea and its resources by man have a long history of international conflict, as well as an equally long history of international cooperation.[1] The future can bring only a deepening of this dichotomy. Scientific progress and technological advances allow mankind to make the most efficient use of the ocean and its resources in history.[2] This will undoubtedly intensify the confrontation among the nations of the world over the exploration and exploitation of these resources. It will also greatly increase the need for effective international cooperation.

[1] J K Oudendyk, *Status and extent of adjacent waters. A historical orientation*, Leyden 1970. C J Colombos, *The international law of the sea*, 6th ed. London 1967. D M Johnston, *The international law of marine fisheries. A framework for policy-oriented inquiries*, New Haven and London 1965. F V Garcia Amador, *The exploitation and conservation of the resources of the sea. A study of contemporary international law*, 2nd ed. 2nd enl. printing, Leyden 1963. S Oda, *International control of sea resources*, Leyden 1963. M S McDougal and W T Burke, *The public order of the oceans. A contemporary international law of the sea*, New Haven and London 1962. L L Leonard, *International regulation of fisheries*, Washington 1944. J Tomasevich, *International agreements on conservation of marine resources with special reference to the North Pacific*, Stanford 1943. G Gidel, *Le droit international public de la mer*, Paris 1932–1934, 3 vols. T W Fulton, *The sovereignty of the sea*, Edinburgh and London 1911.
[2] For examples of new technologies, see A Pardo, *The place of fisheries in a future regime for the ocean*, in *Report of the sixth session of the Committee on Fisheries*, FAO Fisheries Reports No. 103, Rome 1971, p. 32. J E Bardach, *Harvest of the sea*, New York 1968. United Nations Economic and Social Council, *Marine science and technology: survey and proposals*, UN Doc. E/4487, 24 April 1968, pp. 18–29.

Conflict and cooperation have also been the major elements contributing to the formulation of a principle which is still a nucleus of the international law of the sea: the freedom of the high seas. After a long period of conflict among the maritime nations of Western Europe this principle found gradually international acceptance in the 18th and 19th century, although subject to the restriction that each coastal State had sovereignty over an area of the sea adjacent to its coast.[3] Nevertheless, the freedom of the high seas continues to be a concept of considerable ambiguity, not only with respect to its territorial applicability, but also with respect to its meaning. It can, for example, be considered an expression of the notion that the resources of the high seas are *res nullius*, but also of the view that these resources are *res communis*. It can also be seen as a consequence of the international public domain character of the high seas.[4] Article 2 of the Convention on the High Seas of Geneva 1958 emphasizes the fact that under the freedom of the high seas no State may validly purport to subject any part of the high seas to its sovereignty. This Article provides that the freedom of the high seas comprises, *inter alia*, both for coastal and non-coastal States: (1) the freedom of navigation; (2) the freedom of fishing; (3) the freedom to lay submarine cables and pipelines; and (4) the freedom to fly over the high seas.[5] States are required to exercise these and other freedoms which are recognized by the general principles of international law with reasonable regard for the interests of other States.

These various ways of using the oceans and their resources can be distinguished in exploitative and non-exploitative

[3]J K Oudendyk, *op. cit.*, note 1.
[4]M Bos, *La liberté de la haute mer: quelques problèmes d'actualité*, *NTIR* 1965, pp. 337–364. R Bierzanek, *La nature juridique de la haute mer*, *RGDIP* 1961, pp. 233–259. H Accioly, *La liberté des mers et le droit de pêche en haute mer*, *RGDIP* 1957, pp. 193–202. Gidel, *op. cit.*, note 1, vol. 1, pp. 213–234.
[5]*UNTS* vol. 450, p. 82.

uses.[6] Fisheries fall within the first category, while navigation belongs to the second group. Traditionally, the freedom of the high seas has been based upon three interrelated assumptions: (1) that the waters of the seas are not susceptible to effective occupation; (2) that the resources of the seas are inexhaustible; and (3) that a specific use of the oceans does not impair other uses.[7] However, these three assumptions are no longer of unquestionable validity, particularly in the context of such an exploitative use of ocean resources as marine fisheries. States have the capability of effectively controlling large areas of the seas, and the fact that many stocks of fish have been seriously overfished obviates the notion that these resources are inexhaustible. Finally, the more intensive utilization of the living resources of the seas has in many cases led to a situation in which one use preempts another use. Consequently, these traditional assumptions no longer fully justify the freedom of fishing on the high seas.

2. RESTRICTIONS ON THE FREEDOM OF FISHING

The international law of marine fisheries has not remained indifferent to these developments. It has modified the freedom of fishing on the high seas by subjecting this general principle to a wide variety of specific conditions and restrictions. These are indeed the two conceptual extremes of the international law of marine fisheries: on the one hand, the freedom of fishing on the high seas and, on the other hand, a complex maze of restrictions imposed upon this freedom. The international law of marine fisheries is largely the outcome of the confrontation between these two extremes.

The most important restrictions on the freedom of fishing

[6] E W Allen, *The freedom of the seas*, *AJIL* 1964, pp. 984–985.
[7] Grotius linked these assumptions most clearly with the freedom of fishing in his *Defensio capitis quinti maris liberi*, in S Muller Fz, *Mare clausum. Bijdrage tot de geschiedenis der rivaliteit van Engeland en Nederland in de zeventiende eeuw*, Amsterdam 1872.

are a direct consequence of the fact that not all waters of the sea are covered by the regime of the high seas.[8] The high seas can be defined as all parts of the sea that are not included in the territorial sea or in the internal waters of a State.[9] Accordingly, the freedom of fishing does not extend to the territorial sea and the maritime internal waters of coastal States. It need not be mentioned here that there is not yet international agreement with respect to the width of the territorial sea. The First Codification Conference of 1930 and the two Geneva Conferences of 1958 and 1960 were unable to settle this issue. Hence, the extent of this particular type of restriction on the freedom of fishing is uncertain. However, it is clear that it forms a very substantial limitation, especially since it eliminates not only the freedom of fishing, but the freedom of the high seas generally. Other limitations are more selective.

A second category of restrictions on the freedom of fishing is also territorial in scope. However, they do not lead to the total disappearance of the freedom of the high seas, but merely of the freedom of fishing. These restrictions result from exclusive fishery zones that extend beyond the territorial sea. The freedom of fishing does not apply to the waters included in these zones because fishing in such a zone is exclusively reserved to the nationals of the coastal State that has established the zone. The breadth of exclusive fishery zones is also the object of international disputes, although most such zones extend up to twelve miles from the baseline of the territorial sea.

Finally, there are non-territorial restrictions on the freedom of fishing.[10] Article 2 of the Convention on the High

[8]S A Riesenfeld, *Protection of coastal fisheries under international law*, Washington 1942. C B V Meyer, *The extent of jurisdiction in coastal waters*, Leyden 1937.
[9]Art. 1 Convention on the High Seas of Geneva 1958, *UNTS* vol. 450, p. 82.
[10]Johnston, *op. cit.*, note 1, pp. 358–440.

Seas of Geneva 1958 outlines the general basis for such limitations: it provides that States must exercise the freedom of fishing with reasonable regard for the interests of other States. Most restrictions in this category can be found in special international fisheries agreements concerned with questions of overfishing and with the protection of stocks of fish in general. These treaty-based limitations alter the freedom of fishing on the high seas. However, they do not yet materially affect the most essential characteristics of this concept. Of these charactcristics, four are of special relevance. These are: (1) that all States have the right to engage in fishing operations on the high seas;[11] (2) that States, in order to share in these resources and in their wealth, must actually engage in such fishing operations; (3) that the living resources of the high seas are not subject to formal ownership until they are captured; and (4) that fishing operations on the high seas are subject to a minimum of regulation.[12] International fisheries agreements have not substantially modified these four elements of the freedom of fishing.[13] The fact that States have, for the most part, an unrestricted right of access to the living resources of the high seas, and must exercise this right in order to share in these resources, is at the root of many of the problems faced by the international law of marine fisheries.

3. INTERNATIONAL FISHERIES ORGANIZATIONS

The freedom of fishing on the high seas and its limitations are in continuous interaction with each other. The mechanisms of this process are extremely varied and include virtually all techniques developed in centuries of international

[11]Art. 1 Convention on Fishing and Conservation of the Living Resources of the High Seas of Geneva 1958, *UNTS* vol. 559, p. 286.
[12]Pardo, *op. cit.*, note 2, pp. 31–32.
[13]The Interim Convention on Conservation of the North Pacific Fur Seals of Washington 1957 incorporates the most radical departures from these characteristics, see *infra* pp. 85–86.

relations.[14] They range from unilateral action by a single State to decisions of international organizations. Territorial restrictions are primarily based upon unilateral assertions by coastal States.[15] The international legal validity of such claims will depend to a large extent upon the response of the community of States. Non-territorial restrictions, on the other hand, are largely the outcome of international agreements and the actions of international fisheries organizations. The present study will focus on the role of international fisheries organizations in the interaction between the freedom of fishing on the high seas and the non-territorial limitations applicable to this principle. These international fisheries organizations differ greatly from each other – in their terms of reference, their powers and their accomplishments, if any. For that reason, generalizations risk becoming oversimplifications. However, international fisheries organizations have in common that they are functional international organizations:[16] they are designed to perform specific tasks. Moreover, the majority of these international fisheries organizations operate on a regional, rather than global, level. Consequently, as a group they can be characterized as examples of functional international cooperation of a regional scope.

There are several reasons for a legal analysis of international fisheries organizations. It must be emphasized that the following Chapters will approach this analysis from a general international law of the sea angle and not from the

[14]D L McKernan, *International fisheries arrangements beyond the twelve mile limit*, in *International rules and organization for the sea*, L M Alexander ed., Kingston, RI 1969, p. 255.
[15]For a survey of these claims, see FAO, *Limits and status of the territorial sea, exclusive fishing zones, fishery conservation zones and the continental shelf*, FAO Legislative Series No. 8, Rome 1969. A more recent version is: FAO Fisheries Circular No. 127, Rome 1971.
[16]E B Haas, *Beyond the nation State. Functionalism and international organization*, Stanford 1964. I Claude, *Swords into plowshares: the problems and progress of international organization*, New York 1959.

perspective of the law of international organizations. Among the reasons for studying international fisheries bodies is, first of all, the fact that they have not received a great deal of scholarly attention. Yet the fact that they are the object of substantial disagreements among States seems to support the desirability of such attention. Secondly, the international law of marine fisheries is in many respects not capable of coping adequately with the problems of marine fisheries. Therefore, the question must be asked if, and to what extent, international fisheries organizations can offer solutions to these problems. This question has not only legal, but also economic and political implications. However, an analysis of the law of international fisheries organizations must certainly form part of the answer. A third reason is related to the law of the sea in general. The international community is involved in an effort to formulate a future international law of the sea. Much of the international debate on these issues is concerned with the need to establish new international structures for organized decision-making with respect to the exploration and exploitation of the sea and its resources. International fisheries organizations represent the only experience with such decision-making within the international community. Therefore, an analysis of the law of these organizations is of interest not only for the future of the international law of marine fisheries, but for the future of the international law of the sea in general.

Chapter I

The Constitutive Elements of the International Law of Marine Fisheries

1. CONSTITUTIVE ELEMENTS

The most fundamental challenge to any system of law is to further justice and equity within its realm. This also applies to the international law of marine fisheries. However, the international law of marine fisheries, like any other system of law, is not a self-serving and self-contained entity. As an instrument of social order, it functions within a context in which biological, technological, economic, social and political factors are predominant elements. These elements define the problems faced by the international law of marine fisheries; they also determine the way in which it can solve these problems. It is beyond the scope of this study to analyze all aspects of this context in detail, but they must be reviewed in general terms for the purpose of obtaining a wider perspective within which the law of international fisheries organizations can be discussed. This perspective is also essential in making suggestions with respect to future arrangements. These constitutive elements will be discussed, first of all, in general terms and then with attention to their significance for specific problem areas.

1.1 Biological Factors

The most important constitutive elements that influence the international law of marine fisheries are probably those directly related to the biological characteristics of the living resources of the oceans. These resources include not only fish, but also such mammals as whales and seals.[1] Tradition-

[1] For a classification of the living resources of the sea, see FAO, *Yearbook of fishery statistics 1969*, Rome 1970, pp. VIII–IX.

ally, the term 'living resources' refers to animal life. However, animal life is only a part of the whole life cycle of the seas, in which plant life provides the basis for animal life. Therefore, the term 'living resources' will be used here in a flexible manner. The sea's living resources have a number of unique characteristics,[2] best illustrated by comparing them with ocean mineral resources.[3]

First of all, fish are mobile and migrate over a certain range; the location of mineral resources, on the other hand, is fixed. This important characteristic[4] means, for example, that land-based jurisdictional concepts that operate with definite boundary lines are much more difficult to apply to the regulation of fisheries than to the regulation of mineral exploitation.[5] Fish do not respect man-made boundaries, but only the natural conditions of their environment, e.g., currents, temperatures, salinities and food supply. In addition, most man-made boundaries assume a two-dimensional world, while the world of fish is a three-dimensional one. This mobile character of the living resources is the major reason why their productivity varies not only in time, but also from area to area.[6] The living resources are, like mineral resources, not evenly distributed over the oceans, but the fact

[2]W M Chapman, Some problems and prospects for the harvest of living marine resources to the year 2000, paper at a meeting of experts at UNITAR, February 25–27, 1970, p. 5. P M Dodyk, Comments on international law and fishery policy, Clearinghouse for Federal Scientific and Technical Information, Doc. PB 179 427, Springfield, Va. 1968, p. 2. F T Christy, Jr. and A Scott, The common wealth in ocean fisheries. Some problems of growth and economic allocation, Baltimore 1965, pp. 6–17. D M Johnston, The international law of marine fisheries. A framework for policy-oriented inquiries, New Haven and London 1965, pp. 4–10.
[3]Obviously, not only the resources differ, but also patterns of exploitation.
[4]W M Chapman, Fishery resources in offshore waters, in Offshore boundaries and zones, L M Alexander, ed., Columbus, Ohio 1967, pp. 93–98.
[5]Chapman, op. cit., note 4, p. 91. M B Schaefer, in The future development of world fisheries (panel), in The future of the sea's resources, L M Alexander ed., Kingston, RI 1968, p. 127.
[6]FAO, The living resources of the seas: an illustrative atlas, FAO Fisheries Circular No. 126, Rome 1971.

that fish migrate makes this pattern of distribution subject to continuous change. However, the most productive areas of the oceans are in general those where upwellings from below or run-offs from the land supply the nutrients on which all living resources ultimately depend.[7] This means that most of the living resources of the oceans are to be found in the relatively shallow waters over the continental shelf and slope, while generally the productivity of mid-ocean areas is much lower. This biological feature of fish is an important reason why the international law of marine fisheries has stressed regional, rather than global, approaches.

A second biological characteristic which distinguishes living resources from mineral resources is that living resources are renewable: they are born and perish within a relatively short period of time.[8] Although the total quantity of mineral resources is also subject to gradual change, they do not have a comparable life-cycle. This characteristic of the sea's living resources has probably had a greater influence on the international law of marine fisheries than any other single factor. It means that the problems of over-exploitation and under-exploitation have completely different implications for fisheries than for ocean mining. If the surplus of a stock of fish is not caught within its lifespan, the result is in physical terms a permanent loss, since exploitation can not be postponed to a future date as would be feasible in the case of mineral resources.[9] Whether or not this loss in physical terms is also a loss in economic terms depends upon such factors as the demand for the fish in question and the cost of catching them. If, for example, there is no demand at all for the non-exploited fish, there is no direct economic loss. This renewable nature of living resources is at the very heart of

[7]Christy and Scott, *op. cit.*, note 2, pp. 56–74. Johnston, *op. cit.*, note 2, pp. 10–17.
[8]Chapman, *op. cit.*, note 2, p. 5.
[9]Dodyk, *op. cit.*, note 2, p. 46.

all those issues and problems which are covered by the term 'conservation'.

A third relevant biological aspect of the living resources is that they are resources of great variety.[10] This does not so much apply to their nutritional value, which is about the same, but it certainly extends to their natural qualities. There are free swimming fishes (pelagic species) and there are fishes that are associated with the bottom (demersal species). There are fishes which dwell in the sea, but spawn in fresh water (anadromous species) and, by contrast, there are fishes which live in fresh water, but spawn at sea (catadromous species). There are free swimmers (nekton) and there are fixed organisms (benthos). Sedentary species fall largely within the latter category. Legal arrangements must reflect this variety, as in point of fact they already do. There are, for example, special arrangements for anadromous species[11] and for sedentary species.[12] However, at the same time there is a close relationship between many species of fish.[13] For example, one species may feed on another or both may depend upon the same source of food. This means that the international law of marine fisheries must take into account both the differences in natural characteristics and the interrelationship between many species.

A last distinction between living resources and mineral resources can be found in a higher sensitivity of living resources to environmental conditions.[14] The formation of

[10]Christy and Scott, *op. cit.*, note 2, pp. 74–87.

[11]See *e.g.*, the abstention clause of the International Convention for the High Seas Fisheries of the North Pacific Ocean of Tokio 1952, *UNTS* vol. 205, p. 80.

[12]See *e.g.*, Art. 2, para. 4 Convention on the Continental Shelf of Geneva 1958, *UNTS* vol. 499, p. 311.

[13]M B Schaefer, *The scientific basis for a conservation programme*, in *Papers presented at the International Technical Conference on the Conservation of the Living Resources of the Sea*, Rome 1955, pp. 19–22.

[14]Chapman, *op. cit.*, note 2, pp. 45–48. G Moore, *The control of marine pollution and the protection of living resources of the sea*, FAO Technical

Continued on next page

oil deposits and of manganese nodules depends on the presence of specific natural conditions, but once formed, they do not respond to changes in such conditions as living resources do. A slight change in their environment might destroy stocks of fish or considerably alter their behaviour. Accordingly, pollution of the oceans presents a real threat to the sea's living resources, while there is virtually no threat to the mineral resources.

1.2 Technological Factors

Technological factors are also important constitutive elements of the international law of marine fisheries. Most of these factors are concerned with fishing methods and fishing equipment, of which there is a great variety.[15] Some of the more modern forms are: purse seines (nets which encircle schools of pelagic species), trawls (nets which are drawn across the bottom), lines, gill nets (nets which are suspended in the water), traps, dredges and harpoons.

A first relevant aspect is that fishing gear is never completely selective. Consequently, fishing for one species usually results in an incidental catch of another species.[16] The international law of marine fisheries must take into account that this lack of gear selectivity may cause the regulation of a specific fishery to have an undesirable effect on other fisheries. Secondly, technological changes strongly influence

Continued from previous page
Conference on Marine Pollution and Its Effect on Living Resources and Fishing, Document FIR: MP/70/R-15, Rome 1970. R I Jackson *International fisheries and marine pollution*, FAO International Conference on Oil Pollution of the Sea 1968, paper No. 1, Rome 1968.
[15]Christy and Scott, *op. cit.*, note 2, pp. 87–104. Johnston, *op. cit.*, note 2, pp. 55–59.
[16]Porpoises, for example, drown in the purse-seining nets used in the tuna fishery, *Ocean Science News* 1971, No. 36, p. 1; *Ocean Science News* 1972, No. 8, p. 5.

international legal arrangements[17] – and fishing techniques have changed drastically in recent years.[18] Use of sonar in fish location, mechanization of net handling, new types of nets, new synthetic fibres for net construction and new freezing and processing techniques are only a few examples of such changes. However, they have not yet altered the fact that large quantity operations are still primarily limited to schooling species. Catches of species that do not school are usually much smaller, although sometimes very valuable. However, it may be possible that such advanced techniques as the use of satellites for fish location will change this situation.[19]

One of the most important effects of these technological improvements has been the emergence of intensive distant water fisheries. Fishermen are now able to operate efficiently for extended periods of time in areas far away from their home ports.[20] This development had several consequences. It greatly increased the total world catch, but it also led to the depletion of several stocks and to a greatly intensified confrontation between the nations involved in such distant water fisheries and the coas al States. These problems continue to be very virulent areas of conflict in the international community. Thus, the law has not yet been able to absorb fully the impact of these technological improvements. A new area of technological changes which may challenge the traditional international law of marine fisheries exists with respect

[17]On the relationship between law and technological innovation, see United Nations General Assembly, *Conservation problems with special reference to new technology*, UN Doc. A/AC. 138/65, 14 March 1972. W T Burke, *Law and the new technologies*, in *Offshore boundaries and zones*, L M Alexander ed., Columbus, Ohio 1967, pp. 204–225.
[18]W M Chapman, *The theory and practice of international fishery development-management*, San Diego Law Review 1970, p. 415. M B Schaefer, *Harvesting food from the sea*, in *Ocean Engineering, Proceedings of a 1968–69 Seminar Series*, University of Delaware, p. 3.
[19]Chapman, *op. cit.*, note 2, p. 51.
[20]Chapman, *op. cit.*, note 4, p. 92.

to maricultural fisheries. Although most experts do not foresee large scale maricultural operations in the near future, it is beyond doubt that the law of marine fisheries will be forced to respond if technological improvements make such operations both feasible and economically attractive.[21]

1.3 Economic Factors

Most marine fishing operations are commercial in nature. This means that economic considerations are a third category of constitutive elements which influence the international law of marine fisheries. However, there are a few exceptions to this commercial character. First of all, commercial considerations are of relatively little importance in sport fisheries.[22] Economic gain is not their major motivating factor. Secondly, economic factors are also not very important to the primitive fisherman whose main interest is to catch his food supply for the day. But with these exceptions, marine fisheries are carried out to make a profit or to obtain at least a return on the invested capital. This implies that the catch must have economic value. Therefore, demand for fishery products is a primary aspect of these economic elements.[23]

A first observation here is that the demand for fish products is not autonomous, but is affected by the many

[21]T E Kane, *Aquaculture and the law*, Sea Grant Bulletin No. 2, Miami 1970. *Our nation and the sea, Report of the Commission on Marine Science, Engineering and Resources*, Washington 1969, pp. 115–120. J E Bardach, *Aquaculture, Science* 1968, pp. 1098–1106. Christy and Scott, *op. cit.*, note 2, pp. 70–71, p. 96, p. 101.

[22]J L McHugh, *Domestic wrangles and international tangles*, Woodrow Wilson International Center for Scholars, Washington 1971, p. 174. *Panel reports of the Commission on Marine Science, Engineering and Resources*, vol. 3, *Marine resources and legal-political arrangements for their development*, Washington 1969, pp. VII 31–37. R H Stroud, *Sport fishery and recreation demands on the continental shelf*, in *International rules and organization for the sea*, L M Alexander ed., Kingston, RI 1969, pp. 239–246.

[23]Chapman, *op. cit.*, note 2, p. 7. Christy and Scott, *op. cit.*, note 2, pp. 17–55.

alternative ways of satisfying the human nutritional needs fulfilled by fishery products.[24] The living resources of the seas are in this respect in direct competition with land resources, since fishing is only one way of producing food. The reality of marine fisheries clearly reflects this fact. For example, the decline of the American whale industry began after the discovery of a substitute for whale oil.[25] This relationship between marine fisheries and other food sources cannot be ignored by the international law of marine fisheries. Measures designed to bring about a fuller exploitation of certain species may, for example, be useless if there is no demand for these species because land-based alternatives are either cheaper or otherwise preferable. Thus, marine fisheries can not be managed in isolation from the exploitation of land resources.[26] A second aspect of the demand for fish products is that essentially it consists of two components:[27] (1) a demand for direct human consumption; and (2) a demand for reduction to oil and fish meal. A major use of fish meal is as feed for poultry and pigs. Thus, ultimately it may become human food as well. Demand for fish for direct human consumption is largely concentrated on a few species groups: cod, haddock, tuna, salmon, shrimp, halibut, ocean perch and a few others. This selectivity is

[24]T Kamenaga, *The management of world fisheries*, in *The future of the sea's resources*, L M Alexander ed., Kingston, RI 1968, p. 122. K O Emery, *Human food from ocean and land*, Science 1967, pp. 1279–1281.
[25]J L McHugh, *Role and history of the International Whaling Commission*, Woodrow Wilson International Center for Scholars, Washington 1971, p. 18.
[26]V L Arnold and D W Bromley, *Social goals, problem perception and public intervention: the fishery*, San Diego Law Review 1970, p. 478. Kamenaga, *op. cit.*, note 24, p. 122. Schaefer, *op. cit.*, note 5, p. 128.
[27]FAO, *The state of world fisheries*, World Food Problems No. 7, Rome 1968, p. 1. FAO, *The management of fishery resources*, Rome 1967, p. 1 (FAO's *The management of fishery resources* is identical to FAO's *The state of world fisheries*; hereinafter *The management of fishery resources* will be used). Schaefer, *op. cit.*, note 5, p. 127. Christy and Scott, *op. cit.*, note 2, pp. 22–45.

caused by relatively strong taste preferences in most countries. Demand for reduction to oil or meal is primarily covered by such smaller, less valuable fish as herrings, anchovies, menhaden and sardines. These two types of demand correspond with two types of fishing operations. One is concerned with the high value species caught for direct human consumption and is essentially a food fishery. The other operation emphasizes the quantity of the catch, rather than the species involved and is essentially an industrial fishery. One of the problems facing the international law of marine fisheries is how to accommodate food and industrial fisheries. Traditionally, the law has given a certain preference to food fisheries.[28] However, the rapid growth of industrial fisheries makes it questionable that such a preference can be maintained.[29]

From this discussion it will be clear that the value of the catch depends upon a great number of factors,[30] of which only a few are directly related to the physical characteristics of the catch. For example, small fish are generally less valuable per unit of weight than larger fish, nor are fish which have just spawned of great value. Among the factors that are not related to the physical characteristics of the catch are: the availability of substitutes, the desirability of such substitutes, taste preferences, the standard of living, etc. This last group appears to be of little direct relevance to the international law of marine fisheries.

Economic elements refer not only to the value of the catch, but also to the cost of taking such catch. These cost-related

[28]Art. 2 Convention on Fishing and Conservation of the Living Resources of the High Seas of Geneva 1958, *UNTS* vol. 559, p. 288.
[29]FAO, *Report of the second session of the FAO Fishery Committee for the Eastern Central Atlantic (CECAF)*, FAO Fisheries Reports No. 107, Rome 1971, p. 3. Commission on Marine Science, Engineering and Resources, *op. cit.*, note 22, p. VIII–46.
[30]FAO, *op. cit.*, note 27, p. 9. Christy and Scott, *op. cit.*, note 2, pp. 17–56.

economic factors are essentially concerned with the question of how manpower and capital can be used most efficiently. Here again, fishing operations compete with land-based alternatives: a certain unit of manpower and capital can be used for marine fisheries, but it can also be used for agriculture. The expansion of Soviet fisheries, for example, was largely a result of the view of the Soviet government that returns to capital and labour would be greater in marine fisheries than in terrestrial animal husbandry.[31] The international law of marine fisheries has come under very severe criticism as far as these cost-related factors are concerned. It has been pointed out that the existing law contributes to the waste of manpower and capital in marine fishing operations. These problems will be discussed in a separate section.[32]

1.4 Social Factors

Social factors also influence the international law of marine fisheries. A first relevant aspect is that there exist extreme differences among the participants in marine fisheries. They range from the primitive fisherman going out to sea in a canoe to catch his family's daily meal to multinational companies with several factory vessels – from fishermen operating as independent entrepreneurs on the basis of private business concepts to fishing operations which are fully State-owned and State-controlled.[33] This diversity must be taken into account by the international law of marine fisheries. Other social factors stem from the fact that marine fishing is an international business,[34] which is clearly demonstrated by

[31]A view largely based on V S Mikhailov, *On the comparative efficiency of production of some products of the land and sea, Okeanologia* 1962, pp. 385–392.
[32]*Infra* pp. 54–63.
[33]Johnston, *op. cit.*, note 2, pp. 22–34.
[34]W M Chapman, in *International fisheries* (discussion), in *National policy recommendations*, L M Alexander ed., Kingston, RI 1970, p. 317. J L Kask, *Tuna – a world resource*, Law of the Sea Institute, University of Rhode Island, Occasional Paper No. 2, May 1969, app. I, p. ii.

the organization of the fishing industry. To give an extreme example: it is conceivable that a company owned by nationals of one country would purchase a vessel in another country, have that vessel manned with a crew from a third country, register the vessel in a fourth country, operate the vessel far from any of these four countries and land the catches in a fifth country for export to a sixth country. More realistically, American owned fishing companies operate extensively from Latin-American ports, and Japanese fishing firms participate in a great number of joint ventures in other countries. That a substantial portion of the catch enters international trade is yet another indication of the international character of marine fishing operations.

1.5 Political Factors

It is difficult to isolate political factors from the other constitutive elements of the international law of marine fisheries. In a sense they absorb all such other factors. Nevertheless, a number of general observations can be made. First of all, it is obvious that marine fisheries are the object of political friction among States. However, within the whole complex of foreign policy, they are of relatively little importance. With a few exceptions,[35] fishing is no longer essential to the national economy.[36] This explains why nations are no longer willing to risk war or violence in fishery disputes.[37] The most severe confrontations between nations over fishery problems have dealt with the extent of the

[35]*E.g.*, Iceland.
[36]FAO, *Fishery country profiles*, FAO Fisheries Circular No. 140, Rome 1972. Christy and Scott, *op. cit.*, note 2, pp. 114–117. Johnston, *op. cit.*, note 2, pp. 34–42.
[37]W T Burke, *Some thoughts on fisheries and a new conference on the law of the sea*, Law of the Sea Institute, University of Rhode Island, Occasional Paper No. 9, March 1971, p. 4. Chapman, *op. cit.*, note 18, p. 454. Dodyk, *op. cit.*, note 2, p. 75. K R Swygard, *Implications for the future distribution of the sea's resources if present regimes continue in force*, in *The future of the sea's resources*, L M Alexander ed., Kingston, RI 1968, p. 67.

exclusive jurisdiction of coastal States, but even here the use of force has been so minimal as to be non-existent. The United States, for example, has fully refrained from using naval power in its conflicts with Peru and Ecuador. A second observation is that nations engage in marine fisheries for a variety of reasons.[38] An important objective of States is to obtain the food required by their people as efficiently as possible. However, this is certainly not the only reason for participating in fishing operations. Another consideration is that States may wish to earn foreign exchange by expanding their exports, or may wish to protect whatever they have in foreign exchange by limiting their imports. Other goals might be to achieve a higher level of employment or to accumulate capital. Finally, States might simply wish to enhance their national prestige. This diversity of national objectives is of direct relevance to the international law of marine fisheries. Nations should not be compelled to accept specific goals, if their objectives do not conflict with the interests of other nations or with the interests of the world community as a whole.[39] A third point is that most political elements that influence the international law of marine fisheries are concerned with the interests of States. These interests differ widely and depend upon the particular situation of each State – a situation that may be perceived quite differently by other States. This makes it very difficult to generalize with respect to the interests of States in the area of marine fisheries, and generalizations are normally a prerequisite for classification. Nevertheless, it is possible to make a distinction among four broad categories of interests without completely ignoring reality.

[38]Arnold and Bromley, *op. cit.*, note 26, p. 472. W M Chapman, in *International fisheries regimes* (discussion), in *National policy recommendations*, L M Alexander ed., Kingston, RI 1970, p. 348. Kamenaga, *op. cit.*, note 24, p. 122. Chapman, *op. cit.*, note 4, p. 95.
[39]J A Crutchfield, in *International fisheries regimes* (panel), in *National policy recommendations*, L M Alexander ed., Kingston, RI 1970, p. 348.

A first distinction can be made between coastal fishing nations and distant water fishing nations.[40] Coastal fishing nations are those States that fish primarily in waters off their own shores, although not necessarily in their own exclusive fishery waters. Their ships are generally dependent upon home ports and their fisheries concentrate traditionally on species which are in demand for direct human consumption; they engage in food fisheries. Distant water fishing nations, on the other hand, operate far from their own coasts and at times close to those of other States. Their fleets can stay away from home ports for a long time and are usually equipped to process the catch at sea; this makes their fisheries industrial in nature. These characteristics are the theoretical extremes: in reality many States belong to both categories. The United States offers an example. Fisheries out of the ports in New England are essentially a coastal fishing operation, while the tuna vessels based in west coast ports fish off the shores of Latin American countries. Japan is also a case in point: it has large scale coastal fisheries, but even more extensive distant water operations. The distinction is, nevertheless, of importance because of the political confrontation between the two categories of States. Coastal fishing nations take the view that distant water fishing nations have expanded the catches at their expense. Statistical evidence supports this view. The catch of Japan, for example, increased from 2·5 million tons in 1948 to 8·6 million tons in 1969. The catch of the Soviet Union increased in the same period from 1·5 million tons to 6·5 million tons. Most of this increase came from distant water operations. Peru is the only nation which has been able to expand its coastal fisheries in an equally

[40]J J Dykstra and A A Holmsen, *Cost of fishing and foreign competition, New England*, in *The future of the fishing industry of the United States*, Seattle 1968, pp. 105–108. J H Wedin, *Impact of distant water on coastal fisheries*, in *The future of the sea's resources*, L M Alexander ed., Kingston, RI 1968, pp. 14–19. S Oda, *International control of sea resources*, Leyden 1963, pp. 21–34.

impressive way: from 0·8 million tons in 1948 to 9·2 million tons in 1969.[41] Distant water fisheries made undoubtedly a greater contribution to the increase of the total world catch than coastal fisheries.

A second distinction can be made between developing fishing nations and developed fishing nations. A problem here is that criteria which were formulated to distinguish between developed and developing nations in general may not be valid in the area of marine fisheries. It is, for instance, common to classify nations on the basis of gross national product per head of the population.[42] However, certain sectors of the fishing industry of the United States are much more primitive than segments of the fishing industry of Peru, which is a country with a much lower GNP *per capita*. Nevertheless, this distinction is quite relevant, particularly since nations perceive their fishery problems in these terms. Developing nations stress the expansion of marine fisheries and their desire to participate in such expansion.[43] Developed nations, on the other hand, tend to emphasize the protection of their already established fisheries.

There are two other political factors which deeply influence the legal regime of marine fisheries. The first factor is that the international community consists of States that to a large extent continue to act as sovereign entities. This is of fundamental importance to international law in general: it is a political reality that States are extremely reluctant to give up any of their prerogatives in favour of international law.[44] The history of the international law of marine fisheries demon-

[41]FAO, *op. cit.*, note 1, pp. a 8–9.
[42]International Bank for Reconstruction and Development, *Population, per capita product and growth rates*, Washington 1970.
[43]FAO, *Report of the consultation on the conservation of fishery resources and the control of fishing in Africa*, FAO Fisheries Reports No. 101, vol. 1, Rome 1971.
[44]S Oda, *Distribution of fish resources of the high seas: free competition or artificial quota?* in *The future of the sea's resources*, L M Alexander ed., Kingston, RI 1968, p. 30.

strates this. Its development was largely a response to necessities and crises.[45] Stocks of fish had to be depleted, incidents among fishermen had to become serious, and international conflicts had to break out before sovereign States were willing to accept the rules and principles of the international law of marine fisheries. In the international community necessity is still the supreme law-maker. The second factor is that the composition of the international community has changed drastically in recent years. The most dramatic change is undoubtedly the increase in the number of States as a result of the de-colonization process. The fact that most of these new States fall in the general category of developing nations greatly alters the political context within which the international law of marine fisheries operates.[46] This and their relative unfamiliarity with the technical problems of marine fisheries add substantially to the difficulties of reaching international agreement on fishery matters. Accordingly, the traditional principles of the international law of marine fisheries must be reconsidered.

1.6 Not a Single Objective but a Series of Challenges

It is clear that the international law of marine fisheries functions within a context of great biological, technological, economic, social and political diversity. Moreover, it is a context subject to rapid and often unpredictable change. This raises the question of which objectives the international law of marine fisheries can seek to realize. This question can be answered in general terms by stating, for example, that its goals are to maximize human welfare, to alleviate inter-

[45]Chapman, *op. cit.*, note 2, p. 35. J A Crutchfield, *National quotas for the North Atlantic fisheries: an exercise in second best*, in *International rules and organization for the sea*, L M Alexander ed., Kingston, RI 1969, p. 273.
[46]Chapman, *op. cit.*, note 18, p. 417. F T Christy, Jr., *Fisheries and the new conventions on the law of the sea*, San Diego Law Review 1970, pp. 462–463.

national conflicts, and to optimize world public order.[47] However, a less abstract answer is desirable.[48] Unfortunately, such an answer is very difficult to give in view of the extreme complexity of the problems. Moreover, there are no accepted procedures for defining the objectives of the international law of marine fisheries, and there is often a paralyzing lack of communication among those who attempt to define such goals.[49] Finally, the fact that the constitutive context of the international law of marine fisheries is subject to continuous change indicates that its objectives must be defined in dynamic, rather than in static, terms. For these reasons, it is more realistic to take the view that the international law of marine fisheries does not have one single objective, but is confronted by a series of challenges.[50] In this approach the need is to determine which challenges the international law of marine fisheries faces in specific areas, rather than what its single objective is. In the following sections these challenges will be discussed within the context of the six most important problem areas in the international law of marine fisheries: (1) the full utilization of the living resources of the high seas; (2) the conservation of these resources; (3) the economic efficiency of marine fisheries; (4) the allocation of the catch; (5) scientific research; and (6) inter-use and intra-use conflicts.

[47]Arnold and Bromley, *op. cit.*, note 26, p. 481. D M Johnston, *New uses of international law in the North Pacific, WLR* 1967, p. 94. M S McDougal and W T Burke, *The public order of the oceans. A contemporary international law of the sea*, New Haven and London 1962, pp. 37–38.
[48]W T Burke, *Aspects of internal decision-making processes in intergovernmental fishery commissions, WLR* 1967, p. 177. Burke, *op. cit.*, note 17, p. 223. J A Crutchfield, *Management of the North Pacific fisheries: economic objectives and issues, WLR* 1967, pp. 287–288.
[49]See the debate on maximum sustainable yield *versus* maximum economic yield, *infra* pp. 57–61.
[50]Arnold and Bromley, *op. cit.*, note 26, p. 469. Crutchfield, *op. cit.*, note 39, p. 346. Crutchfield, *op. cit.*, note 45, p. 266. Dodyk, *op. cit.*, note 2, p. 1.

2. FULL UTILIZATION

A first group of issues in the international law of marine fisheries concerns the full utilization of the ocean's living resources. These problems have many implications outside the area of marine fisheries *per se*.[51] Full utilization is also a matter of processing and distribution. Obviously, it makes little sense to increase catches if processing and distribution systems are so deficient that the higher catch will probably never reach the consumer. The importance of these aspects is illustrated by an estimate that a total annual catch of only 46 million tons could meet the protein needs of 6 billion people, provided it were divided equally.[52] This explains why a great deal of effort is spent on improving the processing and distribution systems. However, these aspects of full utilization are generally outside the scope of the international law of marine fisheries. The legal implications of processing and distribution are primarily issues of domestic law. Therefore, they will not be discussed further.

Statistical evidence supports the view that the present international law of marine fisheries has not been a serious obstacle to full utilization. The total world catch has grown rapidly since World War II: from a total catch of about 20 million tons in 1950 to about 64 million tons in 1968. The average rate of growth was 6·4 per cent in the period between 1949 and 1964 and 7·9 per cent in the years 1958 to 1966. In 1969 the total world catch declined slightly: from 64·3 million tons in 1968 to 63·1 million tons in 1969. However, this trend was reversed in 1970: the total world catch in that year was 69·3 million tons – an increase of more than 10 per cent over

[51]Christy and Scott, *op. cit.*, note 2, pp. 92–96. C J Bottemanne, *Principles of fisheries development*, Amsterdam 1959.
[52]W M Chapman, in *The future development of world fisheries* (panel), in *The future of the sea's resources*, L M Alexander ed., Kingston, RI 1968, p. 121.

1969.[53] The rate of growth of world fisheries after World War II has exceeded the rate of growth of the world population.[54] This expansion of marine fisheries has resulted in a decrease in the number of stocks that are under-exploited or not exploited at all, but that can be harvested with existing equipment and for which there is a demand. There has also been a change in the kind of species under exploitation. Emphasis has shifted from the most desirable, high value species (cod, tuna, hake, halibut, salmon, etc.) to smaller, less valuable species (herring, anchovies, etc.).[55] This is in effect a change from species relatively high in the food chain to species relatively low in that chain. These smaller species are used primarily for the production of oil and fish meal and not for direct human consumption.

It is expected that marine fisheries will continue to expand, although at a much reduced rate. The Food and Agriculture Organization estimates that in 1975 the total world catch will be close to 75 million tons and will approach 100 million tons in 1985.[56] These estimates are based on the assumption that no radical changes will occur in catching techniques and in taste preferences. The heavy exploitation of commercially attractive stocks in the Northern Hemisphere implies that most of the future expansion of marine fisheries must come from stocks in the Southern Hemisphere.[57] This predicted

[53]FAO, *Yearbook of fishery statistics 1970*, Rome 1971. FAO, *op. cit.*, note 27, p. 1. Christy and Scott, *op. cit.*, note 2, pp. 104–117.
[54]R I Jackson, *Some observations on the future growth of world fisheries and the nature of the conservation problem*, in *The future of the sea's resources*, L M Alexander ed., Kingston, RI 1968, p. 10.
[55]Jackson, *op. cit.*, note 54, p. 10. Schaefer, *op. cit.*, note 5, p. 127.
[56]FAO, *The prospects for world fishery development in 1975 and 1985*, FAO Fisheries Circular No. 118, Rome 1969, p. 19. Commission on Marine Science, Engineering and Resources, *op. cit.*, note 22, pp. VII 3–15. Christy and Scott, *op. cit.*, note 2, pp. 138–145.
[57]FAO, *Report of the first session of the Indian Ocean Fishery Commission*, FAO Fisheries Reports No. 60, Rome 1968, p. 3. Chapman, *op. cit.*, note 4, p. 105.

growth raises the question of the total biological potential of the living resources of the seas. Estimates differ widely[58] and range from a high of 2,000 million to a low of 80 million tons annually. This gap can be explained in part by different methods and assumptions, but it also reflects a lack of knowledge. Based on similar assumptions as for the projected actual expansion of marine fisheries, the Food and Agriculture Organization recently estimated the maximum potential world catch to be 120 million tons annually.[59]

If this FAO figure is accepted as a realistic estimate of the maximum biological potential of the sea, it is clear that the present annual salt water catch of about 60 million tons can be expanded considerably without exceeding biological limits. Such further expansion could make an important contribution towards solving the world's food problems and particularly its need for animal protein.[60] Positive characteristics in this respect are the worldwide distribution of the ocean's living resources, their high nutritional value and the relative ease with which they can be produced. However, full utilization of the living resources is also an economic problem. The question is whether or not full utilization up to the maximum biological limits is economically attractive. There is, first of all, the matter of demand for fishery products. However, it is generally agreed that demand will not form any constraint on the ability to expand marine fisheries.[61] The FAO World

[58]M B Schaefer and D L Alverson, *World fish potentials*, in *The future of the fishing industry of the United States*, Seattle 1968, p. 82. Christy and Scott, *op. cit.*, note 2, pp. 67–70.

[59]FAO, *op. cit.*, note 56, p. 8.

[60]D Fraser, *The people problem; what you should know about growing population and vanishing resources*, Bloomington 1971. C P Idyll, *The sea against hunger*, New York 1970. Commission on Marine Science, Engineering and Resources, *op. cit.*, note 21, p. 87. United Nations, *Feeding the expanding world population: international action to avert the impending protein crisis*, New York 1968.

[61]Commission on Marine Science, Engineering and Resources, *op. cit.*, note 22, p. VII-9. Crutchfield, *op. cit.*, note 48, p. 286.

Study of the Indicative World Plan for Agricultural Development, for example, expects demand to outstrip supply.[62] Only radical changes in the growth rate of the world population or in the availability of substitutes seem capable of altering this projection.

A second economic aspect of fishery development concerns the most efficient use of manpower and capital. If the cost of an additional unit of animal protein from the sea would be higher than the cost of an additional unit produced on land, economic rationality dictates that more manpower and capital be used for the land-based production and less for marine fisheries. However, such an approach to the use of manpower and capital presents several problems. First of all, the two units of protein will probably not be completely identical, which might justify the somewhat higher cost of one of the units. Secondly, it will be extremely difficult to compare accurately the cost-factors involved. This is related to a third problem: manpower and capital are never completely mobile.[63] A fisherman can not be transformed overnight into a farmer. Finally, economic efficiency is a matter of priorities. If, for example, preference is given to producing the maximum amount of protein from the sea, cost-related considerations are less important than if priority is given to maximizing the profits of the fishing industry.[64]

Apart from these biological and economic aspects, full utilization problems also have strong political implications. These stem primarily from the fact that all nations want an acceptable share in the expansion of marine fisheries. This implies that the political aspects of full utilization are essentially concerned with the distribution of the living

[62]FAO, *op. cit.*, note 56, p. 19.
[63]*Panel reports of the Commission on Marine Science, Engineering and Resources*, vol. 2, *Industry and technology*, Washington 1969, p. V-39.
[64]*Infra* p. 59.

resources of the sea. Therefore, they will be more fully discussed in the section dealing with allocation problems.[65]

Many factors determining the extent to which the ocean's living resources will be exploited are beyond the control of the international law of marine fisheries. However, it is necessary to discuss the relationship between the principle of the freedom of fishing on the high seas and the problems of full utilization. A first relevant point is that under the freedom of fishing nations are able to develop their fisheries in whatever way and for whatever purpose they deem fit. It has been discussed that nations fish in different ways and for different purposes. Therefore, it is of positive value to the full utilization of the living resources of the sea that the freedom of fishing does not limit the options open to States. It is also important that under this concept the most resourceful and the most interested States are able to develop their fisheries as quickly as they desire, without being restricted by the law. These nations determine the rate of growth of marine fisheries, and not the less resourceful and less interested States. A last point is that the freedom of fishing does not require States to pay fees, etc. in order to gain access to the resources. Thus, they can fully use the available funds for developing their fishing fleets.

However, freedom of fishing on the high seas has also several disadvantages with respect to full utilization. A first difficulty is that it encourages States to invest in the equipment – vessels and gear – to catch the living resources of the high seas at the expense of investments in the resources themselves. An example of the latter type of investment would occur if a State should decide to limit its fisheries in order to build up a high seas stock to a higher level of abundance. Here, the problem would be that under the principle of freedom of fishing all other nations could reap the benefits from this kind of investment. Accordingly, States will be

[65]*Infra* pp. 63–69.

extremely reluctant to make such a decision. Investments in the resources are essential in maricultural fisheries. The fact that the freedom of fishing does not offer adequate security for these investments must be considered a serious impediment to the development of maricultural operations in the waters of the high seas. A second disadvantage of the freedom of fishing in relation to full utilization is a mirror image of one of its advantages, namely that it allows the most resourceful nations to set the pace of the expansion of marine fisheries. This may result in a further deprivation of the less resourceful States, particularly the developing nations. It can be argued that this negative aspect of the freedom of fishing is only theoretical since lower labour costs would allow developing nations to compete effectively with developed States. However, the extremely slow rate at which the share of developing nations in the total world catch has increased seems to indicate that lower labour costs in themselves do not fully ensure that these nations will have an equitable share in the expansion of marine fisheries. It is more likely that the distant water fleets of the developed States will overfish a stock before developing States will be capable of participating in its exploitation. This negative aspect of the freedom of fishing is relevant not only to the problems of full utilization, but also to those associated with the allocation of the catch.

What, then, are the challenges to the international law of marine fisheries and to international fisheries organizations regarding the full utilization of the living resources of the high seas ? The complexity of the biological, economic and political elements discussed in this section emphasizes that the problems of full utilization differ from situation to situation and from fishery to fishery. However, the prevailing challenge to the international law of marine fisheries and to international fisheries organizations appears to be to stimulate the expansion of marine fisheries to the extent that such expansion is biologically possible and economically attractive. A second challenge is to overcome the negative effects of the freedom of fishing on full utilization, which requires arrangements for protecting direct investments in the resources and for ensuring that developing nations will be able to share equitably in the growth of marine fisheries.

3. CONSERVATION

Full utilization and conservation are not opposing concepts. The central concern of conservation is to prevent the waste of the living resources of the sea by over-exploitation and to preserve their productivity for the future. This implies that any long term full utilization programme must take into account the demands of conservation, since the long range productivity of a stock is normally adversely affected by exploitation beyond its maximum biological limits. The existence of these limits is directly related to the renewable nature of the living resources of the sea.

In the absence of fishing, the total biomass of a stock of fish seeks to achieve equilibrium between the growth of individuals and the recruitment of young fish, on the one hand, and the losses due to natural deaths, on the other. When fishing is initiated, it will tend to reduce the abundance of the stock. At such reduced stock levels, losses due to natural deaths may become smaller, while recruitment and growth may increase – hence providing a surplus. If the total catch of the stock is equal to this surplus, the average size of the stock will become stable at a lower level, which implies that the surplus can be constantly harvested. Therefore, it would represent a sustainable yield. This yield would be small if the stock were very large since in this case natural deaths are only a little less than growth and recruitment. The sustainable yield would also be small if the stock size is very limited since then the absolute value of the increase through growth and recruitment is small. Thus, the sustainable yield

45

is at its peak at some intermediate stock level. At this level the stock produces a maximum sustainable yield, *i.e.*, a yield that can be taken year after year without depleting the stock.[66] This extremely simplified theory of conservation can be illustrated by looking at the history of a brood of fish. If fishing is not very intensive, the individuals of such a brood may survive for a long time. Consequently, the average age and size of the fish caught are high, but their total number and their total weight are small. If, on the other hand, fishing is very intensive, fish will not survive long enough to grow very much. Thus, although the number of fish caught will be higher than in the previous situation, the total weight of the catch will remain low. This implies that the greatest catch from a given brood is taken by allowing the fish to grow to a reasonable, intermediate size.[67] The above discussion provides in outline form the background of a diagram that relates fishing effort to the yield produced by such effort from a certain stock of fish.[68]

This diagram shows that when fishing is initiated an additional unit of effort produces a relatively large increase in yield. When fishing develops beyond its initial stages, larger increases in effort are required to produce the same increase in yield. Ultimately, more effort may even result in a decrease in the total yield. This relationship between effort and yield

[66]Commission on Marine Science, Engineering and Resources, *op. cit.*, note 22, p. VIII–46. J A Gulland, *The concept of the maximum sustainable yield and fishery management*, FAO Fisheries Technical Paper No. 70, Rome 1968. M B Schaefer, *Methods of estimating effects of fishing on fish populations*, in *Transactions of the American Fisheries Society* 1968, pp. 231–241. Chapman, *op. cit.*, note 4, pp. 93–94. FAO, *op. cit.*, note 27, pp. 7–9. M Graham, *A first approximation to a modern theory of fishing*, in *Papers presented at the International Technical Conference on the Conservation of the Living Resources of the Sea*, Rome 1955, pp. 56–61. M Graham, *Concepts of conservation*, in *Papers presented at the International Technical Conference on the Conservation of the Living Resources of the Sea*, Rome 1955, pp. 1–14.
[67]FAO, *op. cit.*, note 27, p. 7.
[68]Gulland, *op. cit.*, note 66. FAO, *op. cit.*, note 27, pp. 9–10.

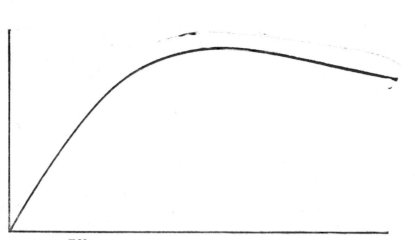

Effort

differs from stock to stock and is unique for each fishery, although the basic shape of the curve applies universally. Therefore, this diagram is probably the most fundamental element of the theory of conservation.

The practical implementation of this theory, however, presents many problems.[69] A first difficulty is that the determination of the maximum sustainable yield and of the yield-effort curve of a specific stock requires a great amount of biological information.[70] Such information consists primarily, but not exclusively, of data concerning: (1) the size of the stock in question; (2) the rate of recruitment and its relation to the parental stock; (3) the rate of growth; and (4) the rate of mortality. In addition, detailed statistical information is required with respect to catches and with respect to the effort that produced such catches. All these data must be collected and interpreted on a continuing basis because the maximum available yield of a stock may change

[69]*Infra* pp. 178–196.
[70]Chapman, *op. cit.*, note 18, p. 411, p. 442, p. 452. FAO, *op. cit.*, note 27, p. 23. Schaefer, *op. cit.*, note 13, pp. 14–56.

from year to year.[71] Nevertheless, maximum sustainable yield estimates are available for many species.[72]

A second difficulty stems from the fact that many species are biologically interrelated.[73] Accordingly, maximizing the yield of one species may result in a lower yield from another species. For example, increasing the size of seal herds in order to achieve a maximum sustainable yield may adversely affect the productivity of the fish resources on which they feed.[74] One way to overcome this problem is to determine the maximum sustainable yield not on a single-species basis, but for a combination of species or even for the living resources of the sea as a whole.[75] Whatever the merits of this approach are, it cannot be denied that the interrelationship between species is a significant obstacle to basing the regulation of marine fisheries exclusively on the biological concept of maximum sustainable yield. These interrelationships present an important reason why the relative economic value of the species involved must be taken into account as well. A similar difficulty may arise from the fact that fishing gear is usually not completely selective.[76] This is another reason

[71]J A Crutchfield, *Overcapitalization of the fishing effort*, in *The future of the sea's resources*, L M Alexander ed., Kingston, RI 1968, p. 25. P Moiseev, *Fluctuations in the commercial fish populations of the North-Western Pacific in relation to environmental and other factors*, in *Papers presented at the International Technical Conference on the Conservation of the Living Resources of the Sea*, Rome 1955, pp. 266–290.

[72]R F Fullenbaum, *A survey of maximum sustainable yield estimates on a world basis for selected fisheries*, Working Paper No. 43, United States Bureau of Commercial Fisheries, Washington 1970.

[73]FAO, *op. cit.*, note 27, pp. 14–15. Christy and Scott, *op. cit.*, note 2, pp. 78–79.

[74]A similar example can be given for whales and krill, see F T Christy, Jr., in *The future development of world fisheries* (panel), in *The future of the sea's resources*, L M Alexander ed., Kingston, RI 1968, p. 137.

[75]P A Larkin, *Critique: fisheries management provisions in the Commission Report*, in *National policy recommendations*, L M Alexander ed., Kingston, RI 1970, p. 303.

[76]FAO, *op. cit.*, note 27, p. 10.

why raising the catch of one species to the maximum sustainable yield level may have an adverse impact on other species. For example, it is quite difficult to separate yellowfin and skipjack tuna in purse-seining operations.[77] This makes it necessary to take special steps to ensure that a desirable increase in skipjack catches does not endanger yellowfin, which is already subject to exploitation at its maximum sustainable yield level.

The question must be asked what the consequences are if catches exceed for some time the maximum sustainable yield of a stock. Fortunately, marine fish produce a very large number of eggs; thus, even a relatively small stock can produce a very large brood. Marine mammals, like whales and seals, do not share this characteristic; their offspring are much smaller in number. With this exception, there is evidence that the size of stocks can be reduced substantially without a significant reduction in the number of young fish produced. This number may fluctuate widely, but is frequently independent from the size of the adult stock.[78] Consequently, most stocks of fish are very resilient to changes in recruitment. In other words, stocks of fish can be overfished, but its consequences are reversible.[79] This seems even to apply to much more vulnerable species like whales. The condition for such a recovery is obviously a strict limitation of catches. However, a stock may not fully recover if the reduction in its size allows competitors and other species to fill the ecological niche that was previously occupied by the larger stock. In such a case, depletion may indeed be irreversible. This might have occurred with the California sardines which did not recover after catches were curtailed.[80] Nonetheless,

[77]IATTC, *Annual Report for the year 1967*, La Jolla 1968, p. 7.
[78]FAO, *op. cit.*, note 27, p. 7.
[79]*Ibidem*, p. 4.
[80]G I Murphy, *Vital statistics of the Pacific sardine and the population consequences*, Ecology 1967, pp. 731–736. FAO, *op. cit.*, note 27, p. 7.

4

it seems to be true that in most cases the fishermen go bankrupt before the fish.[81]

It has been mentioned that the total world catch is still well below what is considered to be the maximum total biological potential of the oceans.[82] Other estimates put the ratio between present landings and the total maximum sustainable yield of all species at 47 per cent.[83] That the living resources of the oceans as a whole are still biologically underexploited does not negate the fact that most commercially valuable species must be protected by conservation measures. The United Nations Conference on the Conservation and Utilization of Resources, held in 1949 at Lake Success, produced a map showing thirty stocks of fish then believed to be under fished.[84] Of these thirty stocks about half are now in need of proper management and substantial exploitation has begun on all of them. If the projections for the expansion of marine fisheries and the estimates of the total biological potential of the sea's living resources prove to be correct, total world catches will rapidly approach the total maximum sustainable yield after 1985. Then the problems of conservation will extend to virtually all species that can be caught with present gear and that are of commercial value.

Several methods are available if conservation measures must be applied to a certain stock. These methods include: (1) limitations on the size of the fish which may be landed; (2) the closure of certain areas to specific fisheries; (3) the closure of certain seasons; (4) restrictions on the type of gear which may be used; (5) limitations on the total catch of a specific stock; and (6) limitations on the total fishing effort applied to a certain stock.[85] Usually, a combination of these

[81]Chapman, *op. cit.*, note 4, p. 102.
[82]*Supra* p. 41.
[83]Fullenbaum, *op. cit.*, note 72, p. ii.
[84]FAO, *op. cit.*, note 27, p. 2.
[85]FAO, *op. cit.*, note 27, pp. 11–15. Johnston, *op. cit.*, note 2, pp. 59–68.

methods is employed. Their general purpose is to control fishing mortality and/or the size of the fish removed from the stock in question.[86] Two of the most widely used techniques prescribe a minimum size for the meshes of fishing nets or provide that fish below a certain minimum size may not be retained. These rules are designed to allow young and immature fish to escape.

The above conservation measures are normally designed to maintain the catch of certain fisheries at a level corresponding with the maximum sustainable yield of the stocks under exploitation. The Convention on Fishing and Conservation of the Living Resources of the High Seas of Geneva 1958 explicitly defines conservation as the aggregate of measures designed to bring about the maximum sustainable yield. It is generally understood that the term optimum sustainable yield in Article 2 of this Convention stands for maximum sustainable yield.[87] Other international fisheries conventions state their objectives in similar terms.[88] Accordingly, most international fisheries agreements and fisheries organizations attempt to maximize the long range physical production of the resources for which they are responsible. It is politically most significant that the *principle* that catches should not exceed the level of maximum sustainable yield has found nearly universal acceptance in the international community.[89] However, the reality of international fisheries regulation suggests that acceptance of this principle should

[86]FAO, *op. cit.*, note 27, p. 11.
[87]W T Burke, *Contemporary legal problems in ocean development*, in *Towards a better use of the ocean*, Stockholm, New York and London 1969, p. 78, note 126. J A Crutchfield, *The Convention on Fishing and Living Resources of the High Seas*, *Natural Resources Lawyer* 1968, p. 114, pp. 116–117. Crutchfield, *op. cit.*, note 48, p. 288.
[88]*Infra* pp. 179–181.
[89]Chapman, *op. cit.*, note 18, p. 411. Burke, *op. cit.*, note 87, p. 78. F V Garcia Amador, *The exploitation and conservation of the resources of the sea. A study of contemporary international law*, 2nd ed. 2nd enl. printing Leyden 1963, pp. 187–201. Oda, *op. cit.*, note 40, pp. 82–86, pp. 111–113.

not be equated with acceptance of concrete conservation measures. The adoption of such specific measures continues to generate international disputes.

There is in this respect an important difference between distant water fishing countries and coastal fishing countries. Distant water fishing States are capable of moving on to other areas or species if a specific stock no longer yields acceptable catches.[90] Their fleets have a great degree of mobility and they fish for quantity rather than for specific species. Coastal fishing operations, on the other hand, depend upon home ports and fish for particular stocks. Consequently, nations involved in such fisheries lack the capability of easily adapting their operations if the traditionally exploited stocks cease to be productive. This explains why coastal fishing nations have generally demonstrated a stronger interest in limiting catches to the level of maximum sustainable yield than distant water fishing countries. Although not explicitly rejecting the concept of maximum sustainable yield, distant water fishing nations have used in some cases pulse-fishing methods, under which stocks were knowingly overfished until they were no longer profitable. If that point had been reached, fishing operations moved on to other stocks to give the over-fished species time to recover.[91] This difference is an important reason for conflicts among States with respect to the implementation of conservation measures. However, pulse-fishing depends upon the availability of commercially attractive species to replace the stocks that have ceased to be profitable because of overfishing. It has been mentioned that more and more commercially attractive stocks are subject to full exploitation.[92] This implies that distant water fishing

[90]D L McKernan, *International fishery regimes – current and future*, in *National policy recommendations*, L M Alexander ed., Kingston, RI 1970, p. 343.
[91]McHugh, *op. cit.*, note 22, pp. 140–141.
[92]*Supra* p. 50.

States are gradually losing the capability of engaging in pulse-fishing.[93] Therefore, their position regarding conservation may become closer to that of coastal fishing nations. If commercially attractive under-exploited stocks are no longer available, distant water fishing countries will have a more direct interest in limiting catches to the maximum sustainable yield level.

From the point of view of conservation, freedom of fishing is a questionable concept. Essentially, it allows States not only to fish, but also to overfish. Most of the existing treaty-based restrictions on the freedom of fishing are already concerned with this problem. Nevertheless, as far as conservation is concerned, the major challenge to international fisheries organizations and to the international law of marine fisheries continues to be the development of effective arrangements for the adoption of conservation measures. This challenge exists on two levels. First of all, on a world community level it is necessary to strengthen the acceptance of the principle that catches should not exceed the maximum sustainable yield of the various species. Secondly, this general principle must be implemented on a regional level. The problems of the conservation of the living resources of the sea differ from fishery to fishery. If they are to be effective, measures dealing with these problems must reflect the specific characteristics of the situation with which they must cope. This strongly suggests that conservation measures can best be adopted on a regional level by the States that are directly concerned with these issues. However, here the problem can arise that with respect to conservation the interests of such States and of the world community are not necessarily identical. It may be in the short range interest of a specific State, or of a group of States, to exceed the maximum sustainable yield of a stock. It is conceivable that under certain exceptional circumstances such overfishing can be

[93]FAO, *op. cit.*, note 27, p. 2.

justified. Yet in almost all cases overfishing infringes upon the interests of the world community,[94] since it results ultimately in the depletion of the living resources of the sea. This means that the international law of marine fisheries is also facing the challenge of finding a balance between the interests of the world community regarding conservation and those of the nations which participate in specific fisheries.

4. ECONOMIC EFFICIENCY

It has been mentioned that the international law of marine fisheries has come under severe criticism with respect to the cost aspects of marine fishing operations.[95] This criticism can be clarified by reference to an extremely simplified economic model of a particular fishery. The simplification of this model stems primarily from these two assumptions: (1) the costs of fishing operations are assumed to be proportional to the amount of fishing effort, measured, *e.g.*, in standard fishing days; and (2) the value of the catch is assumed to be proportional to its weight, which in its turn is related to fishing effort through the yield-effort curve of the stock in question. These assumptions eliminate all variables relating to market conditions, technological advances, etc. The result is the following, well-known diagram.[96]

In this diagram line A represents the total costs of the fishing operations and line B represents the total value of the catch. In spite of the aforementioned simplifications, the model explains several things. At point x^2 the amount of effort produces the maximum value, which under the above assump-

[94]G Hardin, *The tragedy of the commons*, Science 1968, pp. 1243–1248.
[95]F T Christy, Jr., *The distribution of the sea's wealth in fisheries*, in *Offshore boundaries and zones*, L M Alexander ed., Columbus, Ohio 1967, pp. 106–122. Christy and Scott, *op. cit.*, note 2, pp. 6–17. A Scott, *The fishery: the objectives of sole ownership*, *Journal of Political Economy* 1955, pp. 116–124. H S Gordon, *The economic theory of a common property resource: the fishery*, *Journal of Political Economy* 1954, pp. 124–142.
[96]FAO, *op. cit.*, note 27, pp. 9–11.

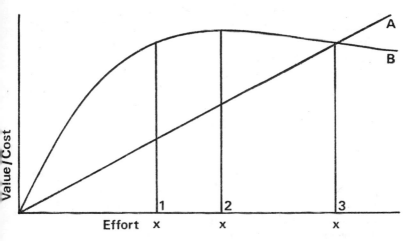

tions coincides with the maximum sustainable yield. However, the diagram also shows that at this point the difference between costs and value is smaller than at point x^1. At point x^1 a maximum economic yield is achieved. Accordingly, point x^1 represents the amount of fishing effort which maximizes the *economic* yield of fisheries, while the *physical* yield reaches its maximum at point x^2.

It is extremely difficult to transform this theoretical model into a realistic description of a specific fishery. Apart from all biological information needed to determine the yield-effort curve, it is necessary to collect and analyze a great deal of economic data. These relate in particular to the cost structure of fishing operations and to the market prices of the product. An additional problem is that these economic data vary with changes in fishing technology and demand. Nevertheless, it is correct to assume that in most fisheries the maximum sustainable yield and the maximum economic yield are achieved at different levels of fishing effort and that generally the maximum economic yield requires a smaller amount of effort than the maximum sustainable yield. It also corresponds with a somewhat reduced catch level.[97]

There is another aspect which must be introduced here.[98] This aspect is a direct consequence of the fact that under the freedom of fishing all nations and all fishermen may enter any fishery which they consider attractive. Accordingly, as long as a specific fishery produces a profit, additional fishermen will be tempted to enter that fishery.[99] This process can continue until the total fishing effort has reached the point at which the total cost of fishing operations is equal to the total value of the catch.[100] In the above diagram this occurs at point x^3. If effort were to increase beyond that point, the total costs of fishing would exceed the total value of the catch. This would result in losses which would force some fishermen out of the fishery in question. Thus, in the absence of management, most high seas fisheries tend to operate at point x^3. At this point they produce no economic rent at all.

Economists criticize the international law of marine fisheries because it treats the living resources of the high seas as common property resources, rather than as private property resources.[101] This is considered the reason why marine fisheries can not operate profitably. However, it is not so much the common property character of the living resources of the sea *per se* that causes this problem, as the fact that under freedom of fishing access to the fisheries is open to all nations and to all fishermen.[102] It is because of this principle of open

[97]M B Schaefer, *Biological and economic aspects of the management of commercial marine fisheries*, in *Transactions of the American Fisheries Society* 1959, p. 103.
[98]Commission on Marine Science, Engineering and Resources, *op. cit.*, note 21, p. 92. Christy, *op. cit.*, note 95, p. 112.
[99]See *e.g.*, for North Sea fisheries, FAO, *op. cit.*, note 27, p. 5.
[100]Commission on Marine Science, Engineering and Resources, *op. cit.*, note 22, p. VIII–47. Christy, *op. cit.*, note 95, p. 112.
[101]F T Christy, Jr., *Fisheries goals and the rights of property*, in *Transactions of the American Fisheries Society* 1969, pp. 369–378. Christy, *op. cit.*, note 95, p. 109. Christy and Scott, *op. cit.*, note 2, pp. 6–17.
[102]A Laing, in *International fisheries regimes* (panel), in *National policy recommendations*, L M Alexander, ed., Kingston, RI 1970, p. 324.

access that entry into a fishery will stop at the point where the total costs of fishing operations are equal to the total value of the catch, rather than, as economic rationale would dictate, at the point where the additional costs of the last unit of effort are equal to the additional value of the catch produced by that last unit of effort.[103] This is the background of a debate between biologists and economists with regard to the objectives of international fisheries regulation.[104] Biologists argue that the objective of fishery management should be to achieve a maximum sustainable yield and to maximize the physical production of the oceans. Economists, on the other hand, reject this and take the view that the objective of fisheries management should be to achieve a maximum economic yield.[105] What is the relevance of this discussion to the international law of marine fisheries?[106]

A first observation is that maximum sustainable yield and maximum economic yield become less irreconcilable if they are approached undogmatically. Both concepts are concerned with the prevention of waste. In the case of maximum sustainable yield, it is the waste of the living resources of the sea that results from overfishing. In the case of maximum economic yield, it is the waste that results from using too much labour and capital in order to produce a certain quantity of fish. Thus, both serve the ulterior objective of furthering human welfare, which may be adversely affected by the waste of the physical resources of the seas and by the waste of the manpower and capital applied to their harvest.

[103]This is point x^1 in the diagram.
[104]Chapman, *op. cit.*, note 18, pp. 412–413. Crutchfield, *op. cit.*, note 71, pp. 23–29. Christy, *op. cit.*, note 95. Christy and Scott, *op. cit.*, note 2. Johnston, *op. cit.*, note 2, pp. 51–54.
[105]Fortunately, lawyers have refrained from defining the objective of the international regulation of marine fisheries as the maximization of justice.
[106]Chapman, *op. cit.*, note 38, p. 348. G Pontecorvo, in *International fisheries regimes* (discussion), in *National policy recommendations*, L M Alexander ed., Kingston, RI 1970, p. 350.

Both goals of fishery regulation also have in common that their practical implementation is very difficult. It has been mentioned that the determination of the maximum sustainable yield of a specific stock requires a great amount of biological data. If maximum economic yield were to be the objective of the international regulation of marine fisheries even more information would be needed. The fact that for many fisheries all these data are simply not available makes the choice between maximum sustainable yield and maximum economic yield somewhat academic.[107] This informational problem becomes even more serious if it is taken into account that stocks and fisheries do not exist in a vacuum. It has been mentioned that reaching the maximum sustainable yield in one fishery may adversely affect the yield of other fisheries. Similarly, maximizing the economic yield of a specific fishery may make the achievement of maximum economic yield in another fishery impossible. An additional complication is caused by the fact that maximum economic yield must consider not only the interrelationships between species, but also the interrelationships between markets and cost structures. As these differ from country to country, it may very well be impossible to determine a single maximum economic yield for all countries.[108]

A third observation is that from the point of view of the world community exceeding the maximum sustainable yield has implications different from those of exceeding the maximum economic yield. In the first case a State, or a group of States, depletes, at least temporarily, a resource which under the freedom of fishing may be harvested by all States. Thus, it gains at the expense of the actual or potential interests of other nations. This is not the case if a State disregards the

[107]Burke, *op. cit.*, note 87, p. 71. Christy, *op. cit.*, note 74, p. 136. Johnston, *op. cit.*, note 47, p. 93.
[108]Commission on Marine Science, Engineering and Resources, *op. cit.*, note 22, p. VIII–62. Kamenaga, *op. cit.*, note 24, p. 123. FAO, *op. cit.*, note 27, p. 10, p. 24.

maximum economic yield. The fact that it does not use the available manpower and capital in the most efficient manner is primarily to its own disadvantage and only indirectly to the disadvantage of other nations. A State may have very valid reasons for a decision not to regulate its fisheries for the purpose of fishing as efficiently as possible. Such a reason could be the protection of employment opportunities. As the maximum economic yield occurs in most fisheries at a lower level of fishing effort than the maximum sustainable yield, economic rationalization may result in unemployment in the fishing industry. States may decide that this is unacceptable, particularly if alternative employment is not available.[109]

Compared with maximum sustainable yield, maximum economic yield will in most fisheries not only result in a reduction of employment opportunities, but also in smaller catches.[110] This may be unacceptable to many States. Moreover, it will reduce the total production of the living resources of the sea measured in physical terms. Consequently, economic rationalization may prevent marine fisheries from making a maximum contribution towards solving the problems of feeding a growing world population. It seems doubtful that the surplus capital and manpower resulting from the economic rationalization of marine fisheries can be used so efficiently in other applications that the gains achieved in these other applications will fully offset the lower productivity of the living resources of the sea.[111] If this is not the case, the net result of economic rationalization can be that marine fisheries have indeed become profitable, but that the total supply of food available to the world population is smaller.

A last relevant point is that maximum sustainable yield is

[109]M B Schaefer, in *International fisheries* (remarks), in *National policy recommendations*, L M Alexander ed., Kingston, RI 1970, p. 306.
[110]*Supra* p. 55.
[111]Schaefer, *op. cit.*, note 5, p. 128.

much more widely accepted than maximum economic yield. It has been mentioned that States have committed themselves to the principle of maximum sustainable yield.[112] This does not yet apply to maximum economic yield. As the international regulation of marine fisheries is the outcome of decisions of States, this difference between the two concepts is of great significance. Among the reasons for the wider acceptance of maximum sustainable yield are the real or perceived differences between the two concepts and the fact that maximum sustainable yield allows States to leave open the question of the distribution of the catch, whereas maximum economic yield forces States to take decisions regarding the allocation of fishing effort. Finally, maximization of economic yield is essentially a concept of profit oriented economies.[113] Other economic systems, particularly those of the socialist countries, also recognize the importance of an efficient use of capital and manpower, but have a different outlook on profits as a mechanism for achieving it. This makes it questionable that these countries will ever fully accept maximum economic yield as the objective of international fisheries regulation. On the other hand, they are in a better position to undertake economic rationalization than many other States, because their fisheries are to a large extent State controlled.

The foregoing suggests that the best approach to these issues is to continue to emphasize maximum sustainable yield as the objective of the international regulation of marine fisheries and to accommodate the problems of economic efficiency within this framework.[114] Accordingly, the question should not be whether the level of the catch must

[112]*Supra* p. 51.
[113]Kamenaga, *op. cit.*, note 24, p. 123.
[114]Chapman, *op. cit.*, note 18, p. 451, p. 453. Chapman, *op. cit.*, note 2, p. 33. V J Norton, in *International fisheries regimes* (panel), in *National policy recommendations*, L M Alexander ed., Kingston, RI 1970, pp. 332–333. Schaefer, *op. cit.*, note 5, p. 128.

be determined on the basis of maximum sustainable yield or on the basis of maximum economic yield, but how a given catch level can be taken as efficiently as possible.[115] If this level corresponds with the maximum sustainable yield, the question is how the maximum sustainable yield can be taken as efficiently as possible. This approach maximizes the food production from the sea, preserves its resources, protects employment opportunities, requires a relative minimum of data, is politically most acceptable and can to a large extent solve the problems of economic efficiency. It attempts to deal with the overcapitalization of marine fishing operations – a problem that occurs if a certain catch is taken by too much manpower and capital.

The reality of marine fisheries demonstrates that over-capitalization is a serious problem.[116] For example, it has been estimated that in the cod and haddock fisheries of the North Atlantic substantially the same catch can be taken with about one half to two thirds of the present fishing effort. If this surplus of manpower and capital could be employed elsewhere, it would produce a total catch close to half a million tons.[117] This catch would be taken at essentially no extra cost. It represents the loss caused by the overcapitalization of the North Atlantic cod and haddock fisheries. Other studies place these losses in the range between $50 and $100 million annually.[118] The North Pacific salmon and halibut fishery[119] and the Eastern Pacific tuna fishery also

[115]Christy, op. cit., note 74, p. 136.
[116]Commission on Marine Science, Engineering and Resources, op. cit., note 22, p. VIII–47. Kask, op. cit., note 34, p. 19. Crutchfield, op. cit., note 71, pp. 24–25. Christy, op. cit., note 95, p. 113.
[117]FAO, op. cit., note 27, p. 6.
[118]Commission on Marine Science, Engineering and Resources, op. cit., note 22, p. VIII–58. ICNAF, Annual Proceedings for the year 1966–1967, Dartmouth 1968, p. 56.
[119]J A Crutchfield and G Pontecorvo, The Pacific salmon fisheries. A study of irrational conservation, Baltimore 1969. Commission on Marine Science, Engineering and Resources, op. cit., note 21, p. 92. FAO, op. cit., note 27, p. 13.

suffer from the same problems. In fact, overcapitalization occurs in virtually all fisheries in which the total catch is limited. Such a limit can be caused by the factual unavailability of more fish, but it may also stem from an internationally agreed to catch limitation. In this situation competition forces nations and fishermen to apply more and more effort to the fishery in question.[120] The result is that the total available catch is taken in shorter and shorter periods of time. For the rest of the year, vessels must be used in fisheries for which they were not designed or must even be tied up in port.

The consequences of overcapitalization are not limited to the waste of manpower and capital, but they extend to the other problem areas of the international law of marine fisheries as well. This applies in particular to conservation. Since most conservation measures restrict fishing operations in one way or another, States have become very reluctant to accept such measures because they would aggravate existing overcapitalization problems. The ineffectiveness of many international fisheries organizations with respect to conservation is a direct result of this relationship. Accordingly, the problems of overcapitalization must be solved, not only because overcapitalization is undesirable, but also because such a solution is a prerequisite for dealing with other marine fisheries problems.

From these observations it will be clear that international fisheries organizations and the international law of marine fisheries are facing a formidable challenge with respect to the economic efficiency of fishing operations. The scope of this challenge is further enhanced by the fact that it is directly related to one of the most basic aspects of the freedom of

---

[120]D L McKernan, in *International fisheries regimes* (discussion), in *National policy recommendations*, L M Alexander ed., Kingston, RI 1970, p. 349. Christy, *op. cit.*, note 74, p. 136. Crutchfield, *op. cit.*, note 71, p. 24. FAO, *op. cit.*, note 27, p. 13.

fishing on the high seas: the fact that access to the living resources of the high seas is open to all nations and to all fishermen. It is this absence of controls over entry which is at the root of the overcapitalization problem. This implies that the challenge to the international law of marine fisheries with regard to economic efficiency involves its most fundamental principles. However, there are also some more positive aspects. A first point is that as far as economic efficiency is concerned, the interests of fishing nations and of the world community do not collide: inefficiency is equally disadvantageous to both. Consequently, the international law of marine fisheries is not required to balance these interests. A second and related point is that economic efficiency should not become a compulsory matter. It has been discussed that if a State fishes inefficiently, it does not gain at the expense of other nations. This means that in relation to economic efficiency the essential challenge to the international law of marine fisheries is to make it possible for States to rationalize their fisheries economically, without, however, forcing them to do so.

5. ALLOCATION

The term allocation refers to the distribution of the living resources of the sea among the nations of the world. Allocation is essentially concerned with the question of who obtains how much. The statistics point out that in the past not all nations have shared equally in marine fisheries and its expansion. Japan, the Soviet Union and Peru are examples of countries that have increased their catches more than proportionately. The established fishing nations of Western Europe and North America, on the other hand, maintained their relative position or have experienced a slight decline.[121] With the exception of Peru, distant water fishing nations have expanded their catches more rapidly than coastal water

[121] FAO, *op. cit.*, note 1, pp. a 4–12.

fishing nations.[122] This has resulted in a great deal of friction between these countries concerning matters of allocation. A similar confrontation exists between developing and developed States. In this respect the statistics are somewhat misleading. A comparison of total catches may give the impression that the catch of the developing nations has grown more rapidly than that of the developed countries. However, most of the increase in the total catch of the developing States must be attributed to a single State: Peru. The share of all other developing nations in the total world catch rose only from 22 per cent in 1958 to 23 per cent in 1968.[123] The developing nations consider this lack of progress unacceptable, particularly in view of the increasingly intensive distant water fisheries of some developed States in waters off their shores.[124]

The allocation of the living resources of the sea is determined by many factors. It is, first of all, fundamentally affected by the fact that the waters of the sea are divided into high seas and into waters subject to the exclusive fisheries jurisdiction of coastal States.[125] The resources in exclusive fishery waters may be harvested only by the coastal State concerned or by States which have its consent.[126] The living resources of the high seas, on the other hand, may be harvested by all States. Thus, by extending the limits of their exclusive fisheries jurisdiction, coastal States are capable of changing the allocation of the living resources of the sea to

[122]*Supra* pp. 35–36.
[123]Chapman, *op. cit.*, note 2, p. 1. Christy, *op. cit.*, note 46, pp. 464–465.
[124]FAO, *op. cit.*, note 43, p. 3.
[125]FAO, *Limits and status of the territorial sea, exclusive fishing zones, fishery conservation zones and the continental shelf*, FAO Legislative Series No. 8, Rome 1969. A more recent version is: FAO Fisheries Circular No. 127, Rome 1971.
[126]D W Windley, *International practice regarding traditional fishing privileges of foreign fishermen in zones of extended maritime jurisdiction*, *AJIL* 1969, pp. 490–503.

their own advantage.[127] The international conflicts provoked by such extensions attest to the importance of these problems. A second fundamental factor that influences allocation is the method by which the living resources of the high seas are apportioned among nations. In this matter there are essentially two alternatives.[128]

The most common method to allocate the living resources of the high seas is to let free competition among fishing nations determine the share of each nation. This approach is closely linked to the principle of freedom of fishing on the high seas, which allows all States to engage in high seas fishing operations.[129] The share of each State is a function of the extent to which it undertakes such operations. Thus, if a nation decides not to develop high seas fisheries, it does not share in the living resources of the high seas. Allocation on the basis of free competition is also closely linked to the problems of overcapitalization reviewed in the previous section. It is essentially competition for a limited quantity of resources that results in overcapitalization problems. It has already been mentioned that free competition may also lead to a further deprivation of the less resourceful countries, i.e., primarily the developing nations.[130]

The second method allocates the living resources of the high seas by international agreement.[131] This can be accomplished in two ways. First of all, it is possible to specify the amount of fishing effort that each State may apply to a fishery. For example, an international agreement can

[127]For a case study of such action, see Ministry for Foreign Affairs of Iceland, *Fisheries jurisdiction in Iceland*, Reykjavik 1972. M Davis, *Iceland extends its fisheries limits: a political analysis*, Oslo 1963.
[128]S Oda, *International law of the resources of the sea*, RdC 1969, vol. 127, p. 405. Oda, *op. cit.*, note 44, p. 30.
[129]It is implicitly adopted in the Convention on Fishing and Conservation of the Living Resources of the High Seas of Geneva 1958.
[130]Christy, *op. cit.*, note 46, p. 463. Oda, *op. cit.*, note 44, p. 29. See *supra* p. 44.
[131]Oda, *op. cit.*, note 40, pp. 65–81.

5

assign a certain number of standard fishing days to each State. Countries would not be allowed to exceed such a limit. However, this approach presents several problems. These originate primarily in the fact that differences in fishing techniques among nations and continuous changes in such techniques make it very difficult to find a standard for measuring fishing effort.[132] Even if such a standard could be found, it would have to be recalibrated frequently. Another difficulty is that the abundance of many stocks is subject to frequent changes and that fishing effort must reflect such changes.[133] This implies that it would be necessary to adjust frequently the effort allocated to a country. This may be difficult to achieve. Finally, allocation on the basis of effort would require a great amount of statistical information, which in many fisheries is not available.[134]

These difficulties explain why the second alternative for determining allocation by international agreement is much more widely accepted. In this approach fishing nations divide the total catch into national quotas. This avoids most of the problems associated with regulating effort;[135] it also is a more direct method. However, national quotas present several problems as well. The most important difficulty is that States are extremely reluctant to accept national quota schemes as long as new States can enter the fisheries to which they apply.[136] Here again, the problem is that under the

[132]J L Kask, *Marine Science Commission recommendations on international fisheries organization*, in *National policy recommendations*, L M Alexander ed., Kingston, RI 1970, p. 291. Crutchfield, *op. cit.*, note 45, p. 267. J A Gulland, *Fisheries management and the limitation of fishing*, FAO Fisheries Technical Paper No. 92, Rome 1969, p. 1. ICNAF, *Annual Proceedings for the year 1966–1967*, Dartmouth 1968, p. 56.
[133]Christy and Scott, *op. cit.*, note 2, p. 77.
[134]FAO, *op. cit.*, note 27, p. 14.
[135]Crutchfield, *op. cit.*, note 45. Commission on Marine Science, Engineering and Resources, *op. cit.*, note 22, p. VIII–64.
[136]Kask, *op. cit.*, note 132, p. 293. Crutchfield, *op. cit.*, note 45, p. 272. Commission on Marine Science, Engineering and Resources, *op. cit.*, note 22, p. VIII–63. Dodyk, *op. cit.*, note 2, pp. 117–118.

freedom of fishing outsiders can reap the benefits of limitations to which other States have committed themselves by international agreement. A second problem is that there are no accepted standards or criteria on which the allocation of the catch can be based.[137] Should allocation be based on past performance? If so, during which period? Should it reflect the special needs and problems of coastal fishing States? If so, to what extent? In the areas of conservation and economic efficiency there is a factual body of knowledge that suggests certain solutions. This is not the case with respect to national quota arrangements. Accordingly, such arrangements are almost exclusively the outcome of political bargaining.[138] In this process each State attempts to maximize its share. As a result, it is extremely difficult to reach agreement. A last problem is that it is essential to ensure that national quotas do not eliminate the incentives for technological innovation[139] and for further expansion of marine fisheries. For this reason, arrangements are necessary which require States to catch their quotas or to transfer them to other States if they are unable or unwilling to do this.[140]

[137]F T Christy, Jr., *Implications for fisheries of the US draft convention on the sea-bed*, paper at Marine Technology Society Symposium on the Law of the Sea: A Year of Crisis, February 1971, p. 13. Commission on Marine Science, Engineering and Resources, *op. cit.*, note 22, pp. VIII 59–60. Dodyk, *op. cit.*, note 2, p. 73, p. 149. F T Christy, Jr., in *A symposium on national interests in coastal waters*, in *Offshore boundaries and zones*, L M Alexander ed., Columbus, Ohio 1967, p. 128. FAO, *op. cit.*, note 27, pp. 13–14.
[138]G Pontecorvo, *Critique on national quotas for the North Atlantic fisheries: an exercise in second best*, in *International rules and organization for the sea*, L M Alexander ed., Kingston, RI 1969, p. 278. FAO, *op. cit.*, note 27, p. 13. S Oda, *Japan and international conventions relating to North Pacific fisheries*, *WLR* 1967, p. 73.
[139]J A Crutchfield, in *Exploitation of the living resources of the high seas* (discussion), in *International rules and organization for the sea*, L M Alexander ed., Kingston, RI 1969, p. 284.
[140]Crutchfield, *op. cit.*, note 45, p. 284. Commission on Marine Science, Engineering and Resources, *op. cit.*, note 22, p. VIII–59.

On the other hand, the advantages of agreement on national quotas would be considerable. Such an agreement would eliminate one of the most virulent sources of conflict among fishing nations. This would greatly alleviate the political confrontation among these nations, particularly between developing and developed fishing nations and between distant water fishing and coastal water fishing States. However, equally important is that agreement on national quotas would be an essential step towards solving other problems of the international law of marine fisheries,[141] especially those of overcapitalization. If fishing nations agree on national quotas, States are no longer forced to compete with each other since they know in advance what their share in the total catch will be.[142] This means that national quotas would enable States to use a minimum of manpower and capital in the fisheries to which such quotas apply, but that States would not be forced to rationalize their fisheries economically.[143] National quotas allow States to fish as inefficiently as other priorities might dictate. Thus, national quotas would solve the problems of overcapitalization outlined in the previous section to a very large extent. In its turn a solution to these problems has become a prerequisite for effective international action with respect to the conservation of the living resources of the high seas. Finally, by taking into account the special problems of developing States, national quotas could make a contribution towards preventing the further deprivation of these countries which could result from allocation on the basis of free competition.

Thus, the essential challenge to international fisheries

[141]Crutchfield, *op. cit.*, note 45, pp. 263–275.
[142]However, fishing nations may continue to compete for the best fishing grounds or the most productive species, see Norton, *op. cit.*, note 114, p. 333.
[143]Commission on Marine Science, Engineering and Resources, *op. cit.*, note 22, p. VIII–63. Crutchfield, *op. cit.*, note 48, p. 304. FAO, *op. cit.*, note 27, p. 13.

organizations and to the international law of marine fisheries with respect to allocation seems to be to work out arrangements for reaching agreement on national quotas, particularly in those fisheries which suffer from overcapitalization and which require conservation measures. This challenge is directly concerned with two fundamental characteristics of the freedom of fishing on the high seas: (1) that all States have access to the fisheries for the living resources of the high seas; and (2) that they must actually engage in such fishing operations in order to share in the wealth of these resources. It seems doubtful that the international law of marine fisheries can solve the problems of allocation without affecting these fundamental features of the freedom of fishing on the high seas. It is extremely difficult to create the conditions that are required for agreement on national quotas among the nations participating in specific fisheries as long as other States can freely enter these fisheries. At the same time, these other States can not give up their right to enter such fisheries, since it constitutes the only way in which they can share in their wealth. Consequently, a most important aspect of the challenge to the international law of marine fisheries in the area of allocation is to work out a distinction between access to fisheries and access to the wealth of the living resources of the high seas.[144] Such a distinction could allow nations with access to the fisheries to agree more easily on national quotas, particularly if other nations without access to the fisheries, but with continuing access to their wealth, would refrain from entering the fisheries in question.

6. RESEARCH

Decisions with respect to full utilization, with respect to conservation, with respect to economic efficiency and with respect to allocation require a great amount of information concerning all aspects of marine fisheries. A first task of

[144]Christy, *op. cit.*, note 46, pp. 463–467. Christy, *op. cit.*, note 95, p. 112.

fisheries research is to make the information available that is necessary for ensuring the rationality of the above decisions.[145] The term research is here being used in its widest possible meaning: it refers to the initial collection of statistical data, to their compilation and interpretation, to biological investigations, to studies concerning the economic aspects of marine fisheries, to legal and political studies, etc. Apart from improving the rationality of decisions, such research may also make regulatory measures much more acceptable to the nations concerned.[146] Therefore, the general functions of fisheries research can be defined as enhancing the rationality and acceptability of the decisions of States concerning the international regulation of marine fisheries.[147] Traditionally, research with respect to the living resources of the seas and their exploitation has been largely biological in nature. This reflects the fact that in the past full utilization and conservation were perceived as the most important questions of marine fisheries. Decisions with respect to these two problem areas require primarily biological information.[148] However, the realization of the importance of the problems of economic efficiency has resulted in a substantial increase in the number of studies concerning these aspects of marine fisheries; it also improved the work done from a legal or political angle. But these developments do not eliminate the fact that biological research is still predominant.

Generally, all research can be divided into two phases: (1) the collection of the basic data; and (2) the interpretation of such data. This distinction is of particular relevance to fisheries research. The collection of basic data concerning marine fisheries can be undertaken by the agencies of fishing nations. It is essentially a technical task without much room

[145]FAO, *op. cit.*, note 27, p. 3.
[146]Chapman, *op. cit.*, note 18, p. 446.
[147]Chapman, *op. cit.*, note 2, p. 45.
[148]*Supra* p. 47.

for subjective interpretation. In this first stage the need for international cooperation is largely limited to the standardization of methods and to the exchange of the collected data. However, additional problems arise in the second phase. The interpretation of basic data must be carried out in such a way that the objectivity of the conclusions is beyond question. Since the interests of fishing States are directly affected by these conclusions, it seems doubtful that this will be the case if this aspect of fisheries research is also entrusted to the agencies of these fishing States. Then, the only guarantee for the objectivity of the scientific conclusions lies in the professional integrity of the scientists involved.[149] Experience shows that this is a guarantee which should not be underestimated. Nevertheless, it seems desirable to handle this second phase of fisheries research internationally, rather than nationally. This could mean that an international forum of experts would interpret the basic information provided by the fishing States. Such an approach could add to the rationality and acceptability of decisions with respect to marine fisheries.[150] However, in reality not only the collection of data, but also their interpretation is primarily the responsibility of the agencies of fishing States. This is a first problem in the area of research.

A second problem is created by the increase in the number of States participating in marine fisheries. Most of these new fishing States are developing nations, which lack the facilities, experts and funds to undertake their own research.[151] This, first of all, hinders the collection of data. Secondly, since

[149]H Kasahara, *International arrangements for fisheries*, in *The United Nations and ocean management*, L M Alexander ed., Kingston, RI 1971, p. 42. Burke, *op. cit.*, note 48, p. 166.
[150]C B Lucas, *International fishery bodies of the North Atlantic*, Law of the Sea Institute, University of Rhode Island, Occasional Paper No. 5, April 1970, p. 18.
[151]FAO, *Report of the first session of the FAO Fishery Committee for the Eastern Central Atlantic (CECAF)*, FAO Fisheries Reports No. 69, Rome 1969, p. 4.

these developing States must rely to a large extent on the investigations of the developed States, credibility problems may arise,[152] particularly if the interests of the developed States differ from those of the developing nations. This fact supports the desirability of internationalizing research,[153] especially as far as the interpretation of data is concerned.

Financial considerations are the main reason why most fisheries research is carried out by the agencies of fishing States. As no State has unlimited financial resources, each State must decide for itself what its priorities are. The most important mechanism for making this decision is the national budget procedure. It is understandable that in the determination of this budget, national needs and national priorities have a much stronger voice than international needs and priorities.[154] Consequently, it is in most cases much more difficult to obtain funding for fisheries research of international bodies than for research of State agencies. This points out that if the international law of marine fisheries is to enhance internationally organized fisheries research, it must develop adequate procedures for its funding.

A final problem stems from the fact that fisheries research is a completely voluntary matter. There is no general obligation for fishing States to undertake certain investigations. If there is any obligation at all, it is based upon special agreements. The absence of such a general obligation is, obviously, no problem as long as research is in the self-interest of States. This is, for example, the case with research that would enable a State to develop new fisheries. However, not all fisheries investigations serve the self-interests of States, particularly if these interests are defined on a short range basis. An example is research which would most likely point

[152]Chapman, *op. cit.*, note 18, p. 453. J L Kask, *Present arrangements for fishery exploitation*, in *The future of the sea's resources*, L M Alexander ed., Kingston, RI 1968, p. 60.
[153]Chapman, *op. cit.*, note 18, p. 443. Kask, *op. cit.*, note 152, p. 60.
[154]Burke, *op. cit.*, note 87, pp. 80–81.

out that catches must be severely restricted. It may be in the short range interest of a State to delay such research for some time, because this could enable it to recover its investment in the fleet without embarrassment. Therefore, it is doubtful that the international law of marine fisheries can continue to respect this voluntary character of fisheries research.[155]

The foregoing outlines the challenge to the international law of marine fisheries in the area of research. Essentially, this challenge is to improve the quality of the information upon which decisions with respect to marine fisheries must be based. However, one *caveat* is in order. It will never be possible to obtain perfect knowledge and complete understanding. There will always be a certain lack of data and their interpretation will always leave room for different opinions. Therefore, the international law of marine fisheries should not require that decisions be supported by absolute scientific evidence. In most situations decisions based upon limited knowledge are better than no decisions at all.[156]

7. INTER-USE AND INTRA-USE CONFLICTS

Fisheries and navigation undoubtedly have the longest history of all human activities at sea. Activities of more recent origin range from oil exploration and exploitation to oceanographic research, from underseas cables to naval manoeuvres, from the dumping of solid waste to the mining of diamonds. This range of uses continues to expand: in the future it may include offshore power stations, global ocean monitoring systems and offshore cities. All these uses of the sea interact with each other. This creates the possibility of inter-use

[155]FAO, *Report of the fifth session of the Advisory Committee on Marine Resources Research*, FAO Fisheries Reports No. 56, Rome 1968, p. 12.
[156]FAO, *op. cit.*, note 29, p. 2. Crutchfield, *op. cit.*, note 39, p. 347. W C Herrington, *The future of the Geneva Convention on Fishing and the Conservation of the Living Resources of the Sea*, in *The future of the sea's resources*, L M Alexander ed., Kingston, RI 1968, p. 64. FAO, *op. cit.*, note 27, p. 3.

conflicts, which may involve marine fisheries as well.[157] Such conflicts may also occur, not between different uses, but within the same use.[158] For example, fishing with fixed gear is largely incompatible with mobile gear fishing. As fishermen have a substantial investment in their equipment, damage to it may provoke serious incidents at sea. The likelihood of these inter-use and intra-use conflicts is increased by the fact that most activities at sea take place in the continental shelf areas. The exploration and exploitation of the oil and other mineral resources of the sea are primarily concerned with the resources of the continental shelf, while ocean navigation converges in these areas in order to reach its destination. Marine fisheries are also concentrated here since most commercially attractive stocks are to be found in relatively shallow waters.

There are several possibilities for minimizing use conflicts. One option is to separate the various uses spatially.[159] The special navigation routes in the Gulf of Mexico, for example, assign different areas to navigation and oil exploitation. However, such an approach presents several problems. First of all, most activities at sea require a large degree of mobility. This is self-evident for navigation and fisheries, but even oil exploitation must be able to move from one location to the other. A second problem is that it will be extremely difficult to reach international agreement on the spatial separation of ocean uses, even if this arrangement were limited to specific areas only. Finally, such a complete physical separation

[157]M B Schaefer, *The resources of the seabed and prospective rates of development as a basis of planning for international management*, in *The United Nations and ocean management*, L M Alexander ed., Kingston, RI 1971, p. 97. L Wakefield, *Fishing interests on the shelf*, in *International rules and organization for the sea*, L M Alexander ed., Kingston, RI 1969, p. 230.
[158]Dodyk, *op. cit.*, note 2, p. 24.
[159]FAO, *Technical Conference on Marine Pollution and Its Effect on Living Resources and Fishing 1970. Conclusions and recommendations as approved*, Document FIR:MP/70/Rec., Rev. 1, Rome 1971, p. 5.

might be unnecessary or undesirable,[160] in which case more flexible alternatives can be followed. In the Gulf of Mexico, for example, fisheries and oil exploitation proved to be quite compatible. Accordingly, if problems did occur, they were accommodated without a spatial separation.

One of the most important sources for inter-use conflicts involving marine fisheries is marine pollution.[161] It has been stated earlier that the changes in the marine environment that result from pollution may have strong effects on the living resources of the high seas. It is quite possible that the extent to which marine pollution can be brought under control is the single most important factor in determining the future of marine fisheries.[162] This applies to pollution originating at sea, but also to pollution originating on land and reaching the sea *via* rivers or the air.

What is the challenge to international fisheries organizations and to the international law of marine fisheries as far as use conflicts are concerned? With respect to conflicts between different forms of marine fisheries, this challenge is to work out arrangements for avoiding such conflicts and for settling them if they occur. However, with respect to those inter-use conflicts that involve marine fisheries, the challenge is less obvious. It is the international law of the sea in general, rather than the international law of marine fisheries, which must deal with this issue. It is beyond doubt that the international law of the sea must develop prescriptions which are more specific than the existing rules and principles, *e.g.*, that States must exercise the freedom of the high seas with reasonable regard for the interests of other States.[163] The

[160]M B Schaefer, in *Competing demands on the shelf* (discussion), in *International rules and organization for the sea*, L M Alexander ed., Kingston, RI 1969, p. 250. Wakefield, *op. cit.*, note 157, p. 231.
[161]Moore, *op. cit.*, note 14. Jackson, *op. cit.*, note 14.
[162]Jackson, *op. cit.*, note 14, p. 1.
[163]Art. 2 Convention on the High Seas of Geneva 1958, *UNTS* vol. 450, p. 82.

international law of marine fisheries and international fisheries organizations could contribute to the formulation of such new rules and principles concerning inter-use conflicts. For example, international fisheries organizations could collect information on those conflicts which involve marine fisheries, particularly between fisheries and marine pollution. To this end, they could participate in the monitoring and evaluation of the impact of pollution on the living resources of the high seas. This would also enable these organizations to articulate the interests of marine fisheries in the more general accommodation of inter-use conflicts by the international law of the sea.

Chapter II

A Chronology of International Fisheries Organizations

International fisheries organizations[1] did not come into existence on the basis of a logically consistent overall design. They appeared over the years as and when States became aware of the need for international cooperation. Thus, the historical development of these organizations is characterized by piecemeal and often *ad hoc* responses to specific problems of marine fisheries. The following sections, which review the history of international fisheries organizations, will clearly demonstrate this characteristic.

1. THE INTERNATIONAL COUNCIL FOR THE EXPLORATION OF THE SEA

After 1850 many countries of Northern Europe developed large, mechanized fishing fleets, which led to a significant expansion of fishing operations in the North Sea and its adjacent waters. This resulted in a series of problems which, among other things, convinced the States in question of the need for joint investigations. After preliminary conferences

[1] Only inter-governmental organizations concerned with marine fisheries will be reviewed; for a survey of such organizations, see FAO, *Report on regulatory fishery bodies*, FAO Fisheries Circular No. 138, Rome 1972, pp. 27–31. W M Chapman, *The theory and practice of international fishery development-management*, San Diego Law Review 1970, pp. 408–455. J L Kask, *Present arrangements for fishery exploitation*, in *The future of the sea's resources*, L M Alexander ed., Kingston, RI 1968, pp. 56–62. FAO, *The management of fishery resources*, Rome 1967, pp. 27–29. For a collection of fisheries agreements, see *Treaties and other international agreements on oceanographic resources, fisheries, and wildlife to which the United States is a party*, by the Legislative Reference Service of the Library of Congress for the use of the Committee on Commerce of the United States Senate, Washington 1970.

in Stockholm (1899) and Christiania (1901), an International Council for the Exploration of the Sea was formally established in Copenhagen in 1902.[2] Although the Statutes of the International Council have been changed from time to time, the Council's functions throughout its existence have been to encourage and coordinate the scientific research of the member States; only occasionally did it conduct its own investigations. The International Council was for a long time a somewhat informally organized body, which could function efficiently through its close contacts with the scientific community in the member States. After World War II it became clear that a more formal organization was desirable. On 12 September 1964 a new Convention for the International Council for the Exploration of the Sea was signed in Copenhagen.[3] It entered into force on 22 July 1968. The present members of the International Council are: Belgium, Canada, Denmark, the Federal Republic of Germany, Finland, France, Iceland, Ireland, Italy, the Netherlands, Norway, Poland, Portugal, Spain, Sweden, the United Kingdom and the USSR; the United States has not yet acted upon a decision in principle to join ICES. The Council's headquarters are in Copenhagen.

Under the new Convention the functions of the International Council are: (1) to promote research for the study

[2]Hereinafter referred to as International Council or ICES; for more information, see C E Lucas, *International fishery bodies of the North Atlantic*, Law of the Sea Institute, University of Rhode Island, Occasional Paper No. 5, April 1970, pp. 2–13. *Panel reports of the Commission on Marine Science, Engineering and Resources*, vol. 3, *Marine resources and legal-political arrangements for their development*, Washington 1969, pp. VIII 148–149. United Nations Economic and Social Council, *Non-United Nations intergovernmental organizations*, UN Doc. E/4487, annex XII, 24 April 1968, pp. 2–10. FAO, *International fisheries bodies*, FAO Fisheries Technical Paper No. 64, Rome 1966, p. 18. D M Johnston, *The international law of marine fisheries. A framework for policy-oriented inquiries*, New Haven and London 1965, pp. 91–92. M K Whiteman, *Digest of international law*, vol. 4, Washington 1965, pp. 1070–1072.
[3]*ILM* 1968, p. 302.

of the sea, particularly with respect to the living resources; (2) to draw up research programmes; and (3) to publish the results. It is concerned with the Atlantic Ocean, but particularly with the North Atlantic. The International Council conducts its business through a number of committees and working groups; at present there are twelve standing committees, each of which deals with a specific subject or with a specific area. A Consultative Committee coordinates the activities of these committees. This structure has enabled ICES to draw a great number of scientists into its work. In addition to the various committees, ICES has a Bureau, which has certain executive functions, and a Secretariat with about eighteen full-time officers. The Council cooperates very closely with a great number of other international organizations, particularly with the North-East Atlantic Fisheries Commission. Apart from its general function of coordinating the marine and fisheries research programmes of its members, the Council's main activities are: (1) the collection and publication of hydrographical data; (2) the standardization of research methods and instruments; (3) the collection and publication of statistical information concerning the fisheries of the member States; and (4) the publication of a wide variety of studies. One of the Council's publications – the *Journal du Conseil* – is a leading journal in its field. It is generally agreed that within its terms of reference the International Council has been a very successful organization. It has made a most impressive contribution to marine science.

2. THE INTERNATIONAL COMMISSION FOR THE SCIENTIFIC EXPLORATION OF THE MEDITERRANEAN SEA, AND, THE NORTH AMERICAN COUNCIL OF FISHERY INVESTIGATIONS

The success of ICES led to the creation of similar research organizations elsewhere. In 1919 an International Commission for the Scientific Exploration of the Mediterranean Sea[4] was established in Madrid in order to promote oceanographic and biological studies in the Mediterranean. Although the organization still exists and although most Mediterranean States are members, it never achieved the success of ICES. The General Fisheries Council for the Mediterranean has in fact taken over most of its work. A second organization inspired by ICES was the North American Council on Fishery Investigations,[5] which was founded in 1920 by Canada, Newfoundland and the United States. This organization was discontinued in 1938, but it laid the foundation for the International Commission for the Northwest Atlantic Fisheries.

3. THE INTERNATIONAL PACIFIC HALIBUT COMMISSION

The construction of a transcontinental railway system in the United States resulted in such a rapid expansion of the Canadian and American halibut fisheries in the Pacific that even before World War I it was clear that these fisheries had to be restricted in order to protect the stocks. After several unsuccessful attempts, the United States and Canada on 2 March 1923 reached agreement on a Convention for the Preservation of the Halibut Fishery of the Northern Pacific Including Bering Sea, which entered into force on 21 October 1924.[6] It made provision for a closed winter season, and it established an International Fisheries Commission. The powers of this Commission were broadened by a Convention of 1930 and by a third Convention of 1937.[7] After World War II a new Convention for the Preservation of the Halibut Fishery of the Northern Pacific Ocean and Bering

[4]FAO, op. cit., note 2, p. 30. Whiteman, op. cit., note 2, pp. 1073–1074.
[5]Whiteman, op. cit., note 2, p. 1072.
[6]LNTS vol. 32, p. 94.
[7]Ibidem, vol. 121, p. 46.

Sea was signed by the United States and Canada on 2 March 1953 in Ottawa;[8] it entered into force on 28 October 1953. Under this Convention the International Fisheries Commission was renamed the International Pacific Halibut Commission.[9]

Throughout its history the Halibut Commission has been responsible not only for investigating the stocks of halibut and the halibut fishery, but also for making proposals to the two member States with regard to the regulation of this fishery. It is one of the few international fisheries organizations that employs its own independent international staff. This staff conducts the necessary investigations and submits regulatory proposals to the Commission. In 1970 it consisted of about nine full-time scientists. The Halibut Commission

[8] *UNTS* vol. 222, p. 78.

[9] Hereinafter referred to as Halibut Commission or IPHC; for more information, see F H Bell, *Agreements, conventions and treaties between Canada and the United States of America with respect to the Pacific halibut fishery*, Report of the International Pacific Halibut Commission No. 50, Seattle 1969. Commission on Marine Science, Engineering and Resources, *op. cit.*, note 2, pp. VIII 136–138. D L Alverson, *Fishery resources in the Northeast Pacific Ocean*, in *The future of the fishing industry of the United States*, Seattle 1968, pp. 86–102. F H Bell, *The Pacific halibut*, in *The future of the fishing industry of the United States*, Seattle 1968, pp. 272–274. J A Crutchfield, *Management of the North Pacific fisheries: economic objectives and issues*, *WLR* 1967, pp. 283–307. FAO, *op. cit.*, note 2, p. 35. R W Johnson, *Fishery developments in the Pacific*, in British Institute of International and Comparative Law, *Developments in the law of the sea 1958–1964*, London 1965, pp. 135–150. Johnston, *op. cit.*, note 2, pp. 374–384. Whiteman, *op. cit.*, note 2, pp. 1017–1020, pp. 1076–1077. R Van Cleve and R W Johnson, *Management of the high seas fisheries of the Northeastern Pacific*, Seattle 1963. S I Shumun, *Pacific fishery conservation conventions. A comparison of organizational structures*, *Sydney Law Review* 1958, pp. 436–459. H A Dunlop, *Management of the halibut fishery of the North-Eastern Pacific Ocean and Bering Sea*, in *Papers presented at the International Technical Conference on the Conservation of the Living Resources of the Sea*, Rome 1955, pp. 222–243. J Tomasevich, *International agreements on conservation of marine resources with special reference to the North Pacific*, Stanford 1943. P C Jessup, *The Pacific coast fisheries*, *AJIL* 1939, pp. 129–138. J W Bingham, *Report on the international law of Pacific coastal fisheries*, Stanford 1938; and IPHC, *Annual Reports*, 1954 – .

6

has been quite successful in rebuilding the stocks of halibut. In 1931 the total catch was 44 million pounds; in 1962 it had increased to more than 75 million pounds.[10] The Commission estimates that at a total expense of $3 million, it prevented a loss to the fishermen of both countries of at least $100 million.[11]

The Halibut Commission is being criticized on the grounds that it has dealt only with conservation problems and that it has done nothing to prevent the overcapitalization of the fisheries. It has been asserted that the potential gains from regulation have been completely wasted by inefficiency and overcapitalization.[12] A second problem is that in recent years trawling operations for other species have become a threat to the halibut stocks. This undermines the conservation programmes of the Commission. Nevertheless, the Halibut Commission can be considered one of the most successful regulatory fishery bodies. However, its success is largely based upon a combination of rather unique factors: (1) the Commission has its own staff; (2) it has only two members, which, in addition, have a tradition of close cooperation; (3) it is concerned with one species only; (4) the Commission receives active support from the fishing industry; and (5) the Commission started with a non-controversial task: to rebuild a resource which was in obvious danger.

4. THE INTERNATIONAL PACIFIC SALMON FISHERIES COMMISSION

The decline of the Fraser River salmon fisheries after 1913 convinced Canada and the United States of the need for

[10]IPHC, *Regulation and investigation of the Pacific halibut fishery in 1963*, Seattle 1964, p. 5.

[11]*Ibidem, 1961*, Seattle 1962, p. 7.

[12]F T Christy, Jr.,*The distribution of the sea's wealth in fisheries*, in *Offshore boundaries and zones*, L M Alexander ed., Columbus, Ohio 1967, pp. 106–122. J A Crutchfield and A Zellner, *Economic aspects of the Pacific halibut fishery*, Fishery Industrial Research, Washington 1963.

joint investigations to answer the question of why sockeye salmon failed to return to the Fraser River in the usual numbers.[13] Between 1920 and 1930 the two countries drafted several agreements, but did not ratify them. Finally, on 28 July 1937 a Convention for the Protection, Preservation and Extension of the Sockeye Salmon Fishery of the Fraser River system entered into force.[14] This Convention was originally signed on 26 May 1930 at Washington, but a supplementary agreement had to be signed in 1934 before the United States Senate was willing to approve it.[15] The 1930 Convention established an International Pacific Salmon Fisheries Commission.[16] The initial responsibility of the Salmon Commission was to investigate the causes for the post-1913 decline of the Fraser River sockeye salmon fishery. These investigations pointed out that a landslide caused by railroad construction in 1913 made it impossible for certain salmon species to reach their spawning grounds. After the removal of this obstruction in 1944 and 1945, the Salmon Commission made for the first time regulatory proposals in 1946. Throughout

[13]Salmon is an anadromous species which spends most of its life cycle at sea, but which returns to fresh water for spawning.
[14]*LNTS* vol. 184, p. 306.
[15]IPSFC, *Annual Report 1946*, New Westminster 1947, p. 10.
[16]Hereinafter referred to as Salmon Commission or IPSFC; for more information, see Chapman, *op. cit.*, note 1, p. 425. J A Crutchfield and G Pontecorvo, *The Pacific salmon fisheries. A study of irrational conservation*, Baltimore 1969. Commission on Marine Science, Engineering and Resources, *op. cit.*, note 2, pp. VIII 138–141. Alverson, *op. cit.*, note 9. Crutchfield, *op. cit.*, note 9. FAO, *op. cit.*, note 2, p. 36. Johnson, *op. cit.*, note 9. Johnston, *op. cit.*, note 2, pp. 386–390. W F Thompson, *Fishing treaties and salmon of the North Pacific*, *Science* 1965, pp. 1786–1789. Whiteman, *op. cit.*, note 2, pp. 1013–1016, p. 1076. Van Cleve and Johnson, *op. cit.*, note 9. Shuman, *op. cit.*, note 9. L A Royal, *The international Fraser River sockeye salmon fishery*, in *Papers presented at the International Technical Conference on the Conservation of the Living Resources of the Sea*, Rome 1955, pp. 243–256. Tomasevich, *op. cit.*, note 9. J A Craig and R H Hacker, *The history and development of the fisheries of the Columbia River*, Washington 1940. Jessup, *op. cit.*, note 9. Bingham, *op. cit.*, note 9; and IPSFC, *Annual Reports*, 1939 – .

its existence, these proposals have been designed to accomplish two objectives: (1) to ensure an adequate escapement of salmon to the spawning grounds; and (2) to divide the allowable catch equally between the fishermen of the two countries. Since 1957 the IPSFC is also responsible for pink salmon.

The Salmon Commission differs in many respects from other international fisheries organizations. First of all, it is almost exclusively concerned with the regulation of fisheries in internal and territorial waters. However, the migratory characteristics of salmon make it virtually impossible to separate these fisheries from high seas salmon fisheries. Secondly, the Salmon Commission is one of the few organizations with the explicit responsibility of allocating the catch between the fishermen of the two member States. Thirdly, it has the unique power to make certain decisions that are directly binding on the fishermen. Generally, decisions of fisheries organizations must be implemented by the member States in order to become binding. Finally, this Commission is also one of the few fishery bodies with an independent international research staff. In 1970 it employed more than fifty scientists.

The Salmon Commission has been quite successful in rebuilding the stocks of Fraser River sockeye salmon. The Commission estimates that its work has resulted in an annual increase of the catch worth approximately $9 million to the fishermen. [17] However, the Salmon Commission has been criticized on the same grounds as the Halibut Commission: it, too, has not dealt with questions of economic efficiency and overcapitalization. [18] Other problems confronting the Commission result from the industrial development of the Fraser River region – logging, industrial pollution, municipal sewage and hydro-electric dams are to a large extent incom-

[17]IPSFC, *Annual Report 1968*, New Westminster 1969, p. 5.
[18]Crutchfield and Pontecorvo, *op. cit.*, note 16.

patible with salmon. The Salmon Commission is reviewing the effects of these developments on the salmon stocks.

5. THE NORTH PACIFIC FUR SEAL COMMISSION

The second part of the nineteenth century witnessed a great deal of conflict among the nations participating in the capture of fur seals in the North Pacific.[19] These disputes were concerned in particular with the extent of the waters in which the United States could prohibit the killing of seals. The Bering Sea Arbitration of 1893 between the United States and Great Britain (on behalf of Canada) dealt primarily with this issue, but the arbitral award also made provision for a joint regulation of fur seal operations. In 1911 Great Britain, Japan, Russia and the United States signed a Convention for the Preservation and Protection of Fur Seals.[20] This Convention produced most favourable results[21] until it was terminated by Japan in 1940. After World War II preliminary investigations to assess the relationship between fur seals and commercially valuable fish led to the Interim Convention on the Conservation of North Pacific Fur Seals, which was signed on 9 February 1957 in Washington by Canada, Japan, the United States and the USSR.[22] It entered into force on 14 October 1957, and it was extended with amendments in 1963 and 1969.[23]

In many respects the 1957 Convention follows the same approach as the 1911 Convention. It prohibits the capture of fur seals at sea (pelagic sealing); it makes the United States and the USSR responsible for regulating the exploitation of the herds on their respective islands; and it compensates Canada and Japan for their losses from the prohibition of

[19]Johnston, *op. cit.*, note 2, pp. 205–212.
[20]*British and Foreign State Papers*, vol. 104, p. 175.
[21]The herds on Pribilof Island, for example, had already doubled in size in 1916.
[22]*UNTS* vol. 314, p. 106.
[23]*Ibidem*, vol. 494, p. 303.

pelagic sealing by providing that the United States and the USSR must each deliver a certain number of skins to these two countries. However, the 1957 Convention differs from the 1911 Convention in one important aspect: it established a North Pacific Fur Seal Commission.[24] The main responsibilities of this Commission are the coordination of the research programmes of the member States, which are designed to find the herds' maximum sustainable yield. It also determines the number of seals to be taken at sea for research purposes. Finally, since the amendment of the Convention in 1963, the Commission studies the question of whether or not pelagic sealing should be permitted again.

These arrangements with respect to fur sealing are unique, particularly since two countries – Japan and Canada – share in the wealth of the seal resources without engaging in their harvest. It is the only case in which the international law of marine fisheries has separated access to the wealth of a resource from access to the harvest of such a resource. This arrangement has been quite successful: it has worked to the satisfaction of the four Contracting Parties and it has resulted in the restoration of the most important Asian as well as Alaskan fur seal herds.[25] No other international conservation agreement has functioned so effectively for so many years.[26] However, this success is based upon a number of unique factors. First of all, fur seal operations no longer involve private entrepreneurs, but are carried out by government agencies. This greatly facilitates their regulation. Secondly,

[24]Hereinafter referred to as Fur Seal Commission or NPFSC; for more information, see Chapman, *op. cit.*, note 1, pp. 420–422. Commission on Marine Science, Engineering and Resources, *op. cit.*, note 2, pp. VIII 116–120. FAO, *op. cit.*, note 2, p. 39. Johnston, *op. cit.*, note 2, pp. 264–269. Whiteman, *op. cit.*, note 2, pp. 1042–1048, p. 1084; and NPFSC, *Annual Reports*, 1958 – . For Rules of Procedure, see NPFSC, *Report of the first meeting*, Washington, DC 1958, Appendix 4.
[25]D L McKernan, *International fishery policy and the US fishing industry*, in *The future of the fishing industry of the United States*, Seattle 1968, p. 2.
[26]Chapman, *op. cit.*, note 1, p. 422.

although there are no formal barriers, no new States have attempted to enter the fur seal business in the Northeast Pacific, primarily because of its modest financial and economic value. This absence of new entrants is probably the most important factor in the continued viability of the fur seal arrangements. It is likely that the 1957 Convention would be discontinued if new States would succeed in beginning fur seal operations.

6. THE INTERNATIONAL WHALING COMMISSION

Already prior to World War II several species of whales were in need of protection. The League of Nations was the first organization to initiate action, but its efforts in 1924 and 1927 failed to produce results. The first agreement with regard to whaling was reached in 1931.[27] Although this agreement was revised in 1937, 1938 and 1939, it did not result in an effective protection of whales.[28] The suspension of operations during World War II gave the Antarctic whaling nations additional time for working out adequate arrangements. In 1944 they were able to reach agreement on a seasonal limit of 16,000 blue whale units for all waters south of 40° South latitude. One blue whale unit was equal to: one blue whale, two fin whales, two and a half humpback whales, or six sei whales. This total catch limit for Antarctic pelagic whaling became part of the International Convention for the Regulation of Whaling, which was signed on 2 December 1946 in Washington.[29] It entered into force on 10 November 1948. The Convention established

[27]*LNTS* vol. 155, p. 351.
[28]Johnston, *op. cit.*, note 2, pp. 396–401. L L Leonard, *Recent negotiations toward the international regulation of whaling*, *AJIL* 1941, pp. 30–113. P C Jessup, *The international protection of whales*, *AJIL* 1930, pp. 751–752. A Raestad, *La chasse à la baleine en mer libre*, *Revue de Droit International* 1928, pp. 595–642.
[29]*UNTS* vol. 161, p. 74.

the International Whaling Commission.[30] The present members of the Commission are: Argentina, Australia, Canada, Denmark, France, Iceland, Japan, Mexico, Norway, Panama, South Africa, the United Kingdom, the United States and the USSR.

The major responsibilities of the Whaling Commission throughout its existence have been to propose amendments to the Whaling Convention and to promote the scientific investigations of the member States. A Schedule attached to, but part of, the Convention contains the international regulations that apply to whaling. The 1946 Convention made the Commission responsible for protecting the stocks by keeping these regulations up-to-date. Fisheries organizations preceding the IWC were established to achieve essentially non-controversial tasks: to promote research (ICES) or to rebuild stocks which had been depleted (IPHC and IPSFC). Under the 1946 Convention the Whaling Commission was concerned with the *prevention* of overfishing. Here, the interests of nations do not coincide. Accordingly, the Whaling Commission was the first international fisheries organization to deal with problems that were inherently controversial in nature.

Many observers consider the Whaling Commission the apex of failure in the international regulation of marine

[30]Hereinafter referred to as Whaling Commission or IWC; for more information, see J L McHugh, *Role and history of the International Whaling Commission*, Woodrow Wilson International Center for Scholars, Washington 1971. Chapman, *op. cit.*, note 1, pp. 427–430. Commission on Marine Science, Engineering and Resources, *op. cit.*, note 2, pp. VIII 122–126. FAO, *op. cit.*, note 2, pp. 21–22. Johnston, *op. cit.*, note 2, pp. 396–411. Whiteman, *op. cit.*, note 2, pp. 1048–1070, pp. 1084–1085. S Oda, *International control of sea resources*, Leyden 1963, pp. 78–82. P. Hansen, *The importance of conservation of stocks of fish and sea mammals in Arctic waters*, in *Papers presented at the International Technical Conference on the Conservation of the Living Resources of the Sea*, Rome 1955, pp. 322–326. R Kellogg, *The International Whaling Commission*, in *Papers presented at the International Technical Conference on the Conservation of the Living Resources of the Sea*, Rome 1955, pp. 243–256; and IWC, *Annual Reports*, 1950 – .

fisheries and there is much which supports this view. Soon after the first meeting of the Commission in 1949, it became clear that the total catch limit for Antarctic pelagic whaling of 16,000 units was excessively high. Nevertheless, the Whaling Commission was unable to reduce this limit substantially until 1965.[31] At that time, some stocks had been depleted to such an extent that it was feared that they would never recover. The major obstacle to a more timely reduction of the catch limit was the fact that such a reduction would prevent the whaling companies from recovering their investment in modern fishing vessels. A 1962 Agreement in which the Antarctic whaling countries divided the total allowable catch into national quotas was a first step in removing this obstacle.[32] However, the Agreement came after a serious crisis: Norway and the Netherlands withdrew temporarily from the Commission, which in order to prevent its collapse even suspended all quota limitations for two seasons.[33] Other factors which induced the Antarctic whaling countries to accept a substantial reduction of the catch were the improved scientific knowledge of the resource and the influence of public opinion. In 1960 the Whaling Commission appointed a group of three independent scientists to assess the condition of the stocks. Their reports, which clearly demonstrated that most whale stocks in the Antarctic were seriously overharvested, laid the foundation for the 1963 and 1965 quota reductions. Since 1965 the IWC has generally succeeded in limiting catches to scientifically acceptable levels.

It is beyond any doubt that until 1965 the Whaling Commission was one of the most ineffective international fisheries organizations. However, the main reason for its inability to prevent the overharvesting of the resource was the unwillingness of the whaling States, especially those involved in An-

[31]IWC, *Seventeenth Report of the Commission*, London 1967, p. 20.
[32]*UNTS* vol. 486, p. 264.
[33]IWC, *Twelfth Report of the Commission*, London 1961, p. 17.

tarctic pelagic operations, to accept effective conservation measures. Like all such bodies, the IWC can only do what its members allow it to do. Consequently, these nations, rather than the IWC as such, are responsible for the overharvesting of whales. It is also true that the Commission's activities were never completely inconsequential. Otherwise, there would not have been a number of countries that have consistently refused to join the Commission. [34] Moreover, throughout its existence, the IWC has been required to function under a Convention with a number of serious weaknesses. Among these are: (1) the fact that the IWC must regulate whaling on the basis of artificial blue whale units, rather than on the basis of individual stocks; and (2) the fact that it has no authority with respect to a most fundamental problem of whaling: the allocation of the catch. [35] In view of these constitutional limitations it is clear that the IWC deserves particular credit for functioning effectively since 1965. A last relevant consideration is that the mere fact that there existed a Whaling Commission gave world public opinion a channel through which it could influence the whaling nations. Without such a channel, it would have been much more difficult to persuade these nations to accept a reduction of the total catch. Therefore, it is evident that without the Whaling Commission whales would have been brought much closer to total extinction.

7. THE NORTH-EAST ATLANTIC FISHERIES COMMISSION

On 5 April 1946 the fishing nations of Northern Europe signed a Convention for the Regulation of the Meshes of Fishing Nets and the Size Limits of Fish. [36] Its objective was to prevent the catch of young and immature fish. To accomplish this, the Convention made provision for minimum

[34]Chapman, *op. cit.*, note 1, p. 429.
[35]*Infra* p. 204.
[36]*UNTS* vol. 231, p. 200.

mesh sizes and for a minimum size for specific species. A Permanent Commission was established to administer these provisions. However, this Convention proved to be unsatisfactory, primarily because it was an obstacle to the development of fisheries for smaller species.[37] A new Convention was signed on 24 January 1959 in London. This North-East Atlantic Fisheries Convention entered into force on 27 June 1963.[38] It established the North-East Atlantic Fisheries Commission.[39] Present members of NEAFC are: Belgium, Denmark, France, the Federal Republic of Germany, Iceland, Ireland, the Netherlands, Norway, Poland, Portugal, Spain, Sweden, the United Kingdom and the USSR. The North-East Atlantic Commission is concerned with all species and all fisheries in its area of competence. In this respect it differs from the commissions discussed in the previous sections, which are responsible for one species only. The North-East Atlantic Commission may make recommendations to its member States for the general purpose of achieving a rational exploitation of the fisheries in the North-East Atlantic. These recommendations continue to be primarily concerned with minimum mesh size and minimum fish size regulations. In formulating its proposals the Commission relies on the International Council for scientific advice. This is the reason why the North-East Atlantic Commission is one of the few international fisheries organizations with no explicit responsibilities concerning fisheries research.

[37]Lucas, *op. cit.*, note 2, p. 14.
[38]*UNTS* vol. 486, p. 158.
[39]Hereinafter referred to as North-East Atlantic Commission or NEAFC; for more information, see Lucas, *op. cit.*, note 2, pp. 13–18, FAO, *op. cit.*, note 2, pp. 23–24. Johnston, *op. cit.*, note 2, pp. 361–365. Whiteman, *op. cit.*, note 2, pp. 977–981, pp. 1072–1073. L M Alexander, *Offshore geography of Northwestern Europe: the political and economic problems of delimitation and control*, Chicago 1963; and NEAFC, *Annual Reports*, 1964 – . For Rules of Procedure, see NEAFC, *Report of the seventh meeting*, London 1969, pp. 76–79.

The North-East Atlantic Commission has not been as successful as the International Council. In some fisheries it did not succeed in limiting catches to the level of maximum sustainable yield. As a result, several stocks have been seriously overfished. One of the weaknesses of the Commission is that it does not yet have the power to make recommendations with regard to national quotas, although agreement with respect to the allocation of the catch seems to be a prerequisite for agreement on the conservation of several species for which it is responsible. The Commission has proposed that it be given more adequate powers in this area.[40] A similar situation exists regarding the overcapitalization of the fisheries of the North-East Atlantic. The Commission may discuss these problems, but it lacks adequate powers concerning the regulation of effort. NEAFC has also requested additional authority in this respect. On the other hand, many NEAFC fisheries have produced steadily increasing yields, while the formulation of an arrangement for the joint enforcement of its regulations is also an accomplishment of the Commission.

8. THE INTERNATIONAL COMMISSION FOR THE NORTHWEST ATLANTIC FISHERIES

An International Convention for the Northwest Atlantic Fisheries was signed on 8 February 1949 at Washington[41] and came into force on 3 July 1950. It established the International Commission for the Northwest Atlantic Fisheries.[42]

[40]NEAFC, *Report of the eighth meeting*, London 1970, p. 12.
[41]*UNTS* vol. 157, p. 158.
[42]Hereinafter referred to as Northwest Atlantic Commission or ICNAF; for more information, see W L Sullivan, *A warning: the decline of international fisheries management looking particularly at the North Atlantic Ocean*, in *The United Nations and ocean management*, L M Alexander ed., Kingston, RI 1971, pp. 43–49. Chapman, *op. cit.*, note 1, pp. 434–437. A Laing, in *International fisheries regimes* (panel), in *National policy recommendations*, L M Alexander ed., Kingston, RI 1970, pp. 324–326.

Continued on next page

Its present members are: Canada, Denmark, France, the Federal Republic of Germany, Iceland, Italy, Japan, Norway, Poland, Portugal, Romania, Spain, the United Kingdom, the United States and the USSR. ICNAF's functions are essentially a combination of those of the International Council and the North-East Atlantic Commission. With respect to research the Northwest Atlantic Commission is responsible for obtaining and collating the necessary information. The Commission could have employed its own research staff, but decided instead to rely on the investigations of the member States.[43] Accordingly, throughout its existence, the Commission has restricted its role in research to the development of programmes, to the coordination of the national participation in these programmes and to the publication of the results. This research work provides the basis for the second function of ICNAF: the regulation of the fisheries in the Northwest Atlantic. ICNAF must keep the stocks of fish in its area of competence at a level which permits their maximum sustainable yield. The Commission may recommend certain regulatory measures to its member States in order to achieve this. Until recently, these measures were primarily minimum mesh size regulations.

The Northwest Atlantic Commission has been very

Continued from previous page
Lucas, *op. cit.*, note 2, pp. 18–26. Commission on Marine Science, Engineering and Resources, *op. cit.*, note 2, pp. VIII 108–110. R L Edwards, *Fishery resources of the North Atlantic region*, in *The future of the fishing industry of the United States*, Seattle 1968, pp. 52–61. United Nations Economic and Social Council, *op. cit.*, note 2, pp. 12–18. FAO, *op. cit.*, note 2, pp. 19–20. Johnston, *op. cit.*, note 2, pp. 365–370. Whiteman, *op. cit.*, note 2, pp. 982–988, p. 1073. E M Poulsen, *Conservation problems in the North Western Atlantic*, in *Papers presented at the International Technical Conference on the Conservation of the Living Resources of the Sea*, Rome 1955, pp. 183–194; and ICNAF, *Annual Proceedings*, 1951 – . For Rules of Procedure, see ICNAF, *Annual Proceedings for the year 1968–1969*, Dartmouth 1969, pp. 35–38.
[43] ICNAF, *Annual Proceedings for the year 1952–1953*, Halifax 1953, p. 23.

successful as far as research is concerned. The activities of the Commission substantially improved the quality and quantity of investigations with respect to the fisheries of the Northwest Atlantic. Its impressive publication programme clearly demonstrates this. However, ICNAF has not been equally successful in discharging its regulatory responsibilities. Its minimum mesh size regulations could not prevent the overfishing of several species – especially the haddock stocks of Georges Bank – largely because these could not cope with the distant water fisheries of the Soviet Union and several other nations. As a result, ICNAF suffers from a great deal of friction between these distant water fishing countries and the two most important coastal States of the ICNAF area, the United States and Canada. A partial solution was reached at the 1969 meeting of the Commission in the form of an overall quota for haddock.[44] At subsequent meetings, similar quotas were set for yellowtail flounder and salmon.

One of the reasons for ICNAF's regulatory ineffectiveness was the time-consuming procedure adopted in the 1949 Convention for implementing recommendations.[45] However, a 1964 Protocol relating to the Entry into Force of Proposals Adopted by the Commission became effective in December 1969.[46] It provides that recommendations become binding after a certain period, except for States which have lodged a formal objection. Another reason for the ineffectiveness of ICNAF – the fact that it could not deal with problems of overcapitalization and allocation – was corrected on 15 December 1971. On that date a Protocol entered into force that gave ICNAF the necessary powers in this respect. At its next annual meeting ICNAF used this new authority most effectively by adopting a number of national quota

[44]*Ibidem, 1968–1969*, Dartmouth 1969, p. 27.
[45]Art. VIII, para. 8 ICNAF Convention.
[46]*ILM* 1966, p. 718.

arrangements. Thus, ICNAF may very well be on its way towards becoming much more successful in regulatory matters.

9. THE INTER-AMERICAN TROPICAL TUNA COMMISSION

In 1949 two agreements were signed with respect to the tuna fisheries of the Eastern Pacific. On 25 January 1949 a Convention Relating to the Establishment of an International Commission for the Scientific Investigations of Tuna was adopted by the United States and Mexico,[47] and on 31 May 1949 a Convention for the Establishment of an Inter-American Tropical Tuna Commission was signed by the United States and Costa Rica[48] at Washington. The latter agreement proved to be the most viable one. It entered into force on 3 March 1950. Present members of the Inter-American Tropical Tuna Commission[49] are: Canada, Costa Rica, Japan, Mexico, Panama and the United States. Ecuador was a member from 1961 to 1968.

Throughout its existence, the Pacific Tuna Commission has been responsible for investigating the stocks of tuna in

[47]*UNTS* vol. 99, p. 4.
[48]*Ibidem*, vol. 80, p. 4.
[49]Hereinafter referred to as Pacific Tuna Commission or IATTC; for more information, see Chapman, *op. cit.*, note 1, pp. 426–427. J L Kask, *Tuna – a world resource*, Law of the Sea Institute, University of Rhode Island, Occasional Paper No. 2, May 1969. Commission on Marine Science, Engineering and Resources, *op. cit.*, note 2, pp. VIII 120 122. United Nations Economic and Social Council, *op. cit.*, note 2, pp. 18–20. FAO, *op. cit.*, note 2, p. 33. J E Carroz, *Establishment, structure, functions and activities of international fisheries bodies – Inter-American Tropical Tuna Commission (IATTC)*, FAO Fisheries Technical Paper No. 58, Rome 1965. Johnston, *op. cit.*, note 2, pp. 436–438. Whiteman, *op. cit.*, note 2, pp. 1029–1034, p. 1083. M B Schaefer, *Scientific investigation of the tropical tuna resources of the Eastern Pacific*, in *Papers presented at the International Technical Conference on the Conservation of the Living Resources of the Sea*, Rome 1955, pp. 194–222; and IATTC, *Annual Reports*, 1953 – . For Rules of Procedure, see Carroz, *op. cit.*, this note, pp. 26–29.

the Eastern Pacific and for recommending conservation measures in order to maintain these stocks at the level of their maximum sustainable yield. It is the third, and last, regulatory fisheries organization that employs its own staff to carry out the necessary investigations. In 1969 this staff consisted of approximately twenty-five scientists. Apart from its headquarters in La Jolla, California, the IATTC has several field offices in the major tuna ports of the Eastern Pacific.

The international staff of the IATTC has been quite successful in its research work. In 1960 IATTC investigations pointed out that the catches of yellowfin tuna had reached the level of the maximum sustainable yield. Accordingly, in 1961 the Commission recommended restricting these catches to an overall limit of 83,000 tons annually. This recommendation did not enter into force until 1967, primarily because domestic legislation in the United States made approval of the recommendation conditional upon its acceptance by all Eastern Pacific tuna fishing nations, regardless of whether or not they were members of the Commission.[50] Since 1967, however, overall quotas have applied to the yellowfin tuna fishery of the Eastern Pacific.

The Pacific Tuna Commission is confronted by several problems. The first is financial: the Commission's investigations suffer from a lack of funds, particularly for sea-going work. A second and more critical problem is that, partly as a consequence of the overall quotas, the season for the yellowfin tuna fishery is becoming shorter and shorter. This has resulted in a serious overcapitalization problem in this fishery. It has also led to political difficulties, since the less efficient fishermen of Mexico and some other member States are unable to take their traditional catch in these shorter seasons. The IATTC is currently trying to solve this problem by setting aside a certain tonnage for smaller fishing vessels.

[50] *United States Code* vol. 16, para. 955.

A third problem is that it is difficult for the Commission to stimulate an expansion of the catches of skipjack tuna while, at the same time, protecting yellowfin tuna. This difficulty is caused by the fact that fishermen cannot easily distinguish between the two species. Finally, tuna migrate over such long distances that it is questionable whether the IATTC's area of competence is large enough. It has been suggested that it would be beneficial to establish a single, worldwide tuna organization to replace the various regional commissions now concerned with tuna fisheries.[51]

10. THE INTERNATIONAL NORTH PACIFIC FISHERIES COMMISSION

After the Treaty of Peace[52] Japan invited Canada and the United States to a conference on fisheries problems. This conference produced the International Convention for the High Seas Fisheries of the North Pacific,[53] which was signed on 9 May 1952 and which entered into force on 12 June 1953. It established the International North Pacific Fisheries Commission.[54] Although more States now participate in the

[51]Kask, *op. cit.*, note 49, Appendix I.
[52]*UNTS* vol. 136, p. 46.
[53]*Ibidem*, vol. 205, p. 80.
[54]Hereinafter referred to as North Pacific Commission or INPFC; for more information, see H Kasahara, *International arrangements for fisheries*, in *The United Nations and ocean management*, L M Alexander ed., Kingston, RI 1971, p 41. Commission on Marine Science, Engineering and Resources, *op. cit.*, note 2, pp. VIII 110–116. R W Johnson, *The Japan-United States salmon conflict*, WLR 1967, pp. 1–43. D M Johnston, *New uses of international law in the North Pacific*, WLR 1967, pp. 77–114. F Nagasaki, *Some Japanese far-sea fisheries*, WLR 1967, pp. 197–230. S Oda, *Japan and international conventions relating to North Pacific fisheries*, WLR 1967, pp. 63–75. S Yamamoto, *The abstention principle and its relation to the evolving international law of the sea*, WLR 1967, pp. 45–62. FAO, *op. cit.*, note 2, p. 34. W C Herrington, *International issues of Pacific fisheries*, Department of State Bulletin 1966, vol. 55, pp. 500–504. Johnston, *op. cit.*, note 9. Johnston, *op. cit.*, note 2, pp. 275–282. Whiteman, *op. cit.*, note 2, pp. 988–1013, pp. 1075–1076. G H J van der
Continued on next page

7

North Pacific fisheries, INPFC's members are still limited to the three original signatories: Canada, Japan and the United States.

The most important function of the North Pacific Commission is to administer the so-called abstention provisions of the 1952 Convention. Under these provisions Japan had originally agreed to abstain from fishing for certain stocks of salmon, halibut and herring on the ground that they are found off the coasts of North America and/or are of North American origin. Canada had agreed to abstain from fishing for salmon originating in the rivers of the United States. The Commission is responsible for determining whether or not the stocks under abstention continue to qualify for such abstention, and whether or not new stocks must be made subject to abstention by one or two of the member States.[55] The 1952 Convention outlines the criteria which the Commission must use in this determination.[56] With respect to stocks not subject to other conservation schemes, but fished by at least two of the members, the Commission has an additional function. At the request of any of its members, it must study these stocks in order to determine the need for joint conservation measures. Such joint conservation measures were adopted for the first time in 1963 when certain stocks

Continued from previous page

Molen, *The principle of abstention and the freedom of the seas*, NTIR Special Issue 1959, pp. 203–212. Shuman, *op. cit.*, note 9. W C Herrington, *Comments on the principle of abstention*, in *Papers presented at the International Technical Conference on the Conservation of the Living Resources of the Sea*, Rome 1955, pp. 344–350. E W Allen, *A new concept for fishery treaties*, AJIL 1952, pp. 319–323. W C Herrington, *Problems affecting North Pacific fisheries*, Department of State Bulletin 1952, vol. 26, pp. 340–342. C B Selak, *Proposed International Convention for the High Seas Fisheries of the North Pacific Ocean*, AJIL 1952, pp. 323–330. W W Bishop, *The need for a Japanese fisheries agreement*, AJIL 1951, pp. 712–719; and INPFC, *Annual Reports*, 1954 – . For Rules of Procedure, see INPFC, *Annual Report for the year 1955*, Vancouver 1956, pp. 9–12.

[55] Art. III INPFC Convention.
[56] Art. IV INPFC Convention.

of halibut were removed from abstention. A third function of the INPFC originates in a Protocol to the 1952 Convention. Under this Protocol the Commission is charged with the responsibility of determining the accuracy of a line that in 1952 was considered accurate in separating salmon of American origin from salmon of Asian origin. If areas of intermingling were found, the Commission was required to recommend a more precise line. This provision led to extensive research, which proved that indeed there are areas of intermingling. However, the Commission has been unable to agree on a new dividing line.

The North Pacific Commission is one of the few international fisheries organizations with direct responsibilities concerning the allocation of the catch. These stem primarily from its administration of the abstention clauses. As allocation is one of the most controversial problems of international fisheries, it is not surprising that the INPFC's meetings witness a great deal of disagreement. Nevertheless, the North Pacific Commission has been able to adapt the abstention provisions from time to time to new realities by recommending that certain stocks be removed from abstention. No new stocks have been added. The Commission has been relatively less effective with respect to conservation. Its 1963 halibut measures did not prevent this species from being severely overfished. Currently, the INPFC is trying to rebuild the halibut stocks in cooperation with the Halibut Commission. The North Pacific Commission has also been unable to formulate conservation measures for king crab in the Bering Sea, although it investigated these stocks for many years. As far as research is concerned, the Commission did much better. Apart from a small secretariat, the INPFC does not employ its own research staff. Its role with respect to research is limited to the drafting of joint programmes, to the co-ordination of the contributions of member States to such programmes and to the exchange of their results.[57] Many of the national programmes are interest-oriented in the sense that they are designed to support, or negate, certain national positions, *e.g.*, that stocks continue to qualify for abstention, that the line separating Asian from American salmon must be moved westward, etc. Nevertheless, the Commission's efforts have greatly increased the knowledge of the resources and the fisheries of the North Pacific.

The original 1952 Convention expired in 1962, but attempts to draft a new convention have been unsuccessful. Japan no longer wishes to accept abstention, whereas the United States insists on its inclusion in any new arrangement. An additional problem is that other States have entered the fisheries of the North Pacific, particularly the Soviet Union and South Korea. It will be difficult to draw up a new agreement without the cooperation of these countries. However, the fact that since 1962 the North Pacific Commission has been able to extend its existence on a year by year basis supports the view that it continues to be a viable organization.

11. THE PERMANENT COMMISSION OF THE CONFERENCE ON THE USE AND CONSERVATION OF THE MARINE RESOURCES OF THE SOUTH PACIFIC

The Permanent Commission of the Conference on the Use and Conservation of the Marine Resources of the South Pacific[58] was established by an agreement which was signed

[57]INPFC, *Annual Report for the year 1955*, Vancouver 1956, p. 4.
[58]Hereinafter referred to as South Pacific Commission; for more information, see Chapman, *op. cit.*, note 1, p. 438. F B Zenny, *Establishment, structure, functions and activities of international fisheries bodies – Permanent Commission of the Conference on the Use and Conservation of the Marine Resources of the South Pacific*, FAO Fisheries Technical Paper No. 77, Rome 1968. Whiteman, *op. cit.*, note 2, p. 1082.

on 18 August 1952 at Santiago by Chili, Ecuador and Peru.[59] The major concern of the Commission is to achieve the objectives of the 1952 Declaration on the Maritime Zone, under which the three countries extended their maritime jurisdiction and sovereignty up to 200 miles from their coasts. In addition, the South Pacific Commission has been required throughout its existence to study the fisheries in this 200 mile zone and to propose conservation measures. It has given special attention to whales, tunas and anchovies, and it has cooperated with the Pacific Tuna Commission and the Whaling Commission. However, its members did not accept an invitation to join the Whaling Commission. The South Pacific Commission has primarily functioned as an organization in which Chile, Peru, and Ecuador have coordinated their policies with respect to the 200 mile zone.

12. THE JAPAN-SOVIET FISHERIES COMMISSION FOR THE NORTHWEST PACIFIC

The closure by the Soviet Union of a certain sea area off its Kamchatka coast to Japanese high seas salmon fisheries[60] in 1956 resulted in negotiations between the two countries. These produced a Convention concerning the High Seas Fisheries of the Northwest Pacific Ocean,[61] which was signed on 14 May 1956 at Moscow and which entered into force on 12 December 1956. It established the Japan-Soviet Northwest Pacific Fisheries Commission.[62] The major

[59]For text, see Zenny, *op. cit.*, note 58, pp. 21–42. S A Bayitch, *Interamerican law of fisheries. An introduction with documents*, New York 1957, pp. 42–47. For Rules of Procedure, see Zenny, *op. cit.*, note 58, pp. 42–44.
[60]Johnston, *op. cit.*, note 2, p. 392.
[61]*AJIL* 1959, p. 763.
[62]Hereinafter referred to as Japan-Soviet Commission; for more information, see Chapman, *op. cit.*, note 1, p. 440. Oda, *op. cit.*, note 54, pp. 67–70. Johnston, *op. cit.*, note 2, pp. 391–396. Whiteman, *op. cit.*, note 2, pp. 1020–1023, p. 1077, pp. 1146–1154. Oda, *op. cit.*, note 30, pp. 72–76. Z Ohira, *Fishery problems between Soviet Russia and Japan*, in *Japanese Annual of International Law* 1958, pp. 1–18.

responsibilities of this Commission are: (1) to periodically review the conservation measures in force; (2) to determine the annual catch of certain species (salmon); and (3) to coordinate research programmes. The determination of the annual salmon catch has led to a great deal of conflict, particularly with respect to the allocation of the total quotas. It has often been necessary to settle this issue outside the Commission on a ministerial level. A second source of friction is that the high seas salmon conservation measures affect Japanese fisheries only, since the Soviet Union does not fish for salmon on the high seas, but catches salmon only in its internal and territorial waters.

13. THE COMMISSION FOR FISHERIES RESEARCH IN THE WESTERN PACIFIC

A Convention for Cooperation in the Execution of Fisheries, Oceanological and Limnological Research in the Western Pacific was signed on 12 June 1956 at Peking by the Chinese People's Republic, the Democratic Republic of Vietnam, the Korean Democratic People's Republic and the USSR. It created a Commission for Fisheries Research in the Western Pacific.[63] The Mongolian People's Republic became a member of this Commission in 1959. The Western Pacific Commission prepares plans for joint research, organizes the exchange of the results, promotes scientific conferences, etc. In addition, it may elaborate measures for the conservation and increase of the fishery resources of the Western Pacific.

---

[63]Hereinafter referred to as Western Pacific Commission; for more information, see Chapman, *op. cit.*, note 1, p. 420. FAO, *op. cit.*, note 2, p. 31. FAO, *Convention, statutes and rules of procedure of the Commission for Fisheries Research in the Western Pacific*, FAO Fisheries Technical Paper No. 50, Rome 1965.

14. THE JOINT COMMISSION FOR THE BLACK SEA

A Convention concerning Fishing in the Black Sea,[64] which was signed by Bulgaria, Romania and the USSR on 7 July 1959 at Varna and which entered into force on 21 March 1960, established a Mixed Commission.[65] The Convention itself makes provision for a minimum size below which certain species must be returned to sea. The major responsibility of the Black Sea Commission is to amend from time to time these minimum fish size regulations. In addition, it is involved in the coordination of national fisheries research programmes and in the exchange of their results.

15. THE MIXED COMMISSION OF 1962

On 28 July 1962 the German Democratic Republic, Poland and the USSR signed an Agreement concerning Cooperation in Marine Fishing,[66] which entered into force on 22 February 1963. It founded a Mixed Commission.[67] The general objective of this Agreement is to provide for cooperation among the three States in the development of marine fishing. To that end the three States will coordinate their investigations and exchange their experiences. The task of the Mixed Commission is to draw up plans for such cooperation and to assist in the exchange of the results. Although more fundamental biological research is not explicitly excluded, the Mixed Commission has been primarily concerned with the expansion of the distant water fisheries of its member States.

[64]*UNTS* vol. 377, p. 220.
[65]Hereinafter referred to as Black Sea Commission; for more information, see FAO, *op. cit.*, note 2, p. 27. FAO, *Establishment, structure, functions and activities of the Mixed Commission for Black Sea Fisheries*, FAO Fisheries Technical Paper, unpublished monograph.
[66]*UNTS* vol. 460, p. 230.
[67]Hereinafter referred to as Mixed Commission 1962.

16. THE JAPAN-REPUBLIC OF KOREA JOINT FISHERIES COMMISSION

Japan and the Republic of Korea ended a long period of fisheries conflicts[68] with an Agreement concerning Fisheries that was signed at Tokyo on 22 June 1965.[69] It created the Japan-Republic of Korea Joint Fisheries Commission.[70] The Agreement establishes joint control zones in the waters of the high seas between the two countries, while the Annex to the Agreement makes provision for certain measures to control the fisheries in these zones. The Commission is responsible for making recommendations to its two member States for the purpose of revising the control measures. It is also responsible for recommending research programmes.

17. THE FOOD AND AGRICULTURE ORGANIZATION

The Preamble to the Constitution[71] of the Food and Agriculture Organization of the United Nations[72] states that the two most important goals of the Organization are to raise levels of nutrition and standards of living and to improve the efficiency of the production and distribution of food and

[68]G Weissberg, *Recent developments in the law of sea and the Japanese-Korean fishery dispute*, The Hague 1966.
[69]*ILM* 1965, p. 1128.
[70]Hereinafter referred to as Japan-Korea Commission; for more information, see Weissberg, *op. cit.*, note 68, pp. 86–97. Whiteman, *op. cit.*, note 2, pp. 1184–1188.
[71]A J Peaslee, *International governmental organizations. Constitutional documents*, 2nd ed. The Hague 1961, vol. I, p. 664.
[72]Hereinafter referred to as FAO; for more information concerning its activities regarding marine fisheries, see United Nations Economic and Social Council, *The sea – exploitation and conservation of living marine resources*, UN Doc. E/4842, 12 May 1970, pp. 2–6. FAO, *Work of FAO and related organizations concerning marine science and its applications*, FAO Fisheries Technical Paper No. 74, Rome 1968. United Nations Economic and Social Council, *Activities of the organizations of the United Nations system*, UN Doc. E/4487, annex XI, 24 April 1968, corr. 1, pp. 2–19.

agricultural products. FAO's functions concerning marine and inland fisheries are based on Article 1 of its Constitution. It provides, *inter alia*, that the term 'agriculture' includes fisheries and marine products. As suggested by the Preamble of its Constitution, FAO's work with respect to marine fisheries tends to emphasize the expansion and development of these fisheries, rather than their conservation and preservation. The three major elements in the organizational structure of FAO are: (1) the Conference, in which all member States are represented; (2) the Council, which is composed of thirty-four States elected by the Conference; and (3) the Staff, which is headed by a Director-General. As the Organization's decision-making organs, the Conference and the Council determine the role of FAO in the area of marine fisheries. However, it is to a large extent the Staff and the FAO-related fisheries bodies that are responsible for carrying out this role.

17.1 The Department of Fisheries

At its 13th Session the FAO Conference decided to upgrade the Staff's Fisheries Division. On 1 January 1966 it was replaced by a Department of Fisheries, whose budget was scheduled to double during the period 1966 to 1971. The Department's central function is to promote national and international action with respect to the development and rational utilization of the living resources of marine and inland waters. [73] In 1969 the structure of the Department of Fisheries was revised. As a result, it now has the following three sections: (1) a Fishery Resources Division; (2) a Fishery Economics and Institutions Division; and (3) a

[73]For more information, see FAO, *Report of the fifth session of the Committee on Fisheries*, FAO Fisheries Report No. 86, Rome 1970, p. 11. Commission on Marine Science, Engineering and Resources, *op. cit.*, note 2, pp. 129–130. FAO, *op. cit.*, note 72. J L Kask, *op. cit.*, note 1, p. 60; and FAO, *Reports of the sessions of COFI*.

Fishery Industry Division. The first Division is primarily concerned with matters of stock assessment and with the scientific base of fisheries management. The second Division deals with the economic aspects of fishery exploitation, with investment criteria for fishery development projects and with problems of government administration. Finally, the Fishery Industry Division provides advisory services to the fishing industry, particularly in the developing countries. FAO's Department of Fisheries also administers the fishery development projects of the United Nations Development Programme. Its work is handicapped by the fact that its budget did not increase as was anticipated at the time of its creation.

17.2 The Committee on Fisheries

The reorganization of 1966 also resulted in a Committee on Fisheries,[74] which was established under Article 5, para. 6 of the FAO Constitution. Originally, it consisted of thirty States that were elected by the Council. However, a recent constitutional change has temporarily opened membership to all interested FAO member States. Most nations send senior fishery officials to the meetings of COFI. Its general functions are to review the fisheries programmes of FAO and to conduct periodic reviews of all fishery problems of an international character; it may also consider the desirability of establishing new international fisheries organizations. COFI is essentially a forum for discussion, and, as such, it is

[74]Hereinafter referred to as COFI; for more information, see J E Carroz, in *Management of international fisheries arrangements* (discussion), in *The United Nations and ocean management*, L M Alexander ed., Kingston, RI 1971, pp. 66–67. W M Chapman, *Some problems and prospects for the harvest of living marine resources to the year 2000*, paper at a meeting of experts at UNITAR, February 25–27, 1970, p. 42. Commission on Marine Science, Engineering and Resources, *op. cit.*, note 2, p. VIII–67, p. VIII–130; and FAO, *Reports of the sessions of COFI*, 1966 – . For Statutes, see FAO, *Report of the first session of the Committee on Fisheries*, FAO Fisheries Reports No. 33, Rome 1966, Appendix C, pp. 1–4.

very successful. This is evident from the fact that the Soviet Union, which is not a member of FAO, sends observers to COFI's meetings. Among the factors which contribute to this success are: (1) the expertise of the persons serving on the Committee; and (2) the fact that it is the only forum in which marine fishery problems can be discussed on a world-wide basis. In its short history, COFI has been instrumental in the establishment of several new fisheries bodies. This is principally the result of a programme under which COFI assesses the effectiveness of the existing international arrangements for fisheries regulation. COFI also participated in the reorganization of the Department of Fisheries and it assists in the formulation of the Department's programme. Finally, by reviewing at its annual meetings the activities of other international organizations in the area of marine fisheries, COFI makes a substantial contribution towards the co-ordination of these activities.

17.3 The Advisory Committee on Marine Resources Research

An Advisory Committee on Marine Resources Research was created in 1962.[75] It consists of fifteen fisheries experts appointed in their individual capacity by the Director-General of FAO. This Committee has a dual responsibility: it is an advisory body to the Director-General with respect to FAO's research on fishery resources and it advises the Inter-governmental Oceanographic Commission of UNESCO on the fisheries aspects of oceanography. ACMRR constitutes a very useful link between the scientific community and FAO; its primary function is to identify research priorities.

[75]Hereinafter referred to as ACMRR; for more information, see Commission on Marine Science, Engineering and Resources, *op. cit.*, note 2, pp. VIII 132–133. FAO, *op. cit.*, note 72; and FAO, *Reports of the sessions of ACMRR*, 1963 – . For Statutes, see FAO, *Report of the first session of the Advisory Committee on Marine Resources Research*, FAO Fisheries Reports No. 14, Rome 1963, Annex III, pp. 27–28.

The Advisory Committee took the initiative for the re-organization which resulted in the Department of Fisheries and COFI. A functional difference between ACMRR and COFI is that ACMRR is exclusively concerned with research, while COFI also deals with regulatory and policy matters.

17.4 The Indo-Pacific Fisheries Council

The FAO Constitution offers several opportunities for creating subsidiary bodies. Article 14 of the Constitution provides, for example, that the Conference and the Council may submit draft conventions to the member States. The Indo-Pacific Fisheries Council[76] was the first organization to be created under this provision. It was established by a convention that was signed on 26 February 1948 at Baguio;[77] this agreement was substantially amended in 1961.[78] The present members of the Council are: Australia, Burma, Ceylon, France, India, Indonesia, Japan, Khmer Republic, the Republic of Korea, Malaysia, the Netherlands, New Zealand, Pakistan, the Philippines, Thailand, the United Kingdom, the United States and the Republic of Vietnam. The Council's responsibilities are advisory in character. It discusses oceanographical, biological, technical and other investigations; it coordinates the research programmes of its member States; and it assembles and disseminates relevant information. IPFC exercises these functions not only with respect to the marine waters of the Indo-Pacific region, but

[76]Hereinafter referred to as Indo-Pacific Council or IPFC; for more information, see Chapman, *op. cit.*, note 1, pp. 430–432. Commission on Marine Science, Engineering and Resources, *op. cit.*, note 2, pp. VIII 131–132. FAO, *op. cit.*, note 2, p. 28. J E Carroz, *Establishment, structure, functions and activities of international fisheries bodies – Indo-Pacific Fisheries Council (IPFC)*, FAO Fisheries Technical Paper No. 57, Rome 1965. Whiteman, *op. cit.*, note 2, pp. 1077–1082; and FAO, *Reports of the sessions of IPFC*, 1955 – . For Rules of Procedure, see Carroz, *op. cit.*, this note, pp. 26–35.
[77]*UNTS* vol. 120, p. 60.
[78]*Ibidem,* vol. 418, p. 348.

also with respect to inland waters. Most of its activities are concerned with fishery development programmes. Although the Council has a certain degree of autonomy, it functions within the general framework of FAO. FAO provides secretarial services and funds the Council's operations. In addition, membership in the Council is linked to membership in FAO. The Indo-Pacific Council has not been very successful. It has an abundance of study groups and working parties and it is involved in a wide range of topics. Unfortunately, all these activities are to a large extent inconsequential: the Council adopts resolution after resolution, but they are rarely implemented. However, in recent years the IPFC has shown signs of improving in this respect. Another problem is that FAO is not in a position to fund the Council very generously.

17.5 The General Fisheries Council for the Mediterranean

Another organization created under Article 14 of the FAO Constitution is the General Fisheries Council for the Mediterranean,[79] which was established by an agreement of 24 September 1949.[80] Its present members are: Algeria, Bulgaria, Cyprus, Egypt, France, Greece, Israel, Italy, Lebanon, Libya, Malta, Monaco, Morocco, Romania, Spain, Tunisia, Turkey and Yugoslavia. The structure and functions of the Mediterranean Council are virtually identical to

[79]Hereinafter referred to as Mediterranean Council or GFCM; for more information, see Chapman, *op. cit.*, note 1, p. 432. F B Zenny, *Establishment, structure, functions and activities of international fisheries bodies – General Fisheries Council for the Mediterranean (GFCM)*, FAO Fisheries Technical Paper No. 78, Rome 1968. FAO, *op. cit.*, note 2, p. 29. Whiteman, *op. cit.*, note 2, pp. 1074–1075. M J Girard, *Note on the General Fisheries Council for the Mediterranean*, in *Papers presented at the International Technical Conference on the Conservation of the Living Resources of the Sea*, Rome 1955, pp. 262–266. For Rules of Procedure, see Zenny, *op. cit.*, this note, pp. 31–37.
[80]*UNTS* vol. 126, p. 239; this Agreement was revised in 1963, *UNTS* vol. 490, p. 444.

those of the Indo-Pacific Council. It is also primarily an organization with advisory functions in the area of marine research and more specifically fisheries research. Its problems, too, are similar to those of the Indo-Pacific Council: the Mediterranean Council has also diluted its limited resources over too many projects.

17.6 The Latin-American Fisheries Council

The fact that membership would be open to non-Latin American States was the main reason why a third attempt to establish a fishery body under Article 14 of the FAO Constitution failed.[81] An Agreement to Establish a Latin American Fisheries Council was signed on 22 September 1951.[82] However, this Council never came into existence because the agreement failed to obtain the required ratifications. In 1959 the Conference of FAO acknowledged the failure of the Latin American Fisheries Council and authorized the creation of fishery bodies under Article 6, para. 1 of the FAO Constitution. This provision allows the FAO Conference or the FAO Council to establish: (1) commissions whose membership is open to all FAO members; or (2) regional commissions whose membership is open to those FAO members whose territory is situated, wholly or partly, within that region.

17.7 The Regional Fisheries Advisory Commission for the South West Atlantic

The first organization to be established under this clause of the FAO Constitution was the Regional Fisheries Advisory

[81]Chapman, *op. cit.*, note 1, p. 432. J E Carroz, *Establishment, structure, functions and activities of international fisheries bodies – Regional Fisheries Advisory Commission for the South West Atlantic (CARPAS)*, FAO Fisheries Technical Paper No. 60, Rome 1966, pp. 1–2.
[82]FAO, *Report of the sixth session of the Conference*, Rome 1951, p. 104.

Commission for the South West Atlantic.[83] An attempt to establish a Regional Fisheries Commission for West Africa failed.[84] The Statutes of CARPAS were promulgated by the Director-General of FAO on 17 May 1962 on the basis of a resolution of the FAO Conference. Its members are: Argentina, Brazil and Uruguay. CARPAS advises FAO on fishery matters concerning the South West Atlantic and it promotes cooperation in these matters among its members. CARPAS is essentially an advisory body within the FAO structure. It lacks the relative autonomy of the Indo-Pacific and Mediterranean Councils. Unlike those bodies, it is not based upon a separate international agreement and it can not have a budget of its own. A problem exists in connection with the requirement of Article 1 of the CARPAS Statutes that the territory of the members of the commission must be situated, wholly or partly, within the region in question. This prevents Paraguay from joining CARPAS. A suggestion by COFI to open membership to all interested States has never been implemented.

17.8 The Indian Ocean Fishery Commission

At the suggestion of COFI,[85] a second organization was established in 1967 under Article 6, para. 1. Resolution 2/48 of the FAO Council created an Indian Ocean Fishery Commission.[86] The members of the IOFC are: Australia,

[83]Hereinafter referred to as CARPAS (Comisión Asesora Regional de Pesca para el Atlántico Sudoccidental); for more information, see Carroz, *op. cit.*, note 81; and FAO, *Reports of the sessions of CARPAS*, 1963 — . For Statutes, see Carroz, *op. cit.*, note 81, pp. 21–24. For Rules of Procedure, see Carroz, *op. cit.*, note 81, pp. 24–28.
[84]Chapman, *op. cit.*, note 1, p. 433. FAO, *op. cit.*, note 2, pp. 25–26.
[85]FAO, *Report of the second session of the Committee on Fisheries*, FAO Fisheries Reports No. 46, Rome 1967, p. 13.
[86]Hereinafter referred to as IOFC; for more information, see FAO, *Reports of the sessions of IOFC*, 1969 — . For Resolution see FAO, *Report of the first session of the Indian Ocean Fishery Commission*, FAO Fisheries Reports No. 60, Rome 1968, pp. 12–13. For Rules of Procedure, see FAO, *op. cit.*, this note 1968, pp. 14–19.

Bahrain, Ceylon, Cuba, Ethiopia, France, Greece, India, Indonesia, Iraq, Israel, Japan, Jordan, Kenya, the Republic of Korea, Kuwait, Madagascar, Malaysia, Mauritius, the Netherlands, Oman, Pakistan, Portugal, Qatar, Tanzania, Thailand, the United Kingdom, the United States and the Republic of Vietnam. With the exception of the Arab States and the nations of East Africa, several IOFC members are also members of the Indo-Pacific Council. The functions of the Indian Ocean Commission are to promote, assist and co-ordinate national programmes of fishery development. To that end it encourages research and development activities through international sources. It may also examine management problems. As an advisory body within the FAO structure, the IOFC makes recommendations to the FAO Conference. Within its relatively short history, the IOFC has been quite productive. It is actively involved in improving the collection of statistical data concerning the fisheries in the Indian Ocean, and it critically reviews these fisheries. It has been instrumental in the formulation of the Indian Ocean Fishery and Development Programme.[87] Since their responsibilities are very similar and concern to a large extent the same ocean areas, the Indo-Pacific Council and the IOFC are faced with the need to coordinate their activities rather closely. A more serious problem is that several stocks in the IOFC area are in need of proper conservation measures, but that the Indian Ocean Commission has only minimal powers to deal with conservation problems. Its terms of reference merely authorize it to 'examine' management problems.[88]

17.9 The Fishery Committee for the Eastern Central Atlantic

Another FAO-related fishery body created at the initiative of COFI is the Fishery Committee for the Eastern Central

[87]FAO, *Report of the second session of the Indian Ocean Fishery Commission*, FAO Fisheries Reports No. 95, Rome 1970, pp. 4–6.
[88]Art. 2, para. c IOFC Resolution.

Atlantic.[89] It was established by the FAO Director-General on 19 September 1967 in view of a resolution of the FAO Council. Its terms of reference make CECAF responsible for promoting national and regional research and development programmes leading to the rational utilization of the fishery resources in the Eastern Central Atlantic. Its present members are: Cameroon, the People's Republic of Congo, Cuba, Dahomey, France, Gabon, Gambia, Ghana, Greece, Guinea, Italy, Ivory Coast, Japan, the Republic of Korea, Liberia, Mauretania, Morocco, Nigeria, Poland, Romania, Senegal, Sierra Leone, Spain, Togo, the United Kingdom, the United States and the Republic of Zaire. A major part of CECAF's activities is concerned with technical assistance for the development of marine fisheries and for the training of scientists and technicians. As far as regulation is concerned, CECAF has the same problems as the IOFC: it, too, has only minimal powers to deal with conservation problems.[90]

18. THE INTERNATIONAL COMMISSION FOR THE CONSERVATION OF ATLANTIC TUNAS

Since 1960 FAO has been involved in the problems of the tuna fisheries of the Atlantic Ocean.[91] Its activities resulted in an International Convention for the Conservation of Atlantic Tunas, which was adopted on 14 May 1966 at a FAO sponsored conference in Rio de Janeiro.[92] It established the International Commission for the Conservation of

[89]Hereinafter referred to as CECAF; for more information, see FAO, *Reports of the sessions of CECAF*, 1969 – . For Statutes, see FAO, *Report of the first session of the FAO Fishery Committee for the Eastern Central Atlantic (CECAF)*, FAO Fisheries Reports No. 69, Rome 1969, pp. 37–39. For Rules of Procedure, see FAO, *op. cit.*, this note 1969, pp. 16–20.
[90]FAO, *Report of the first session of the FAO Fishery Committee for the Eastern Central Atlantic (CECAF)*, FAO Fisheries Reports No. 69, Rome 1969, p. 3.
[91]Kask, *op. cit.*, note 49, p. 22.
[92]*ILM* 1967, p. 293.

8

Atlantic Tunas,[93] whose present members are: Brazil, Canada, France, Ghana, Japan, the Republic of Korea, Morocco, Portugal, Senegal, South Africa, Spain and the United States. It held its first meeting in December 1969. Although it was established at the initiative of FAO, ICCAT is an independent organization which is responsible for maintaining the stocks of tuna in the Atlantic Ocean at the level of their maximum sustainable yield. In order to achieve this, ICCAT may recommend certain regulatory measures to its member States. In addition, the Commission is charged with the collection and analysis of information concerning the Atlantic tuna fishery and with the publication of the results of scientific investigations. The 1966 Convention indicates that certain reservations with respect to the future performance of the Atlantic Tuna Commission may be appropriate. For example, the financial provisions suggest that ICCAT will not be able to appoint an independent international research staff, while its responsibilities are rather vaguely defined.[94]

19. THE INTERNATIONAL COMMISSION FOR THE SOUTHEAST ATLANTIC FISHERIES

On 23 October 1969 a Convention on the Conservation of the Living Resources of the Southeast Atlantic was signed in Rome. This Convention entered into force on 24 October 1971[95] and established the International Commission for the

[93]Hereinafter referred to as Atlantic Tuna Commission or ICCAT; for more information, see Chapman, *op. cit.*, note 1, p. 437. Commission on Marine Science, Engineering and Resources, *op. cit.*, note 2, pp. VIII 126–129. J E Carroz and A G Roche, *The proposed International Commission for the Conservation of Atlantic Tunas*, AJIL 1967, pp. 673–702.
[94]W T Burke, *Aspects of internal decision-making processes in intergovernmental fishery commissions*, WLR 1967, p. 178.
[95]Press release FAO/2297 L/T/766 of 18 October 1971.

Southeast Atlantic Fisheries.[96] Its creation is also largely the result of the initiatives of COFI. The present members of ICSEAF are: Bulgaria, Japan, Poland, Portugal, South Africa, Spain and the USSR. ICSEAF must, first of all, coordinate the research programmes of the member States with respect to the living resources of the Southeast Atlantic. Within the limits of a supplementary budget, it may undertake its own investigations. The second major responsibility of ICSEAF is to make recommendations to its members in order to achieve a rational utilization of the fishery resources of its area of competence.

20. OTHER INTERNATIONAL FISHERIES ORGANIZATIONS

This chronology of international fisheries organizations is not complete.[97] Among the intergovernmental marine fisheries organizations that were not reviewed[98] are: (1) the Commission established by the Agreement concerning Measures for the Protection of the Stocks of Deep Sea Prawns, European Lobsters, Norway Lobsters and Crabs, which was signed on 7 March 1952 at Oslo by Denmark, Norway and Sweden;[99] (2) the Commission established by the Agreement on Measures for Regulating the Catch and Conserving Stocks of Seals in the Northeastern Part of the Atlantic Ocean, which was signed on 22 November 1957 at Oslo by Norway and the USSR,[100] and (3) the Commission

[96]Hereinafter referred to as Southeast Atlantic Commission or ICSEAF; for text Convention, see FAO, *Final Act of the Conference of Plenipotentiaries on the Conservation of the Living Resources of the Southeast Atlantic 1969*, Rome 1970.

[97]Non-governmental organizations concerned with marine fisheries and inter-governmental organizations dealing with inland water fisheries have not been discussed. See United Nations Economic and Social Council, *Non-governmental organizations*, UN Doc. E/4487, annex X, 24 April 1968.

[98]This also applies to the Baltic Sea Salmon Standing Committee and the Shellfish Commission for the Skagerrak-Kattegat.

[99]*UNTS* vol. 175, p. 208.

[100]*Ibidem*, vol. 309, p. 280.

for the Conservation of Shrimp established by the Convention for the Conservation of Shrimp, which was signed on 15 August 1958 at Havana by Cuba and the United States.[101] The information that is available with respect to these organizations is very limited, while the third Commission never became operative. The Organization for Economic Co-operation and Development will not be discussed since it is primarily concerned with the economic aspects of the fisheries policies of its member States, rather than with the legal regime of high seas fishing and the international regulation of marine fisheries.[102] However, the institutions that have been reviewed are a representative selection of the existing types of international fisheries organizations.

21. THE CONVENTION ON FISHING AND CONSERVATION OF THE LIVING RESOURCES OF THE HIGH SEAS

The question arises of what the relationship is between all these international fisheries organizations and the Convention on Fishing and Conservation of the Living Resources of the High Seas, which was signed on 29 April 1958 and which entered into force 20 March 1966.[103] The history and the provisions of this Convention have been discussed in great detail elsewhere.[104] Essentially, it declares that all States

[101]*Ibidem*, vol. 358, p. 64.
[102]United Nations Economic and Social Council, *op. cit.*, note 2, pp. 22–23.
[103]*UNTS* vol. 559, p. 286.
[104]Hereinafter referred to as 1958 Fisheries Convention; for more information, see W M Chapman, *The United States fish industry and the 1958 and 1960 United Nations conferences on the law of the sea*, in *International rules and organization for the sea*, L M Alexander ed., Kingston, RI 1969, pp. 35–64. Commission on Marine Science, Engineering and Resources, *op. cit.*, note 2, pp. VIII 105–107. J A Crutchfield, *The Convention on Fishing and Living Resources of the High Seas*, *Natural Resources Lawyer* 1968, pp. 114–124. W C Herrington, *The future of the Geneva Convention on Fishing and the Conservation of the Living Resources of the Sea*, in *The future of the sea's resources*, L M Alexander ed.,

Continued on next page

have the right to engage in fishing on the high seas, subject to: (1) their treaty obligations; (2) the interests and rights of coastal States as provided for in the Convention; and (3) the provisions of the Convention concerning the conservation of the living resources of the high seas.[105] Conservation is defined in terms of achieving the maximum sustainable yield of the resources.[106] The 1958 Fisheries Convention requires States to adopt all necessary conservation measures.[107] If two or more States fish for a stock in need of such measures, these States must act jointly by international agreement.[108] If negotiations fail, coastal States may, under certain conditions, adopt unilateral high seas conservation measures.[109] Disputes concerning the application of these provisions are subject to compulsory arbitration.[110]

The major goals of the 1958 Fisheries Convention were to make the adoption of conservation measures an international obligation of all States and to create a general framework within which such measures could be formulated. International fisheries bodies were deemed very important ele-

Continued from previous page
Kingston, RI 1968, pp. 62–65. W C Herrington, *The Convention on Fisheries and Conservation of Living Resources: accomplishments of the 1958 Geneva Conference*, in *Offshore boundaries and zones*, L M Alexander ed., Columbus, Ohio 1967, pp. 26–36. Johnston, *op. cit.*, note 2, pp. 488–495. Whiteman, *op. cit.*, note 2, pp. 1140–1146. F V Garcia Amador, *The exploitation and conservation of the resources of the sea. A study of contemporary international law*, 2nd ed. 2nd enl. printing, Leyden 1963, pp. 187–194. W W Bishop, *The 1958 Geneva Convention on Fishing and Conservation of the Living Resources of the High Seas*, Columbia Law Review 1962, pp. 1206–1230. S Oda, *The 1958 Geneva Convention on the fisheries: its immaturities*, Die Friedens-Warte 1960, pp. 317–339. A H Dean, *The Geneva Conference on the Law of the Sea: what was accomplished*, AJIL 1958, pp. 607–628. H Ph V Visser 't Hooft, *Les Nations Unies et la conservation des ressources de la mer*, The Hague 1958.

[105] Art. 1 1958 Fisheries Convention.
[106] Art. 2 1958 Fisheries Convention.
[107] Art. 3 1958 Fisheries Convention.
[108] Art. 4 and Art. 5 1958 Fisheries Convention.
[109] Art. 6 and Art. 7 1958 Fisheries Convention.
[110] Art. 9, Art. 10 and Art. 11 1958 Fisheries Convention.

ments of this framework.[111] However, the 1958 Fisheries Convention has not achieved its objectives. The main reason for this failure is that some of the most important fishing nations have not ratified the Convention. Among these States are Japan and the USSR. The non-ratification of the USSR is primarily the result of the general unwillingness of this country to accept any system of compulsory arbitration. The combined catches of all nations that have ratified the Convention account for only fourteen per cent of the total world catch.[112] Other problems of the 1958 Fisheries Convention are that it does not deal adequately with the allocation of the catch and with the enforcement of conservation measures. However, all these shortcomings do not negate the fact that the Convention has become a moral code which fishing nations prefer not to violate.

[111]See the Resolution on International Fishery Conservation Conventions which was adopted by the 1958 Geneva Conference, *UNTS* vol. 450, p. 60.
[112]Herrington, *op. cit.*, note 104, p. 62.

Chapter III

The Structure of International Fisheries Organizations

1. SOURCES

Legal provisions concerning the organizational or institutional law[1] of international fisheries organizations can be found in a variety of sources. Probably the most important source is the legal document[2] by which the organization was established. This can be a bilateral or multilateral international agreement, but it can also be a resolution promulgated by another international organization. This latter approach is largely limited to the FAO-related fisheries bodies. A second source for the organizational law is the rules of procedure[3] adopted by international fisheries organizations on the basis of the more general provisions of the legal act by which they were established. Such rules of procedure must be consistent with the general provisions, but they are usually much more detailed. Finally, there is a third, less formal, source for the organizational law of international fisheries commissions. These bodies are not only the subjects of their organizational law; they also create it: the rules of procedure

---

[1] FAO, *Report on regulatory fishery bodies*, FAO Fisheries Circular No. 138, Rome 1972. W T Burke, *Aspects of internal decision-making processes in intergovernmental fishery commissions*, *WLR* 1967, pp. 115–178. FAO, *International fisheries bodies*, FAO Fisheries Technical Paper No. 64, Rome 1966.

[2] Hereinafter this document will be indicated by reference to the organization it established: the International Convention for the Northwest Atlantic Fisheries, for example, will be referred to as ICNAF Convention. Further information concerning such agreements can be found in Chapter II under the fisheries commission in question.

[3] Hereinafter these rules of procedure will be indicated by reference to the organization which adopted them. Further information can be found in Chapter II under the commission in question.

are here a prime example. However, equally important is the continuous interpretation of the organizational law in their activities.[4] Consequently, an analysis of the organization of international fisheries commissions can not limit itself to the legal acts by which they were established and to the rules of procedure, but must also include their activities.

2. MEMBERSHIP

2.1 Eligibility[5]

The legal provisions concerning eligibility for membership in international fisheries organizations can be distinguished in three categories. These are: (1) closed membership: membership is limited to the States which ratified the agreement establishing the organization; (2) conditionally open membership: other States may become members, provided they meet certain conditions; and (3) unconditionally open membership: any State which is interested may become a member.

The Conventions establishing the Halibut Commission, the Salmon Commission, the Fur Seal Commission and the North Pacific Commission do not contain any provisions on accession by new States. Membership is limited to two, two, four and three States respectively. In addition, the Halibut and Salmon Commissions were established for the explicit purpose of rebuilding stocks which were depleted by the fishermen of the two member States, while the Conventions creating the Fur Seal Commission and the North Pacific Commission deal not only with conservation problems, but also with the allocation of the catch among the member States. These considerations strongly suggest that the absence of provisions on accession by new States must be

---

[4]These activities are recorded in the annual reports of the various international fisheries organizations.
[5]FAO, *op. cit.*, note 1, 1972, pp. 7–8. Burke, *op. cit.*, note 1, pp. 120–124. FAO, *op. cit.*, note 1, 1966, pp. 6-7.

interpreted as restricting membership to the original signatories of the respective Conventions.[6]

Several international fisheries organizations belong to the second category: other States may become members, provided they meet certain conditions. The most common requirements are: (1) the consent of the existing members; (2) membership in FAO, the United Nations or any other specialized agency of the United Nations; (3) a coastline in the area with which the organization is concerned; and (4) participation in the fisheries for which the organization is responsible. The first condition can be found in the ICES Convention[7] and IATTC Convention[8]. States may accede to the International Council if three quarters of the existing members give their consent. In the Pacific Tuna Commission accession is subject to the unanimous approval by all existing members. The second condition is generally used in the FAO-related organizations.[9] Eligibility for membership in the IOFC, CARPAS, and CECAF is strictly limited to members and associate members of FAO. In the GFCM and the IPFC, other States may be admitted by the FAO Council, provided that these States are members of the United Nations. Membership in the Atlantic Tuna Commission and the Southeast Atlantic Commission is also conditional upon United Nations membership,[10] although the wording of the ICSEAF provision may make it possible for the Commission to invite non-United Nations members. The third condition is a characteristic of CECAF, CARPAS and the IOFC. As far as CARPAS and CECAF are concerned, their respective Statutes provide that members must be selected from among

[6]But see FAO, *op. cit.*, note 1, 1972, p. 8.
[7]Art. 16, para. 4 ICES Convention.
[8]Art. V, para. 3 IATTC Convention.
[9]Art. 2 CECAF Statutes. Art. 3 IOFC Resolution. Art. 1 CARPAS Statutes. Art. IX, para. 1 and 2 IPFC and GFCM Agreements.
[10]Art. XVII, para. 1 ICSEAF Convention. Art. XIV, para. 1 ICCAT Convention.

States whose territory borders the ocean area with which the commission is concerned.[11] This requirement prevented Paraguay from joining CARPAS. Although the IOFC Resolution is silent on this matter, it must be assumed that a similar condition applies to membership in that organization: the IOFC has been created under Article 6, para. 1 of the FAO Constitution which authorizes the FAO Council and the FAO Conference to establish regional bodies composed of FAO member States whose territory is, wholly or partly, situated within the region in question. Finally, the fourth condition concerning eligibility for membership can be found in the IATTC Convention, which stipulates that any State whose nationals participate in the fisheries covered by the Convention may apply for membership.

The third category of membership provisions – unconditionally open – is a feature of most of the important multilateral conventions. Membership in the Whaling Commission, the North-East Atlantic Commission and the Northwest Atlantic Commission, for example, is open to all interested States.[12] A State wishing to become a member of these organizations has merely to submit a notification to that effect.

2.2 Termination[13]

As far as termination of membership is concerned, it will be obvious that membership ends if the organization ceases to exist. This occurs if the agreement on which the organization is based expires without being extended, either by a *tacit* understanding among the parties,[14] or by an explicit agreement.[15] It can also occur if the organization which established

[11]Art. 1 CARPAS and CECAF Statutes.
[12]Art. 15, para. 3 NEAFC Convention. Art. XV, para. 3 ICNAF Convention. Art. X, para. 2 IWC Convention.
[13]Burke, *op. cit.*, note 1, pp. 124–125.
[14]Art. V, para. 2 IPHC Convention. Art. XI, para. 2 INPFC Convention.
[15]Art. XI NPFSC Convention.

the fishery body in question decides to discontinue it. As FAO created CARPAS, the IOFC and CECAF, it is also FAO which may decide to terminate these bodies. Membership in an international fisheries organization can also end if a State decides to withdraw from that organization. Several conventions allow such withdrawal,[16] provided that States respect certain procedural requirements with respect to notification, etc. Withdrawal usually takes effect one year after notification. If a State withdraws from an organization based upon a bilateral agreement, that organization will cease to exist. However, the situation is less clear with respect to fishery bodies established by multilateral conventions. The Whaling Commission, for example, continued to function after the withdrawal of Norway and the Netherlands.[17] Some multilateral agreements provide that the organization will cease to function if the number of members drops below a certain minimum.[18] In the absence of such provisions, it must be assumed that the remaining member States may decide whether or not they wish to continue the organization after the withdrawal of one or more members. Finally, membership in international fisheries organizations can end if a State no longer fulfills the conditions for membership. If, for example, a State withdraws from FAO, it automatically ceases to be a member of the Indo-Pacific Council and the Mediterranean Council.[19] The same situation exists with respect to CARPAS, the IOFC and CECAF, although their Statutes are silent on this matter.

2.3 Evaluation

It has already been mentioned that some regional fisheries

[16]Art. XX ICSEAF Convention. Art. XII ICCAT Convention. Art. 17 NEAFC Convention. Art. V, para. 4 IATTC Convention. Art. XVI ICNAF Convention.
[17]IWC, *Eleventh Report of the Commission*, London 1960, p. 3.
[18]Art. XIV IPFC Agreement.
[19]Art. XII, para. 3 IPFC and GFCM Agreements.

organizations must approve the admission of new member States. Apart from this responsibility, they have other, more informal, functions with respect to membership. The Whaling Commission, for example, has on several occasions invited non-member States to join the Commission.[20] Other commissions have done the same. In addition, they often maintain extensive relations with such non-member States. These relations will be discussed in more detail in reviewing the external organization of fisheries bodies,[21] but it must be pointed out here that the activities of international fisheries organizations have frequently crossed the boundary line between member and non-member States. Thus, one reason for establishing a fisheries organization is that it becomes easier to draw non-parties into the sphere of influence of the agreement concerned.

Nevertheless, a basic feature of membership is that it reflects the fact that under the principle of the freedom of fishing on the high seas, participation in international fisheries agreements is entirely voluntary. No State is obliged to become a member of an international fisheries organization in order to have the right to engage in the fisheries for which such organization is responsible. Consequently, States will only join a fishery body if they consider this in their self-interest, or at least not in conflict with such interest. The 1958 Fisheries Convention attempted to make participation in international conservation arrangements compulsory, but it failed to achieve this objective.[22] As a result, there is not yet a widely accepted international agreement or a rule of customary international law which requires

[20]IWC, *Fourth Report of the Commission*, London 1953, p. 3.
[21]*Infra* pp. 153–155.
[22]The 1958 Geneva Law of the Sea Conference, however, did adopt a Resolution on International Fishery Conservation Conventions and a Resolution on Cooperation in Conservation Measures which stressed the need for the States concerned to participate in such organizations, *UNTS* vol. 450, p. 60.

States to join the international fisheries commission which regulates a fishery in which they participate. A related point is that States are under no obligation to establish such an organization. The result is that existing international fisheries organizations are entirely dependent upon voluntary cooperation among States.

As far as the three categories of existing membership provisions are concerned, there are two possible points of view. One viewpoint is that membership in international fisheries organizations should include as many States as possible. The second viewpoint is that membership must be limited to those States which have an active interest in the fisheries concerned, because non-interested States would unnecessarily complicate the decision-making process. Restrictions upon membership on the basis of conditions *unrelated* to the fishery are undesirable in either approach. This refers in particular to the requirement that a State can only become a member of a fishery body if it is a member of another international organization. The fact that CARPAS, the IOFC and CECAF are fully incorporated in the FAO structure may justify such provisions in their Statutes. However, since the Indo-Pacific Council and the Mediterranean Council are semi-autonomous, there is less justification for including this requirement in their respective Agreements. There is even less reason for making membership in such fully autonomous bodies as ICCAT and ICSEAF conditional upon membership in the United Nations. As almost all States are members of the United Nations, these requirements will probably not result in any serious difficulties. However, they may cause problems – for example, if a member of the fisheries organizations in question withdraws for some reason temporarily from the United Nations. In addition, no specific benefits seem to result from such requirements.

As far as conditions limiting membership on the basis of

criteria *related* to the fisheries are concerned, the second viewpoint would justify such restrictions. Accordingly, membership should be limited to States which have a coastline in the area with which the organization is concerned, or which participate in the fisheries for which the organization is responsible. However, the fact that membership usually entails certain financial obligations is in itself a sufficient guarantee that a State without any interest at all will refrain from becoming a member. In addition, all States have a general interest in protecting the living resources of the high seas, irrespective of the question of whether or not they fish for a specific stock; these resources may be caught by all nations. Consequently, conditions which limit membership to the States with a direct interest in the fisheries involved are both unnecessary and undesirable, particularly since the efficiency of the decision-making process can be ensured by other means.[23] Such restrictions on membership may also result in the organization becoming an instrument to further the interests of its members, rather than an instrument to regulate marine fisheries rationally. The conclusion must be that unconditionally open membership is preferable.

3. AREA AND SPECIES COVERED

3.1 Legal Provisions[24]

With the exception of COFI, no international fisheries organization is concerned with all fisheries in all parts of the seas. Fisheries commissions deal with specific areas and/or specific species. This reflects the fact that fisheries problems do not occur in general, but arise with respect to certain stocks and in certain areas. A few international fisheries organizations are responsible for a precisely defined area. The areas of competence of the North-East Atlantic Commission and of

[23] *Infra* pp. 186–188.
[24] FAO, *op. cit.*, note 1, 1972, pp. 4–6. FAO, *op. cit.*, note 1, 1966, pp. 5–7.

the Northwest Atlantic Commission are, for instance, delineated in degrees longitude and latitude and complement each other accurately.[25] However, most international fisheries conventions are considerably less precise.[26] The International Council, for example, is concerned with the Atlantic Ocean as a whole.[27] Although vaguely defined, most fisheries organizations are regional in scope. The only other global organization besides COFI is the Whaling Commission since its area of competence extends to 'all waters in which whaling is prosecuted'.[28]

Vaguely defined areas of competence are sometimes clarified elsewhere. It is possible that the fisheries convention itself indicates the area in rather vague terms, but that a separate annex to the agreement is much more precise.[29] As such an annex can usually be amended more easily than the convention itself, this technique results in a precisely defined, but flexible, area of competence. A second way in which such areas can be clarified is by reference to the preparatory documents of the fisheries convention in question. For example, the area of the Indo-Pacific Council is broadly defined as the Indo-Pacific area,[30] but documents submitted to the Baguio conference indicate that the Council is primarily interested in the waters of the Southwestern Pacific and Indian Ocean.[31] Finally, the area of competence of a fisheries organization can also be defined more precisely by the activities of the organization itself. Although the Pacific Tuna

[25]Art. 1, para. 1 NEAFC Convention. Art. I, para. 1 ICNAF Convention.
[26]Art. I ICCAT Convention. Art. I INPFC Convention. Art. II IATTC Convention.
[27]Art. 2 ICES Convention.
[28]Art. I, para. 2 IWC Convention.
[29]Art. 1, para. 1 and Annex I Convention on Conduct of Fishing Operations in the North Atlantic of London 1967, *ILM* 1967, p. 760.
[30]Art. V IPFC Agreement.
[31]J E Carroz, *Establishment, structure, functions and activities of international fisheries bodies – Indo-Pacific Fisheries Council (IPFC)*, FAO Fisheries Technical Paper No. 57, Rome 1965, p. 3.

Commission is concerned with the Eastern Pacific as a whole, its regulations apply to an area which is delineated in degrees longitude and latitude.[32] In a similar fashion, CARPAS adopted a precisely defined statistical area, although it deals with the South West Atlantic in general.[33] Several fisheries conventions provide that the general areas of competence are divided into sub-areas. Article I, para. 3 of the ICNAF Convention, for example, provides that the convention area will be divided into five sub-areas, the boundaries of which are determined in an Annex to the Convention. ICNAF has special subsidiary bodies which are responsible for the fisheries in these five areas. Most fisheries organizations have similar committees to deal with specific regions within their overall area of competence.[34]

Some international fisheries agreements explicitly include the territorial waters of the Contracting Parties in their area of competence,[35] while others explicitly exclude these territorial waters from the area to which they apply.[36] However, most fisheries agreements are silent on this matter, although several contain a provision to the effect that nothing in the convention will prejudice the rights, claims and views of the Contracting Parties in respect of the extent of their fisheries jurisdiction.[37] This silence may raise questions with respect to the applicability of earlier international regulations in those areas of the high seas which have been claimed subsequently by coastal States as exclusive fishery zones. The general

[32]IATTC, *Annual Report for the year 1962*, La Jolla 1963, p. 15.
[33]J E Carroz, *Establishment, structure, functions and activities of international fisheries bodies – Regional Fisheries Advisory Commission for the South West Atlantic (CARPAS)*, FAO Fisheries Technical Paper No. 60, Rome 1966, p. 8.
[34]*Infra* pp. 140–144.
[35]Art. I, para. 2 IPHC Convention.
[36]Art. I, para. 1 Japan-Soviet Commission Convention. Art 1, para. 1 INPFC Convention. Art. I, para. 1 ICNAF Convention.
[37]Art. II ICCAT Convention. Art 1 Black Sea Commission Convention. Art. 2 NEAFC Convention. Art 1, para. 2 Western Pacific Commission Convention. Art. I, para. 2 ICNAF Convention.

principle governing such a situation should be that no later unilateral act can derogate a preceding international agreement, unless the unilateral act is justified by the terms of that agreement.

Several international fisheries organizations do not deal with all species within their area of competence, but are solely concerned with a specific stock. The Whaling Commission is the only organization which is exclusively species-based: it is concerned with whales wherever they are caught. Some of these single-species fisheries commissions have their origin in the period before World War II,[38] while others were established immediately after World War II.[39] However, with the exception of the Atlantic Tuna Commission, most modern international fisheries organizations are multi-species, rather than single-species, bodies.

3.2 Evaluation

A first observation is that fisheries organizations should be able to accommodate changes in the fisheries for which they are responsible. This suggests that a certain degree of vagueness in the delimitation of the areas of competence is not undesirable. Such vagueness allows an organization, for example, to cope with the expansion of the geographical range of the fishing operations with which it is concerned. However, this vagueness should not result in jurisdictional conflicts between fisheries commissions. If this seems likely, a more precise delimitation of the areas of competence is necessary. This has been done with respect to the two North Atlantic Commissions. A second observation is that in most fisheries multi-species bodies are to be preferred over single-species bodies. Fishing for a certain species has always some effects on other stocks and, conversely, fishing for other species affects the specific stock under regulation.[40] In

[38] The Halibut Commission and the Salmon Commission.
[39] The Pacific Tuna Commission and the Whaling Commission.
[40] *Supra* p. 27.

9

addition, as most stocks migrate within a limited range, an area-based approach is quite feasible. However, those species which migrate over extended distances, *e.g.*, whales and tuna, are exceptions here. For these stocks single-species organizations with no area limitations may be preferable. The provisions on the area and species coverage of most recent international fisheries organizations are quite consistent with these observations.

4. INTERNAL STRUCTURE[41]

The internal structure of international fisheries organizations consists of three major elements: (1) a plenary group; (2) subsidiary bodies; and (3) a staff. The following sections will concentrate on the organization of these three basic elements. Their interaction will be reviewed in the following Chapter dealing with the functions of international fisheries organizations.

4.1 The Plenary Group

4.1.1 Composition

The central element in the organizational structure of most international fisheries organizations is a plenary group in which all member States are represented. As far as the composition of this plenary group is concerned, international fisheries agreements usually provide that the member States must appoint one or more delegates. Some conventions stipulate that each State appoints a fixed number of delegates,[42] but others merely give a maximum number.[43] Usually, this number is limited to two or three representatives. A few international fisheries conventions follow a slightly different approach. They provide that the plenary group is composed of national sections and that each member State appoints

[41]Burke, *op. cit.*, note 1, pp. 125–145.
[42]Art. III, para. 1 IWC Convention. IWC Rules of Procedure, Rule I.
[43]Art. 3, para. 2 NEAFC Convention. Art. II, para. 2 ICNAF Convention.

their members.[44] Here again, some agreements specify the number of persons serving on the national sections, while others only indicate a maximum number. It is generally provided that the names of the delegates and of the members of the national sections must be sent to the secretary of the organization in question.[45]

Most fisheries conventions are silent with respect to such questions as the procedure for appointing delegates, their terms of office and their qualifications. Apparently, these questions are to be decided by the member States. However, a few agreements are more detailed. The IPSFC Convention, for example, provides that the United States representatives must be appointed by the President of the United States and the Canadian representatives by His Majesty on the recommendation of the Governor in Council.[46] These representatives hold office during the pleasure of the member State by which they were appointed. As far as the qualifications or background of the representatives are concerned, the Rules of Procedure of CARPAS, the IOFC and CECAF require member States to appoint delegates who are responsible for the formulation and implementation of the fishery policy of the appointing State.[47] A 1952 fisheries agreement between the three Scandinavian countries provides that each member State appoints two delegates to the Commission established by that agreement: one for scientific research and one for the fishing industry.[48] The qualifications of

[44]Art. III, para. 2 Japan-Soviet Commission Convention. Art. II, para. 2 INPFC Convention. Art. I, para. 1 IATTC Convention.
[45]NEAFC Rules of Procedure, Rule 1. INPFC Rules of Procedure, Rule 1.
[46]Art. II IPSFC Convention.
[47]CARPAS, IOFC and CECAF Rules of Procedure, Rule I, para. 2.
[48]Art. 7 Agreement concerning Measures for the Protection of the Stocks of Deep Sea Prawns, European Lobsters, Norway Lobsters and Crabs, *UNTS* vol. 175, p. 210; it is interesting that the French translation of the original text speaks of: 'un représentant *de* l'industrie de la pêche', which suggests that the delegate must actually come from the industry and is not a government official representing the industry.

the delegates are also sometimes specified in national legislation which implements a certain fisheries convention. For example, the United States Tuna Conventions Act of 1950[49] provides that one United States representative to the Pacific Tuna Commission must be an officer of the Fish and Wildlife Service, that at least one must be a person from the public at large, and that of the four, at least three must reside in a state whose vessels participate in the tuna fishery. Similar provisions exist for the United States delegation to the North Pacific Commission.[50]

These official delegates are not the only persons attending the meetings of the plenary group of international fisheries organizations. Almost all fisheries conventions allow the official representatives to be accompanied by experts and advisers.[51] These experts and advisers may attend the meetings of the plenary group and, at the discretion of the Chairman,[52] may address these meetings. They have no vote in the plenary group, although they may usually vote in the various committees and working groups of the organization. A special category of advisers are the members of so-called Advisory Committees, which may be established by the Contracting Parties of several fisheries agreements.[53] These Advisory Committees are composed of persons well informed concerning the fisheries covered by the convention in question. The members of such Advisory Committees may attend all meetings of the plenary group, except when it meets *in camera*.[54] A last group attending the meetings of fisheries

[49]*United States Code* vol. 16, para. 952(c).
[50]*Ibidem*, para. 1022.
[51]Art. III, para. 2 ICCAT Convention. Art. 6, para. 3 ICES Convention. Art. 3, para. 2 NEAFC Convention. Art. II, para. 2 ICNAF Convention. Art. III, para. 1 IWC Convention.
[52]INPFC Rules of Procedure, Rule 8.
[53]Art. 12 ICES Convention. Art. II, para. 8 INPFC Convention. Art. I, para. 11 IATTC Convention. Art. V, para. 1 ICNAF Convention.
[54]INPFC Rules of Procedure, Rule 5. IATTC Rules of Procedure, Rule II.

commissions consists of the observers from other international organizations or from non-member States.[55] There is a frequent exchange of observers among the various international fisheries organizations.[56]

4.1.2 Chairman

A Chairman usually presides over the deliberations of the plenary group. In most organizations he is elected at the end of the annual meeting and his term of office covers the period from his election to the end of the following annual meeting.[57] However, there are exceptions: in the North-East Atlantic Commission, for example, the Chairman holds office for three years.[58] Under some arrangements the Chairman must be selected from among the delegates,[59] while other arrangements do not require this.[60] If selected from among the delegates, the person elected normally ceases to be a delegate. Several fisheries conventions require the office of Chairman to rotate among the member States.[61] His responsibilities include: (1) to preside at all meetings; (2) to decide all questions of order; (3) to call for votes and to announce the results; (4) to determine a provisional agenda; (5) to sign certain documents; and (6) to carry on the business of the organization in the intervals between its meetings.[62] In

[55]INPFC Rules of Procedure, Rule 7. IWC Rules of Procedure, Rule III.
[56]However, at its seventh meeting NEAFC decided to stop sending observers to the meetings of other fisheries organizations since other channels of communication were deemed adequate, NEAFC, *Report of the seventh meeting*, London 1969, p. 25.
[57]CECAF, IOFC and CARPAS Rules of Procedure, Rule II, para. 1. ICNAF Rules of Procedure, Rule 3, para. 1. IPFC Rules of Procedure, Rule VII, para. 1.
[58]NEAFC Rules of Procedure, Rule 3.
[59]Art. III, para. 5 ICCAT Convention. Art. 10, para. 1 ICES Convention. Art. III, para. 2 IWC Convention.
[60]Art. 3, para. 3 NEAFC Convention.
[61]Art. II, para. 6 INPFC Convention. Art. I, para. 7 IATTC Convention. Art. II, para. 3 ICNAF Convention.
[62]NEAFC Rules of Procedure, Rule 4. INPFC Rules of Procedure, Rule 14. IWC Rules of Procedure, Rule VIII.

carrying out these responsibilities, he is usually assisted by one or more Vice-Chairmen.[63]

4.1.3 Meetings

It will be clear from the foregoing that quite a number of people may attend the meetings of the plenary group of international fisheries organizations. The 1968 annual meeting of the North Pacific Commission, for example, had a total of 117 accredited participants. The 1968 ICNAF meeting was attended by 95 delegates, advisers and observers, and at the 1968 NEAFC meeting about 85 participants were present. Obviously, the annual meetings of bilateral organizations normally involve a smaller number of persons. Most fisheries commissions meet once a year, but there are exceptions in both directions. The Indo-Pacific Council, for example, meets once every two years, while in 1970 the Salmon Commission held as many as nineteen formal sessions.[64] As far as legal provisions are concerned, some fisheries agreements prescribe a fixed number of regular meetings,[65] but other conventions merely indicate the minimum number of meetings which must be held in a certain period.[66] However, the Whaling Commission is completely free with respect to the frequency of its sessions.[67] Most fisheries commissions determine the time and place of their next meeting at the end of each annual conference, except CARPAS, the IOFC and CECAF which convene at the discretion of the Director-General of FAO.[68] Attendance by a majority of the members

[63]Art. III, para. 5 ICCAT Convention. Art. 10 ICES Convention.
[64]IPSFC, *Annual Report 1970*, New Westminster 1971, p. 5.
[65]Art. 7, para. 1 ICES Convention. Art. 3, para. 5 NEAFC Convention. Art. V, para. 6 NPFSC Convention.
[66]Art. III, para. 5 Japan-Soviet Commission Convention. Art. I, para. 6 IATTC Convention.
[67]Art. III, para. 8 IWC Convention.
[68]CECAF and IOFC Rules of Procedure, Rule IV, para. 2. CARPAS Rules of Procedure, Rule III, para. 1.

is usually considered the required *quorum*.[69] Almost all fisheries organizations may hold extraordinary meetings.[70] Although the details differ from commission to commission, most special meetings are convened by the Chairman at the request of a majority of the member States. Several fisheries organizations have used this option quite frequently. For example, most of the nineteen sessions of the Salmon Commission in 1970 were extraordinary meetings. Other commissions were able to reach agreement on critical regulatory problems by convening a special meeting. The INPFC, for example, formulated its first halibut conservation proposals at a special meeting in 1963; and the IWC finally reduced the total quotas for Antarctic pelagic whaling at an extraordinary meeting in 1965.

Several commissions have a tradition of beginning each annual meeting with a session open to the general public.[71] The following sessions are open to accredited participants only. Some commissions may even meet in an executive or *in camera* session, which is restricted to the official delegates and specifically invited advisers.[72] At the annual meeting most fisheries organizations conduct much of their work in committees and working groups, which convene in the intervals between the plenary sessions. As a result, such annual meetings consist of a few sessions of the plenary group and a great number of committee sessions. The most important committees meet quite often prior to the first plenary session in order to prepare their reports for the

[69]NEAFC Rules of Procedure, Rule 10. IWC Rules of Procedure, Rule XVII.
[70]Art. V, para. 1 ICSEAF Convention. Art. III, para. 5 Japan-Soviet Commission Convention. Art. II, para. 5 INPFC Convention. Art. II, para. 6 ICNAF Convention.
[71]IPHC, *Annual Report 1969*, Seattle 1970, p. 8. INPFC, *Annual Report 1968*, Vancouver 1970, p. 1.
[72]INPFC Rules of Procedure, Rule 4, 5 and 6. INPFC, *Annual Report 1968*, Vancouver 1970, p. 5.

plenary group.[73] Committees may also meet in the intervals between two annual meetings. International fisheries organizations rotate the location of their annual meetings usually among the Contracting Parties. This is largely a matter of practice, since only a few international fisheries conventions require such rotation explicitly.[74] Most conventions simply provide that the commission meets at its headquarters unless it determines otherwise.[75] The FAO Director-General decides with respect to the location of the meetings of CARPAS, the IOFC and CECAF, and advises the IPFC and the GFCM on this question.

4.1.4 *Voting*

As far as the voting arrangements of the plenary group are concerned, the almost universal rule is that each member State has one vote, irrespective of the number of official representatives. However, the Halibut and Salmon Commissions are exceptions. Article III, para. 1 of the IPHC Convention provides, *inter alia*, that the Commission will make its decisions '. . . by a concurring vote of at least two of the Commissioners of each Contracting Party'. The total number of Commissioners is six.[76] This provision is a departure from the one nation-one vote system of other fisheries commissions, since the vote is linked to an individual, rather than to a member State. Other fisheries conventions which stipulate that the plenary group decides by a majority of the votes of the delegates, rather than of the member States, also stipulate that each member State has only one representative.[77] Consequently, this delegate does

[73]IWC, *Twenty-first Report of the Commission*, London 1971, p. 7, p. 24. INPFC, *Annual Report 1968*, Vancouver 1970, p. 1. ICNAF, *Annual Proceedings for the year 1968–1969*, Dartmouth 1969, p. 14.
[74]Art. 8 Black Sea Commission Convention.
[75]Art. 7, para. 1 ICES Convention. Art. II, para. 5 ICNAF Convention.
[76]Art. VI IPSFC Convention is similar.
[77]Art. III, para. 1 and 2 IWC Convention.

not vote in an individual capacity as the Commissioners of the Halibut Commission and Salmon Commission seem to do.

Several fisheries organizations are required to take all decisions by an unanimous vote of all member States.[78] Some conventions waive this requirement of unanimity for certain types of decisions, or limit its applicability to those member States which are directly affected by a certain decision. In the Fur Seal Commission, for example, decisions concerning the size and the sex and age composition of the seasonal commercial kill from a herd are taken by an unanimous vote of those member States which share in the sealskins from that herd.[79] Most commissions in which a small number of States participate decide by unanimity. The larger fisheries organizations have more flexible arrangements. Some of these even vote by simple majority.[80] If a plenary group votes in principle by simple majority, the convention may provide that certain types of decisions require a two-thirds majority or even unanimity. The North-East Atlantic Commission, for example, may change the boundaries of the sub-areas into which the Convention waters have been divided by an unanimous vote only,[81] although it usually decides by a majority vote. Finally, a third category of fisheries organizations decides as a general rule on the basis of a two-thirds majority.[82]

[78] Art. 10 Black Sea Commission Convention. Art. III, para. 3 Japan-Soviet Commission Convention. Art. II, para. 3 INPFC Convention. Art. I, para. 8 IATTC Convention.

[79] Art. V, para. 4 NPFSC Convention. Art. III, para. 1 (c) (ii) INPFC Convention.

[80] CECAF and IOFC Rules of Procedure, Rule VI, para. 2. Art. III, para. 3 ICCAT Convention. Art. 8, para. 2 ICES Convention. Art 3, para. 8 NEAFC Convention. Art. III, para. 2 IWC Convention.

[81] Art. 5, para. 4 NEAFC Convention.

[82] Art. V, para. 3 ICSEAF Convention. Art. IV, para. 4 ICNAF Convention.

4.2 Subsidiary Bodies

4.2.1 Establishment and Composition

Almost all fisheries conventions[83] authorize international fisheries organizations to establish subsidiary bodies or committees.[84] Such committees have also been established without explicit authorization: the North Pacific Commission, for example, has several committees,[85] but the INPFC Convention itself is silent on this matter. The only general restriction on the establishment of subsidiary bodies seems to be that their terms of reference must fall within those of the organization itself. Other, more practical, restrictions may stem from financial considerations. The budget of the organization must allow it to bear the expenses of the sessions of its committees, particularly if these convene in the intervals between two annual meetings. As the FAO is responsible for their expenses, establishment of subsidiary bodies in the FAO-related commissions is conditional upon the approval of the FAO Director-General.[86]

The procedures for creating subsidiary bodies differ from organization to organization. However, the three most generally accepted methods are: (1) the fisheries convention itself provides that the plenary group has certain subsidiary bodies; (2) the plenary group itself may establish committees; and (3) a subsidiary body may establish sub-committees. The ICNAF Convention exemplifies the first approach: it provides that there will be a special panel for each of the sub-areas

---

[83]Art. VI ICCAT Convention. Art. 12 ICES Convention. Art. 3, para. 7 NEAFC Convention. Art. IV ICNAF Convention. Art. III, para. 2 and 3 IPFC Agreement. Art. III, para. 4 IWC Convention.

[84]Hereinafter the term 'commission' will refer to the organization itself or to the plenary group, while the term 'committee' is used for all subsidiary bodies.

[85]INPFC, *Annual Report 1969*, Vancouver 1971, *passim*.

[86]Art. 4, para. ii CECAF Statutes. Art. 4 IOFC Resolution. Art. 8, para. iii CARPAS Statutes. Art. III, para. 4 IPFC and GFCM Agreements.

into which the Convention waters have been divided. These panels review the fisheries in their sub-area and report to the plenary group.[87] The second procedure is the most common one. Almost all plenary groups of international fisheries organizations have used their authority to establish committees, which perform a variety of functions. These will be discussed in more detail in the following section. Finally, an example of the third method is offered by the NEAFC Convention which provides that the panels for the sub-areas may establish such sub-committees as are necessary.[88]

The composition of committees and other subsidiary bodies is usually not the object of any special rules. The result is that on most committees all member States will be represented by an expert in the area of concern to the committee in question. However, if a subsidiary group is not a committee of the whole, there are essentially two methods to determine its composition: (1) by appointing selected member States to that committee; or (2) by simply inviting interested member States to appoint a representative. The Whaling Commission illustrates both approaches. Under the IWC Rules of Procedure, the Chairman appoints five member States to the Finance Committee of the Commission,[89] but he polls all Commissioners to determine if they desire representation on the Scientific and Technical Committees.[90] The latter system is also used to determine the composition of the committees of the Indo-Pacific Council.[91] A few international fisheries conventions contain explicit provisions with respect to the composition of particular subsidiary bodies. Although the sub-area panels of the Northwest Atlantic Commission are established by the Convention itself, the Commission is responsible for deter-

[87]Art. VII ICNAF Convention.
[88]Art. 6, para. 4 NEAFC Convention.
[89]IWC Rules of Procedure, Rule XVIII.
[90]*Ibidem*.
[91]IPFC Rules of Procedure, Rule X, para. 2(a).

mining representation on each panel on the basis of current substantial exploitation of certain species of the sub-area in question. In addition, States with a coastline adjacent to a sub-area have a right to be represented on the panel for such area.[92] The NEAFC Convention contains similar provisions.[93]

4.2.2 Categories

A first classification of subsidiary bodies would distinguish between *ad hoc* and standing committees. Most international fisheries organizations have a relatively small number of standing committees, but a much larger number of *ad hoc* committees.[94] The *ad hoc* groups usually study a specific problem with which the organization is concerned, while the standing committees have the task of coordinating these activities. However, it is also possible to distinguish subsidiary bodies on the basis of functional, rather than formal, criteria. From such a functional point of view, subsidiary bodies can be divided into five general categories: scientific, regulatory, administrative, enforcement and executive committees.

Most subsidiary bodies are concerned with the scientific aspects of the activities of the commission in question. Several fisheries organizations have a standing scientific committee with a variety of scientific sub-committees. The Northwest Atlantic Commission, for example, has a Standing Committee on Research and Statistics;[95] the North Pacific Commission has a Standing Committee on Biology and Research;[96] and the Whaling Commission has a Scientific

[92]Art. IV, para. 2 ICNAF Convention; for proposed amendment, see ICNAF, *Annual Proceedings for the year 1968–1969*, Dartmouth 1969, p. 21.
[93]Art. 5, para. 2 NEAFC Convention.
[94]ICNAF, *Annual Proceedings for the year 1970–1971*, Dartmouth 1971, *passim*. INPFC, *Annual Report 1969*, Vancouver 1971, *passim*.
[95]ICNAF, *Annual Proceedings for the year 1970–1971*, Dartmouth 1971, p. 16.
[96]INPFC, *Annual Report 1969*, Vancouver 1971, p. 1.

Committee and a Technical Committee.[97] An exception is the North-East Atlantic Commission which has no scientific committees since it relies completely on the scientific advice of the International Council.[98] The responsibilities of ICNAF's Standing Committee on Research and Statistics are characteristic of those of other scientific committees. They are: (1) to make recommendations to the plenary group concerning the collection, compilation and analysis of fishery statistics; (2) to keep under review the research programmes in progress in the convention area, and to recommend changes in existing programmes or to recommend such new programmes as may be deemed desirable; and (3) to keep under review the condition of the stocks and the effects of fishing on these stocks.[99] This Standing Committee oversees and coordinates the work of a great number of sub-committees and working parties which study specific scientific problems of relevance to ICNAF. The reports of the Standing Committee present all these activities to the plenary group in an unified and easily accessible manner. Other international fisheries organizations have a similar structure of scientific subsidiary bodies.[100]

It is difficult to distinguish between scientific problems and their regulatory implications. Consequently, many scientific committees are concerned not only with purely scientific questions, but also with regulatory matters. Yet there is a category of subsidiary bodies for which regulatory questions are the *raison d'être*. These can be called regulatory committees. The sub-area bodies of the North-East Atlantic and of the Northwest Atlantic Commission fall within this category. Article 6 of the NEAFC Convention, for example, provides that NEAFC's regional committees may initiate

[97]IWC, *Twenty-second Report of the Commission*, London 1972, p. 25.
[98]Art. 11, para. 1 NEAFC Convention.
[99]ICNAF Rules of Procedure, Rule 6, para. 3.
[100]*E.g.*, the North Pacific Commission and the Whaling Commission; see Burke, *op. cit.*, note 1, pp. 140–144.

proposals for regulatory measures in the areas for which they are responsible.[101] Similar arrangements exist in the Northwest Atlantic Commission.[102] A slightly different approach to regulatory committees can be found in the North Pacific Commission. In 1958 it established an *Ad hoc* Committee on Abstention,[103] which is responsible for determining whether or not stocks under abstention continue to qualify for such abstention.[104] This is clearly a regulatory function. The importance of this Committee is demonstrated by the fact that usually all four representatives of the three member States attend its meetings. It is also evident from the fact that the Commission does not report on the deliberations within the Committee, but only on the outcome of such deliberations.[105] Another INPFC committee with direct regulatory functions is the *Ad hoc* Committee on the Protocol, which is responsible for adjusting the provisional line separating salmon of American origin from salmon of Asian origin. [106]

A third category of subsidiary bodies is involved in administrative and financial problems. Several international fisheries organizations have a standing committee to deal with these questions. The Northwest Atlantic Commission, for example, has a Standing Committee on Finance and Administration;[107] the North Pacific Commission has an identically named Committee;[108] and the Whaling Commission has a Finance and Administration Committee.[109] These committees are primarily responsible for the internal functioning of the fisheries commission in question, and they advise the

[101]Art. 6, para. 2 NEAFC Convention.
[102]Art. 7 NEAFC Convention.
[103]INPFC, *Annual Report for the year 1958*, Vancouver 1959, p. 11.
[104]Art. III, para. 1(a) INPFC Convention.
[105]INPFC, *Annual Report 1964*, Vancouver 1966, p. 9.
[106]*Ibidem, 1958*, Vancouver 1959, p. 8.
[107]ICNAF, *Annual Proceedings for the year 1970–1971*, Dartmouth 1971, p. 16.
[108]INPFC, *Annual Report 1969*, Vancouver 1971, p. 5.
[109]IWC, *Twenty-second Report of the Commission*, London 1972, p. 25.

plenary group on expenditures, budgets, contributions, financial regulations, staff questions, procedural matters, etc.[110]

A few fisheries organizations have committees which are concerned with the enforcement of fisheries regulations. The Whaling Commission, for example, has a special Infractions Sub-Committee which reports to the Technical Committee.[111] The North-East Atlantic Commission has a similar body.[112] The primary responsibility of these committees is to review the reports which member States must submit concerning infractions of the regulations of these organizations and concerning their inspection efforts.

A last category of subsidiary bodies consists of executive committees. The IPFC Agreement, for example, establishes a committee composed of the Chairman, the Vice-Chairman and the immediately retired Chairman.[113] Its function is to conduct the business of the Indo-Pacific Council between the biennial meetings of the plenary group. To that end it must meet at least once a year in this inter-session period. The Atlantic Tuna Commission has a similar subsidiary body.[114]

This classification of subsidiary bodies is not exhaustive and, as has been mentioned, it is often difficult to distinguish between the various categories. In addition, the role of a specific committee varies with the importance of the problems with which it is concerned. In their initial stages such problems might be largely scientific in scope, but after some time their regulatory implications may very well become more predominant. However, in most international fisheries organizations, subsidiary bodies are essentially forums in which experts discuss specific questions. They have advisory functions and they report to the plenary group or, in the case

[110]IWC Rules of Procedure, Rule XVIII.
[111]IWC, *Twenty-second Report of the Commission*, London 1972, p. 24.
[112]NEAFC, *Report of the ninth meeting*, London 1971, p. 26.
[113]Art. III, para. 1 IPFC Agreement.
[114]Art. V ICCAT Convention.

of sub-committees, to the committee which established them.[115]

4.3 Staff

4.3.1 Legal Provisions

The third basic element in the organizational structure of international fisheries organizations is the staff. The North Pacific Commission and the Pacific Tuna Commission have not an appointed, but an elected Secretary,[116] whose office must rotate among the member States. However, with these exceptions, the staff of international fisheries organizations consists of appointed officials. It seems that even in the INPFC and the IATTC, the appointed Director has taken over most of the responsibilities of the elected Secretary.[117] Most international fisheries conventions authorize the commission to appoint one official,[118] who appoints and heads the staff in accordance with rules and conditions laid down by the commission.[119] Apart from a permanent staff, a few fisheries organizations are also explicitly authorized to employ experts on a temporary basis.[120]

[115]*Infra* pp. 186–188.

[116]Art. II, para. 6 INPFC Convention. INPFC Rules of Procedure, Rule 13. Art. I, para. 7 IATTC Convention. IATTC Rules of Procedure, Rule VI.

[117]In 1958 the INPFC Secretary declared, for example, that he did not submit a special report since the report of the Executive Director covered the functions of his office, INPFC, *Annual Report for the year 1958*, Vancouver 1959, p. 2.

[118]His title usually is: Executive Director, Director of Investigations, Secretary or Executive Secretary.

[119]Art. XII ICSEAF Convention. Art. VII ICCAT Convention. Art. 13, para. 1 ICES Convention. Art. 3, para. 6 NEAFC Convention. Art. II, para. 13 INPFC Convention. Art. I, para. 10 and 13 IATTC Convention. Art. III ICNAF Convention. Art. III, para. 3 IWC Convention.

[120]Art. III, para. 3 GFCM Agreement.

Some international fisheries organizations employ only a small secretarial staff. The Whaling Commission, for example, has a Secretary, whose offices are in the Ministry of Agriculture, Fisheries and Food of the United Kingdom. For his part-time services the Commission pays about £750.[121] The North-East Atlantic Commission also relies on an official of this Ministry for secretarial assistance, and it pays the Ministry £2,750 for the salary of a Secretary, for administrative and clerical help, and for overhead.[122] The Fur Seal Commission has a similar arrangement with the National Marine Fisheries Service of the United States. The FAO handles the secretarial work of all FAO-related fisheries organizations. Its Director-General appoints, for example, a Secretary for the Indo-Pacific Council and for the Mediterranean Council, who is responsible to him.[123] These arrangements also exist for CARPAS, the IOFC and CECAF.[124] The responsibilities of such secretarial staffs are limited to: (1) receiving the contributions and disbursing the funds in accordance with the instructions of the commission; (2) maintaining the files of the commission; (3) preparing the meetings of the commission; (4) preparing certain reports; (5) submitting budget estimates; and (6) conducting routine correspondence.[125]

A few international fisheries organizations have staffs which perform not only these secretarial functions, but which have certain research-oriented tasks as well. This is largely a practical difference, which is not related to specific legal provisions. For example, the responsibilities of the Executive Director of the North Pacific Commission are described[126] in

[121]IWC, *Twenty-first Report of the Commission*, London 1971, p. 109.
[122]NEAFC, *Report of the eighth meeting*, London 1970, p. 72.
[123]Art. II, para. 6 IPFC and GFCM Agreements.
[124]Art. 7 CARPAS Statutes.
[125]NEAFC Rules of Procedure, Rule 6. IWC Rules of Procedure, Rule XI.
[126]INPFC Rules of Procedure, Rule 18.

terms that are very similar to those used to describe the responsibilities of the Secretary of the Fur Seal Commission.[127] Yet there is a very distinct difference between their activities. In addition to secretarial work, the Executive Director of the North Pacific Commission and his staff are also involved in: (1) the compilation of statistical data; (2) the publication of a statistical yearbook; (3) the preparation of other scientific publications; and (4) maintaining contact with other organizations in scientific matters.[128] These additional responsibilities are research-oriented, although they do not involve actual investigations. The staff of the Northwest Atlantic Commission and of the International Council has similar responsibilities. The publications of these organizations are essentially the result of research by member States, but their staff is instrumental in compiling scientific information and in preparing it for publication.[129] Two of the commissions in this category could have employed a permanent staff to conduct their own investigations.[130] However, both the Northwest Atlantic Commission and the North Pacific Commission decided at an early stage in their development to leave the actual investigations to the agencies of the member States and to limit their own role to the coordination of research programmes and the exchange of the results.[131] The provisions of the ICCAT Convention[132] also authorize the Atlantic Tuna Commission to employ a research staff, but the financial limitations imposed upon the Commission make it questionable that it will be able to use this authority.[133]

There are only three international fisheries organizations

[127]NPFSC Rules of Procedure, Rule 13.
[128]INPFC, *Annual Report 1968*, Vancouver 1970, p. 31.
[129]ICNAF, *Annual Proceedings for the year 1970–1971*, Dartmouth 1971, pp. 6–7.
[130]Art. II, para. 13 INPFC Convention. Art. III ICNAF Convention.
[131]INPFC, *Annual Report for the year 1955*, Vancouver 1956, p. 4.ICNAF, *Report of the first annual meeting*, Washington, D.C. 1951, p. 24.
[132]Art. VII ICCAT Convention.
[133]Art. X ICCAT Convention.

with a staff that is responsible for carrying out the actual scientific studies. These are: the Halibut Commission, the Salmon Commission and the Pacific Tuna Commission. The IPHC Convention and the IPSFC Convention require the respective commissions to undertake the necessary investigations, but do not elaborate upon the responsibilities and organization of the research staff.[134] The IATTC Convention is more detailed. The IATTC Director of Investigations is in charge of: (1) the drafting of research programmes and the preparation of budget estimates; (2) the disbursement of the funds of the Commission; (3) the accounting of these funds; (4) the appointment and immediate direction of personnel; (5) the arrangements for cooperation with other organizations; and (6) the drafting of administrative and scientific reports.[135] As a result, the IATTC staff is involved not only in secretarial and research-oriented work, but in conducting scientific investigations as well. The same applies to the staff and the Directors of Investigation of the Halibut Commission and Salmon Commission. It has been mentioned that the research programmes of these three commissions have been very successful.[136]

4.4 Evaluation

Most international fisheries commissions are modest entities when compared with other international organizations. This is clearly reflected not only in their limited powers, but also in their internal structure. The most striking characteristic of this structure is informality. The legal provisions of most international fisheries conventions are rather general with respect to the organization of the commissions they establish. The fact that the rules of procedure of a specific organization may add some detail to these general provisions does not

[134]Art. III, para. 1 IPHC Convention. Art. III IPSFC Convention.
[135]Art. I, para. 13 IATTC Convention.
[136]*Supra* p. 80, p. 82, p. 95.

prevent the internal structure of most international fisheries organizations from being rather vaguely defined. However, this informality seems to be more advantageous than disadvantageous. It gives fisheries organizations a degree of flexibility, which enables them to adapt their structure to new developments and new problems. The frequent changes in the committee structure of most fisheries organizations attest to the fact that they utilize this opportunity effectively. Consequently, as long as international fisheries commissions operate within a context which is subject to continuous change, the informality of their internal structure appears to be an asset, rather than a liability.

The effectiveness of fisheries organizations depends in their present stage of development upon the voluntary cooperation of States.[137] In its turn, such cooperation depends in many countries upon the cooperation of the fishing industry. This implies that the influence of the members of the national delegations within their respective countries is an important factor in determining the success of a fisheries commission. Consequently, it should be possible to include in these delegations representatives of those interest groups which will be influential in the process by which a government decides whether or not it will accept a certain recommendation of a fisheries organization. The acceptance of these recommendations on the national level is greatly facilitated if representatives of the fishing industry and the scientific community of the members participate in the international deliberations within international fisheries commissions. The existing legal provisions on the selection of delegates, which give complete freedom to member States, seem quite satisfactory in this respect.

It has been mentioned that with a few exceptions, international fisheries organizations meet once a year. This may be quite adequate if an organization is primarily involved in

[137]*Supra* p. 124.

promoting and coordinating national research programmes. However, if an organization is also concerned with the regulation of marine fisheries, it is questionable whether annual meetings are sufficient. A first indication of the need to meet more frequently is that several commissions have reached critical regulatory decisions at extraordinary sessions, rather than at their regular annual meetings. Another indication is the fact that a few fisheries commissions have deemed it necessary to establish executive committees to conduct the commission's business in the inter-session period. Other fisheries bodies attempt to continue their work in this period by voting through correspondence on certain issues.[138] Nevertheless, the Salmon Commission is the only organization which makes substantive decisions in the period between two formal conferences. The fact that in almost all regulatory fisheries organizations decisions can only be taken at annual meetings undoubtedly contributes to one of their most serious shortcomings: they can often not act in a timely fashion. There are essentially two alternatives to correct this situation: (1) to delegate substantial decision-making authority to permanent committees or to the staff; or (2) to have more frequent meetings of the plenary group. The specific circumstances under which a commission operates will determine which alternative is preferable. However, it is unquestionable that the pace at which marine fisheries are changing has made it unacceptable to restrict the decision-making process of fisheries organizations to an annual conference.

Voting arrangements in international fisheries commissions are not very important: whatever a fishery organization decides, the decision is almost never[139] directly binding on the member States or their fishermen. All decisions are recommendations which, in order to become binding, must

[138]INPFC, *Annual Report 1969*, Vancouver 1971, p. 27.
[139]*Infra* pp. 188–190.

be formally accepted by the States concerned. The most important effect of a decision of a commission is that its member States must decide whether or not they are willing to implement the decision in question. For this reason, it seems rather superfluous to require any fisheries organization with more than two members to decide by an unanimous or by a two-thirds majority vote. Yet there are quite a few international fisheries conventions which contain such a requirement. This may also result in delaying necessary regulatory recommendations.

Most international fisheries organizations have a highly desirable degree of flexibility concerning the creation of subsidiary bodies. They may establish committees whenever they consider it necessary to do so and for whatever purpose they deem fit. The few restrictions imposed upon commissions in this respect do not alter this fact. This flexibility has enabled fisheries commissions to adapt their work to new developments by establishing a special committee to deal with such developments. However, one problem is that no conventions provide for executive committees with more than minimal responsibilities. The use of such committees could be extremely helpful in giving the work of fisheries organizations a larger degree of continuity.

Committees and staff are in essence mutually exclusive. Fisheries organizations with a large number of committees have only a small-sized staff with limited responsibilities, and fisheries organizations with an effective research staff have only a small number of committees, if any at all. The reason for this mutual exclusivity of staff and committee structure is that both serve the same function: to provide the plenary group with scientific advice. The functional aspects of these two alternatives will be discussed in the next Chapter, but they also have different implications concerning the internal structure of fisheries organizations. A first point is that the structure of a commission with a research staff is much simpler than that of a commission with several committees. In the first alternative there is a plenary group and a staff, while the second alternative adds an often confusing number of committees. Secondly, a staff has a degree of permanency which committees lack. As a result, commissions with a research staff can be classified as permanent international organizations much more easily than commissions with a committee structure, which are still very similar to periodic international conferences. In addition, commissions with a staff are a more continuous form of international fisheries regulation than commissions with a committee structure. In the latter type of commissions, the decision-making process is basically confined to the annual meeting, while in the first category of organizations the staff ensures a degree of continuity.

5. EXTERNAL RELATIONS

5.1 Legal Provisions

International fisheries conventions generally authorize fisheries commissions to maintain relations with other organizations.[140] It is usually provided that the commission may establish and maintain working arrangements with any other international organization with related objectives. A few agreements specifically include the public and private agencies of the member States in the organizations with which such a relationship may be established.[141] The IWC and ICNAF Conventions contain a rather unique provision which requires member States to decide within a certain period of time after the entry into force of the conventions whether or not these commissions will be brought within the

[140]Art. XI ICSEAF Convention. Art. XI, para. 2 ICCAT Convention. Art. 4 ICES Convention. Art. 11 NEAFC Convention. Art. X, para. 1 ICNAF Convention. Art. VI IPFC Agreement. Art. IV IWC Convention.
[141]Art. IV, para. 1 IWC Convention.

framework of a specialized agency of the United Nations.[142] When these two commissions were established, it was thought that all regional fisheries organizations could function within the framework of FAO. However, both the Whaling Commission and the Northwest Atlantic Commission decided to remain fully independent.[143] On the basis of the above provisions, most international fisheries commissions maintain extensive relations with a variety of national and international organizations. These relations will be reviewed in the following sections.

5.2 Member State Agencies

It will be clear that the national delegations to the meetings of a fisheries organization are a major channel for communication between the organization and the agencies of its member States. This is also the major reason why it has been suggested that the composition of these delegations is an important factor in determining the organization's effectiveness.[144] In order to facilitate communication between their secretariat and the member States during the inter-session period, some international fisheries commissions have a special correspondent or liaison officer in each State.[145] However, most contacts between fisheries commissions and the member States' agencies are less formal and do not require such a structured approach. This is particularly the case with respect to scientific cooperation between the organization's staff and the scientists working in the research institutions of member States. These contacts are usually quite informal, particularly if the fisheries commission has its headquarters in one

[142]Art. X, para. 2 ICNAF Convention. Art. III, para. 6 IWC Convention.
[143]ICNAF, *Second Annual Report for the year 1951–1952*, St. Andrews 1952, p. 12. IWC, *Second Report of the Commission*, London 1951, p. 4.
[144]*Supra* p. 148.
[145]FAO, *Report of the second session of the Indian Ocean Fishery Commission*, FAO Fisheries Reports No. 95, Rome 1970, p. 9. INPFC Rules of Procedure, Rule 23.

of the research laboratories of a member State.[146] The Halibut Commission, for example, is located in a Marine Sciences Building of the University of Washington in Seattle, and the Pacific Tuna Commission has its headquarters at the United States Fishery-Oceanography Center on the campus of the University of California at San Diego. There is daily contact between the scientists of these two commissions and their national counterparts. More strictly organized is the communication between fishery organizations and member States on regulatory matters. Some conventions stipulate, for example, that a commission must transmit the text of its regulatory proposals to a Depository Government, which in its turn must transmit this document to the other member States.[147]

5.3 Non-Members

International fisheries conventions are generally silent on the matter of relations with non-member States. An exception is the NEAFC Convention, which provides that at the request of any Contracting Party, the North-East Atlantic Commission must consider representations made by non-member States for the opening of negotiations on the conservation of the fish stocks in the Convention area.[148] Obviously, the actual negotiations will take place between delegations consisting of State representatives. Nevertheless, this Article gives the Commission a certain formal role in dealing with non-member States. A different clause has been inserted in the INPFC Convention.[149] It requires the three member States to confer upon steps to obviate the adverse effects which fishing operations of a non-member State might have on the fisheries of a member State. This provision has been

[146]IATTC, *Annual Report for the year 1969*, La Jolla 1970, p. 42.
[147]Art. VIII, para. 1 ICNAF Convention.
[148]Art. 6, para. 1 NEAFC Convention.
[149]Art. VI INPFC Convention.

the basis for frequent discussions in the Commission regarding the North Pacific fisheries of the Soviet Union and the Republic of Korea.

The fact that fisheries agreements do not address themselves to this subject has not prevented fisheries organizations from developing certain relations with non-member States. First of all, observers from such States attend the annual meetings of several commissions. The Northwest Atlantic Commission, for example, has a policy of inviting observers from those non-member States which are members of the North-East Atlantic Commission.[150] The Whaling Commission is also an example here, although in an effort to persuade non-member States to join the commission it considered for a while the idea of no longer inviting their observers. These plans had to be abandoned rather quickly.[151] A second source of contact is that fisheries commissions do not hesitate to call for the voluntary cooperation of non-member States. They have, for example, requested non-member States to adopt their regulatory proposals. This action is sometimes successful: all nations participating in the tuna fishery of the Eastern Pacific have accepted the regulatory proposals of the Pacific Tuna Commission, regardless of their IATTC membership status.[152] Similar requests have been made concerning scientific information. The North Pacific Commission, for instance, has repeatedly asked the Soviet Union to provide information on its fisheries in the INPFC area.[153] The Soviet Union did not respond to these requests. Japan and Cuba, on the other hand, did provide the Northwest Atlantic Commission with statistical information on their fisheries in the ICNAF area, although they were not

[150]ICNAF, *Annual Proceedings for the year 1969–1970*, Dartmouth 1970, p. 7.
[151]IWC, *Second Report of the Commission*, London 1951, p. 4.
[152]In addition, United States legislation required this as a condition for approval.
[153]INPFC, *Annual Report 1968*, Vancouver 1970, p. 30.

members of ICNAF.[154] Finally, a last way in which a fisheries commission might maintain contacts with non-member States is through the exchange of scientists. Before having become a member, Japan exchanged scientists with the Pacific Tuna Commission.[155] The same Commission has field offices in several non-member countries in order to collect data on landings.[156]

5.4 Other International Organizations

International fisheries commissions maintain extensive relations with other international organizations concerned with marine fisheries. These relations are to a large extent rather informal in nature. A first source of informal contact is created by the fact that many persons who are involved in a specific fisheries organization also participate in the work of similar organizations. These personal relationships are a main channel through which international fisheries commissions communicate with each other. This is particularly the case on a scientific level: many scientists work for several organizations at the same time. A somewhat more formal mechanism through which fisheries commissions are in contact with each other is the exchange of observers.[157] Such an exchange of observers exists in particular among those commissions which operate in the same general region. The three North Pacific commissions, for example, usually attend each other's meetings. Another channel for communication is the establishment of joint working groups. These groups are responsible for studying a problem which is of common concern to the sponsoring organizations. The International

[154]ICNAF, *Annual Proceedings for the year 1968–1969*, Dartmouth 1969, p. 7.
[155]IATTC, *Annual Report for the year 1966*, La Jolla 1967, p. 49.
[156]*Ibidem*, p. 47.
[157]See ICNAF, *Annual Proceedings for the year 1970–1971*, Dartmouth 1971, p. 17. INPFC, *Annual Report 1969*, Vancouver 1971, p. 11.

Council, the FAO, the Northwest Atlantic Commission and the North-East Atlantic Commission, for instance, have established several joint study groups.[158] Fisheries bodies also organize joint symposia on specific problems.[159] Finally, if commissions function within the overall structure of the same organization, they communicate with each other through this organization. This is particularly the case with all the fisheries bodies that are established within the framework of FAO: CARPAS, the IOFC, CECAF, the IPFC and the GFCM report to FAO and coordinate their work in this way.

These various mechanisms have resulted in a remarkably close cooperation between several international fisheries organizations. However, the relationship between the International Council and the North-East Atlantic Commission remains unique. Membership in both organizations is nearly identical.[160] This explains Article 11, para. 1 of the NEAFC Convention which requires the North-East Atlantic Commission to seek the scientific advice of the International Council. NEAFC has no functions with regard to research, but relies in this respect completely on the Council. The Council has established a special Liaison Committee, which reports to the annual meetings of NEAFC. Essentially, ICES functions as NEAFC's research arm.[161] It is reimbursed for its work by the Commission. A similar arrangement exists between FAO and some regional fisheries commissions. FAO undertook, for example, stock assessment work for the Whaling Commission. This cooperation was not initiated

[158]ICNAF, *Annual Proceedings for the year 1969–1970*, Dartmouth 1970, p. 7.
[159]*Ibidem.*
[160]Italy and Finland are members of ICES, but not of NEAFC.
[161]C E Lucas, *International fishery bodies of the North Atlantic*, Law of the Sea Institute, University of Rhode Island, Occasional Paper No. 5, April 1970, p. 13.

without any problems,[162] but was, nevertheless, quite productive for several years.[163] Such close contacts are usually limited to research. However, with respect to regulation a rather close collaboration exists between the Halibut Commission and the North Pacific Commission. In 1963 the INPFC removed the halibut stocks of the Eastern Bering Sea from abstention. As these stocks were also of concern to the Halibut Commission, both Commissions decided to cooperate in adopting the necessary conservation measures. The two Commissions have developed an informal procedure under which the United States-Canada Halibut Commission formulates draft halibut conservation regulations and submits these to the United States-Canada-Japan North Pacific Commission. As a result, the halibut stocks of the Eastern Bering Sea are under the joint regulation of both organizations.[164]

5.5 Private Groups

All international fisheries organizations depend upon the acceptance of their recommendations by the member States. This explains the importance of relations with those private groups which are influential in determining such acceptance, and in particular with the fishing industry. Persons associated with the industry can, first of all, be appointed as members of the national delegations to the meetings of a fisheries commission.[165] They may be included in these delegations as

[162]When the IWC first suggested that FAO would carry out these studies, the FAO representative indicated that FAO was not willing to cooperate if the IWC '. . . permitted the results of the scientific studies to be used merely for the organization of the more efficient destruction of the source for which it was responsible', IWC, *Sixteenth Report of the Commission*, London 1966, p. 17.
[163]In 1969 FAO notified the IWC that it considered other commitments more pressing, IWC, *Twenty-first Report of the Commission*, London 1971, p. 9.
[164]IPHC, *Regulation and investigation of the Pacific halibut fishery in 1963*, Seattle 1964, p. 10.
[165]*Supra* pp. 130–133.

experts or advisers; they may even be the official delegates.[166] The fishing industry may also send observers. The meetings of the Whaling Commission, for example, were for several years attended by observers from the Association of Whaling Companies.[167] Another mechanism through which fisheries commissions can maintain relations with the fishing industry is public hearings. The ICNAF Convention, for example, provides that the commissioners of each member State may organize public hearings within their respective countries.[168] Other conventions contain a similar clause.[169] Several agreements go a step further and provide that the Contracting Parties may establish special Advisory Committees.[170] These Committees generally consist of persons who have experience in the fishing industry; their members have the right to attend meetings of the fisheries organization in question. Finally, communication with the fishing industry is also the main reason why several commissions have a practice of beginning each annual meeting with a session open to the general public.[171] These arrangements have led to a great deal of contact between the industry and most international fisheries organizations. The Halibut and Salmon Commissions are especially active in this respect. Both commissions meet frequently with industry representatives in order to discuss the regulatory proposals under consideration.[172] The tradition of industry participation in these two Commissions can in fact be considered as the origin of similar arrangements in other organizations.

[166]ICNAF, *Annual Proceedings for the year 1970–1971*, Dartmouth 1971, pp. 37–42.
[167]IWC, *Seventh Report of the Commission*, London 1956, p. 3.
[168]Art. V, para. 2 ICNAF Convention.
[169]Art. II, para. 9 INPFC Convention. Art. I, para. 12 IATTC Convention.
[170]Art. 12 ICES Convention. Art. II, para. 8 INPFC Convention. Art. I, para. 11 IATTC Convention. Art. V, para. 1 ICNAF Convention.
[171]INPFC, *Annual Report 1969*, Vancouver 1971, p. 1.
[172]IPHC, *Regulation and investigation of the Pacific halibut fishery in 1968*, Seattle 1969, p. 6.

The fishing industry is certainly the most important private group with which international fisheries organizations maintain relations. However, other private groups occasionally attend the meetings of these organizations. An example is the Whaling Commission: its twenty-first meeting was attended by observers from: (1) the International Society for the Protection of Animals; (2) the International Union for the Conservation of Nature and Natural Resources; and (3) the World Federation for the Protection of Animals.[173] The fact that observers from the Association of Whaling Companies have been replaced by observers from these groups is indicative of the performance of the Whaling Commission.

5.6 Evaluation

International fisheries commissions must maintain external relations with other national and international organizations for the following reasons: (1) to coordinate their activities with those of other organizations; (2) to enable these other organizations to participate in their decision-making process; and (3) to achieve a higher degree of effectiveness. The first consideration is the main reason why fisheries commissions maintain relations with other international fisheries organizations. Stocks of fish and fishing fleets are mobile. Consequently, regulations adopted by one commission may have repercussions on the fisheries for which another commission is responsible. If, for example, the North-East Atlantic Commission would restrict catches in its area of competence, it is likely that some of the resulting overcapacity in the fleet would be directed to the Northwest Atlantic Commission's area of competence. A related point is that the functions of several commissions are either complementary or similar. For example, the research functions of ICES complement the regulatory functions of NEAFC, while the functions of the

[173]IWC, *Twenty-first Report of the Commission*, London 1971, p. 17.

IOFC and the IPFC are very similar. Both situations require cooperation and coordination between the organizations in question. The second reason is an important element in the contacts between international fisheries organizations, the fishing industry and other national and international groups. Their participation in the work of a fisheries commission has a positive effect on the quality of its decisions, since it greatly improves the scientific and other advice upon which the commission relies in making such decisions. It also enhances the acceptability of these decisions on the national level. This implies that participation by other groups in the decision-making process of a specific organization also serves the third reason: it makes this organization more effective. This aspect is also of particular importance in the relations between a fisheries commission and non-member States. A major purpose of these contacts is to enhance the organization's effectiveness by drawing non-member States into its work.

Existing legal arrangements have enabled international fisheries commissions to establish satisfactory relations with all relevant national and international organizations. Most commissions have not encountered any problems in this respect. A minor difficulty has been that a few fisheries commissions have preferred not to deal directly with non-member States, but did consider it necessary to act through one of the member States.[174] However, it is doubtful whether the external relations of fisheries organizations will continue to be characterized by such an absence of serious problems. First of all, the problems facing these organizations are not likely to be solved without more radical regulatory measures. This will strain the relations with the fishing industry, member and non-member States. Secondly, if the number of international fisheries organizations increases, it will become more difficult to coordinate their activities. Thirdly, the close personal rapport among the fishery experts involved in the

[174]*Infra* p. 164.

international regulation of marine fisheries is gradually disappearing.[175] This is the result of the entry into marine fisheries of many new States whose representatives no longer know each other on a personal basis. These developments may make it more difficult to maintain satisfactory external relations. This raises the question of the desirability of a more structured approach to these relations, which until now have been almost completely voluntary in nature.

6. LEGAL STATUS

6.1 Legal Provisions

The question of the legal status of international fisheries organizations has two facets: (1) their capacity to act as legal entities under *international* law; and (2) their capacity to act as legal entities under *national* law. Both categories have in common that only a few fisheries conventions contain explicit provisions with respect to these issues. Consequently, the major factors to be considered in defining the legal status of international fisheries organizations are: (1) their functions; (2) their structure; and (3) their activities.

As far as legal capacity under international law is concerned, a first relevant aspect is the degree to which a certain fisheries commission is an independent entity. Several commissions are fully autonomous. They were established by a special international agreement, and they function independently under the terms of that agreement.[176] A second group of international fisheries organizations is semi-independent. The Indo-Pacific Council and the Mediterranean Council, for example, were established by special agreement, but they function within the general framework of FAO.[177] This is

[175]F T Christy, Jr., *Fisheries and the new conventions on the law of the sea, San Diego Law Review* 1970, pp. 462–463.
[176]For example, the NEAFC, the Japan-Soviet Commission, the IPHC, the INPFC, the IATTC, ICNAF and the IPSFC.
[177]Art. I, para. 1 IPFC and GFCM Agreements.

evident from the fact that membership in the two Councils is linked to membership in FAO; that FAO provides their secretariat; that the FAO pays most of their expenses; and by the fact that several of their decisions must be approved by FAO. On the other hand, both Councils may maintain independent relations with other international organizations, and they can have their own budget. Accordingly, they have a certain degree of autonomy. This is not the case with a third group of fisheries commissions. The IOFC, CARPAS and CECAF were created under Article 6 of the FAO Constitution and they are essentially advisory bodies within the FAO structure. Therefore, they can not be considered international legal entities distinct from FAO. Other factors determining the legal capacity of fisheries organizations under international law are related to their internal and external organization. In respect to their external organization the authority to establish and maintain relations with other national and international organizations dealing with marine fisheries is a very essential element of the international legal status of fisheries organizations. As far as their internal structure is concerned, the existence of a permanent research staff is one of the most important aspects: if a commission has a staff, it acquires a degree of permanency which enhances its status under international law. Finally, the absence of explicit provisions causes the international legal capacity of fisheries organizations to depend to a very large extent upon their functions. A commission which is solely responsible for the coordination of national research programmes requires a lesser degree of legal capacity than a commission which is involved in the regulation of marine fisheries. As a general principle, it can be assumed that international fisheries organizations have such legal capacity under international law as is clearly required for the realization of their functions.[178]

The legal status of international fisheries organizations

[178]*ICJ Reports* 1949, *Reparations Case*, p. 180.

under national law is somewhat less ambiguous. A few international agreements even contain an explicit provision in this respect. The ICES Convention, for example, stipulates that in the territory of the Contracting Parties, the Council enjoys such legal capacity as may be agreed upon between the Council and the States concerned.[179] In addition, the Council, the delegates and experts, the General Secretary and other Council officials enjoy in the territory of the member States such privileges and immunities as are necessary for the fulfilment of their functions.[180] A second example is the ICSEAF Convention which confers upon the Southeast Atlantic Commission the capacity to contract and to acquire and dispose of movable and immovable property.[181] Further clarification of the legal capacity of fisheries organizations under national law can be found in the legislation of a few countries. United States domestic legislation, for example, designates the fisheries commissions that have their head-quarters on United States territory[182] as 'public international organizations'. As a result, they have under United States law the capacity to contract, to acquire and dispose of property and to institute legal proceedings.[183] On the basis of these provisions, fisheries commissions engage primarily in the following acts under national law: (1) they receive and disburse funds;[184] (2) they enter into a variety of contracts;[185] (3) they appoint personnel and lease office space; and (4) they

[179]Art. 15 ICES Convention.
[180]*Ibidem*.
[181]Art. XV, para. 2 ICSEAF Convention.
[182]The IPHC and the IATTC.
[183]*United States Code* vol. 22, para. 288a(a).
[184]NEAFC even lends money to a municipal authority in the United Kingdom in order to '. . . take advantage of the high interest rates . . .' in that country, NEAFC, *Report of the eighth meeting*, London 1970, p. 68.
[185]The IPSFC, for example, handled all contracts involved in the removal of the obstruction at Hell's Gate, IPSFC, *Annual Report 1944*, New Westminster 1945, p. 9.

own property.[186] A problem arose in ICNAF with respect to the question of whether or not this Commission had the capacity under Canadian law to enter into a contract with an insurance firm in order to set up a staff pension plan. Canada, on whose territory the Commission has its headquarters, took the view that ICNAF lacked such capacity. An arrangement was worked out under which the Canadian government established a corporation to enter into a contract with the insurance firm on behalf of the Commission.[187]

6.2 Evaluation

The absence of more detailed provisions concerning the legal status of international fisheries organizations has resulted in a few minor problems. One such problem is that some commissions have taken the view that they lack the authority to deal directly with non-member States.[188] However, it seems that this problem stems primarily from an unnecessarily restrictive interpretation of the legal capacity of the commissions in question. Such an interpretation is also the main reason for the rather complex procedure which ICNAF followed in respect to its staff pension plan. It must be assumed that an organization which may employ a staff and which is allowed to establish its headquarters in the territory of one of the member States has an implicit capacity to enter into staff-related contracts under the national law of its host State. The rather vaguely defined status of ICES was also the main reason for the need to draw up the new 1964 Convention. Such problems concerning the legal capacity of fisheries organizations may very well become more serious in the future, particularly if these organizations should develop

[186]Art. VIII of the IPSFC Convention prohibits the Salmon Commission from owning land.
[187]ICNAF, *Annual Proceedings for the year 1956–1957*, Halifax 1957, p. 11.
[188]INPFC, *Annual Report 1969*, Vancouver 1971, p. 5. *Ibidem*, *1960*, Vancouver 1961, p. 12.

into more permanent institutions. This, and the fact that a more precise definition of the legal status of international fisheries organizations presents no theoretical and practical difficulties indicates that it is both desirable and feasible to make international fisheries agreements more specific in this respect.

7. FINANCES

7.1 Legal Provisions[189]

The budgets of international fisheries organizations differ widely: from a low of $8,000 for the NPFSC[190] to a high of $754,000 for the IPSFC.[191] The major elements determining levels of spending are: (1) the number of member States; (2) the functions of the organization; and (3) the size of the staff. Fisheries commissions which carry out their own investigations rank highest on the scale of expenditures. However, almost all fisheries organizations spend certain amounts for: (1) salaries of personnel; (2) other personnel related expenditures (social security, pension funds); (3) office expenses; (4) travel; (5) publications; and (6) meetings.[192] Essentially, there are two ways in which international fisheries organizations finance these expenditures.

Several fisheries commissions receive funds from other international organizations. The North-East Atlantic Commission, for example, makes a contribution to ICES to cover

[189]FAO, *op. cit.*, note 1, 1972, pp. 10-11. FAO, *op. cit.*, note 1, 1966, pp. 10-11.
[190]Fiscal year 1969.
[191]Fiscal year 1969; for more information, see *Panel Reports of the Commission on Marine Science, Engineering and Resources*, vol. 3, *Marine resources and legal-political arrangements for their development*, Washington 1969, p. VIII-52.
[192]NPFSC, *Proceedings of the fourteenth annual meeting*, Washington, D.C. 1971, p. 5. IWC, *Twenty-second Report of the Commission*, London 1972, pp. 147-148.

the expenses which ICES incurs by giving scientific advice to the Commission.[193] Such international funding is especially a feature of the FAO-related commissions. The Director-General of FAO may, within the overall FAO budget, authorize payment of expenses arising out of the activities of CARPAS, the IOFC and CECAF.[194] These bodies are not allowed to have their own budget. This distinguishes them from the two other FAO-related organizations: the Indo-Pacific Council and the Mediterranean Council. Although their operating expenses are part of the FAO budget, both Councils may have an independent budget for cooperative projects.[195] However, such projects were never initiated.[196] If a State which is not a member of FAO joins the IPFC or the GFCM, it is required to assume a proportionate share of its expenses.[197] Some of these FAO-related bodies also receive funds from the United Nations Development Programme.[198] In 1968 COFI requested the FAO Director-General to organize discussions concerning direct UNDP support for the research and fishery development work of the FAO fisheries bodies. COFI invited the commissions concerned to formulate specific proposals for such assistance.[199] One of the first results of these actions was UNDP funding for the International Indian Ocean Fishery Survey and Development Programme of the IOFC.[200]

With these exceptions international fisheries organizations

[193]NEAFC, *Report of the ninth meeting*, London 1971, p. 23.
[194]Art. 10, para. iv CARPAS Statutes.
[195]Art. VII, para. 3 IPFC and GFCM Agreements.
[196]F B Zenny, *Establishment, structure, functions and activities of international fisheries bodies – General Fisheries Council for the Mediterranean (GFCM)*, FAO Fisheries Technical Paper No. 78, Rome 1968, p. 16. Carroz, *op. cit.*, note 31, p. 18.
[197]Art. IX, para. 3 GFCM and Art. IX, para. 2 IPFC Agreement.
[198]FAO, *op. cit.*, note 145, p. 4.
[199]FAO, *Report of the third session of the Committee on Fisheries*, FAO Fisheries Reports No. 58, Rome 1968, p. 3.
[200]FAO, *op. cit.*, note 145, p. 4.

receive their funding directly from the member States.[201] It is universally provided that these member States pay the expenses of their delegations to the meetings of the organization.[202] As far as joint expenses are concerned, there are basically three formulas for their apportionment: (1) all member States pay equal amounts; (2) member States pay in proportion to their share in the total catch; and (3) member States pay in proportion to the number of committees on which they are represented. Examples of the first approach are the Salmon Commission, the Halibut Commission and the North Pacific Commisison. Their members contribute equal amounts—either on the basis of a provision in the Convention,[203] or on the basis of a decision of the organization.[204] The Pacific Tuna Commission offers an illustration of the second formula: the contributions of its member States are proportionate to their share in the tuna catch.[205] This resulted in an arrangement under which the *actual* United States contribution is used as the basis for computing the contributions of the other member States.[206] The North-East Atlantic, the Northwest Atlantic Commission and the Atlantic Tuna Commission exemplify the third formula. In the first two Commissions each member State pays a certain fixed amount and contributes to the remainder of the budget in proportion to the number of regional committees or panels on which it is represented.[207] Since panel representation is

[201]In the FAO-related commissions, members pay *indirectly* through their contributions to FAO.
[202]Art. 4, para. 1 NEAFC Convention. Art. II, para. 11 INPFC Convention. Art. XI, para. 1 ICNAF Convention. Art. I, para. 3 IATTC Convention. Art. III, para. 5 IWC Convention.
[203]Art. III IPHC Convention. Art. II IPSFC Convention.
[204]Art. II, para. 11, 12 and 13 INPFC Convention.
[205]Art. I, para. 3 IATTC Convention; an Exchange of Notes, which defines the share of each country as that part of the tuna catch which is used for domestic consumption, prevents a State from being charged for tuna landed in its ports, but exported to other member States.
[206]IATTC, *Annual Report for the year 1961*, La Jolla 1962, p. 17.
[207]Art. 4 NEAFC Convention. Art. XI, para. 3 ICNAF Convention.

linked to participation in the fisheries of a specific sub-area,[208] this system also relates the apportionment of expenses to the fishing activities of the member States. This is even more clearly stressed in the ICCAT Convention. The Atlantic Tuna Commission must apportion the remainder of its budget on the basis of the share of member States in the total catch if its expenditures exceed income from fixed amounts and from the panel representation fees.[209]

7.2 Evaluation

Most international fisheries organizations are capable of operating on a relatively small budget, largely because their functions are limited. This is undoubtedly the major reason why the existing budget apportionment formulas have worked adequately in most cases. However, a commission's financial needs increase drastically if it conducts its own investigations. Two of the existing organizations with a permanent research staff seem to experience relatively little difficulty in obtaining the necessary funding.[210] The Pacific Tuna Commission, on the other hand, has been forced to operate under severe financial constraints.[211] The main reason for its problems and the fact that only a few fisheries organizations have a permanent research staff is the unwillingness of States to fund internationally organized research when faced with the pressing funding requirements of national research programmes.[212] Consequently, if international fisheries organizations are to expand the scope of their functions and activities, different budget apportionment formulas will be necessary. A major improvement would be to give fisheries organizations a certain financial independence from the member States. This could be

[208]*Supra* p. 139.
[209]Art. I, para. 3 ICCAT Convention.
[210]The Halibut Commission and the Salmon Commission.
[211]IATTC, *Annual Report for the year 1963*, La Jolla 1964, p. 5.
[212]*Supra* p. 72.

accomplished by authorizing commissions to impose a levy on the fisheries for which they are responsible.[213] Another alternative would be to expand financing by such international sources as the UNDP and FAO. This would also insulate fisheries organizations from the uncertainties and pressures of the national budget procedures of their member States.

[213]The Whaling Commission imposed a levy on whaling in order to finance certain research projects, IWC, *Eighteenth Report of the Commission*, London 1968, p. 9.

Chapter IV

The Functions and Powers of International Fisheries Organizations

1. INTRODUCTION

The structural elements of international fisheries organizations that were discussed in the preceding Chapter are not an end in themselves. They are merely instruments for the realization of the functions of these organizations. Such functions fall generally within the following seven categories: (1) functions concerning the full utilization of the living resources of the sea; (2) functions concerning their conservation; (3) functions concerning the economic efficiency of marine fisheries; (4) functions concerning the allocation of the catch; (5) functions concerning research; (6) functions concerning the enforcement of fisheries regulations; and (7) functions concerning inter-use and intra-use conflicts. The discussion of the extra-legal factors involved in marine fisheries[1] has indicated that these seven categories are inter-related: research functions, for example, may support functions with respect to conservation; responsibilities concerning allocation are directly relevant to the problems of economic efficiency. Consequently, the distinction between these seven categories is not absolute. It, nevertheless, provides a framework within which the various functions of international fisheries organizations can be analyzed.

2. FUNCTIONS CONCERNING FULL UTILIZATION[2]

2.1 Indirect Functions

Almost all international fisheries organizations have certain functions with respect to the full utilization of the living

[1]Chapter I.
[2]For a discussion of the extra-legal background of full utilization functions, see *supra* pp. 39–45.

resources of the sea. Essentially, these functions are designed to bring about the fullest desirable use of these resources. However, for most fisheries commissions such functions are merely a consequence of their responsibilities in other areas. If, for example, a fisheries organization is exclusively involved in biological research, the results of its work may very well be used for a fishery development project designed to increase the utilization of specific stocks. In this case a research commission has an indirect function concerning full utilization. This applies even more strongly to those fisheries commissions which are primarily responsible for the conservation of the living resources of the sea. As will be discussed, conservation measures are usually designed to maintain catches at the level of the maximum sustainable yield of the stock in question.[3] Maximum sustainable yield has strong implications for full utilization. First of all, it is designed to maximize the long range physical productivity of the sea's living resources, which also ensures their long range full utilization. Secondly, if a specific stock is exploited below its maximum sustainable yield, the achievement of this objective requires measures to expand, rather than to limit, catches. This implies that a fisheries commission which is responsible for maintaining catches at the level of maximum sustainable yield has in effect full utilization functions regarding biologically under-exploited stocks. Finally, if a fisheries organization limits the catches of a specific stock to its maximum sustainable yield level, the resulting surplus fishing capacity may be directed towards other species. This leads to a fuller utilization of the species involved.[4]

2.2 Direct Functions

Several fisheries organizations have more direct responsibilities concerning full utilization. The Halibut Commission

[3]*Infra* p. 180.
[4]For example, the yellowfin tuna conservation measures of the IATTC contributed to the increase of skipjack tuna catches.

and the Salmon Commission, for example, were established for the explicit purpose of rebuilding stocks which had been depleted prior to international regulation. Apart from its related research and conservation functions, the Salmon Commission is authorized to conduct salmon fish cultural operations, improve spawning grounds, construct and maintain hatcheries, rearing ponds and similar facilities, and stock the waters to which the Convention applies with salmon.[5] The Halibut Commission was made responsible for developing the stocks of halibut in the Northern Pacific Ocean to levels which permit a maximum sustainable yield.[6] As these stocks had been depleted previously, this was essentially a full utilization function. Another fisheries commission with a similar function concerning full utilization is the North-East Atlantic Commission. Under the NEAFC Convention, it has the authority to recommend measures for the improvement and the increase of marine resources.[7] These measures may be concerned with artificial propagation, the transplantation of organisms and the transplantation of young fish. Another organization with substantial full utilization responsibilities is the Mixed Commission of 1962.[8]

However, the most important organizations with direct functions concerning the full utilization of the sea's living resources are the FAO-related fisheries bodies. This is understandable in view of the general nature of FAO's work.[9]

The task of its Department of Fisheries, for example, is to promote national and international action with respect to the development of the world's fisheries.[10] Its three

[5]Art. III IPSFC Convention.
[6]Art. III, para. 2 IPHC Convention.
[7]Art. 7, para. 1 (f) NEAFC Convention.
[8]Art. 3 Mixed Commission 1962 Convention.
[9]*Supra* pp. 104–113.
[10]FAO, *Work of FAO and related organizations concerning marine science and its applications*, FAO Fisheries Technical Paper No. 74, Rome 1968, p. 1.

Divisions carry out such projects as: (1) the location and appraisal of under-exploited stocks; (2) research of the aquatic environment with emphasis on predicting production trends; (3) assistance in production, processing and distribution; (4) fishery education and training; and (5) assistance to developing countries in creating export opportunities for their fishery products.[11] Although many of these activities have little direct relation to the legal regime of marine fisheries, they are all designed to result in a fuller utilization of the living resources of the sea. The same applies to the United Nations Development Programme projects that are administered by FAO's Department of Fisheries. Most of these projects are designed to expand the fisheries of developing nations. COFI evaluates all these programmes and attempts to define their priorities.[12]

This orientation of FAO itself explains the full utilization functions of the Indo-Pacific Council, the Mediterranean Council, CARPAS, the IOFC and CECAF. The Statutes of CECAF, for example, provide that the Commission must give advice on promoting and coordinating national and regional programmes of research and development designed to lead to a rational utilization of the fish resources of CECAF's area of competence.[13] The Terms of Reference of the IOFC contain a similar clause.[14] In addition, the IOFC and CECAF must further research and development activities in their respective areas through international sources, and in particular through international aid programmes.[15] These functions are based on a suggestion of COFI that the FAO bodies should be able to formulate proposals for

[11]FAO, *Report of the fifth session of the Committee on Fisheries*, FAO Fisheries Reports No. 86, Rome 1970, p. 11.
[12]*E.g.*, FAO, *Report of the sixth session of the Committee on Fisheries*, FAO Fisheries Reports No. 103, Rome 1971, pp. 5–7.
[13]Art. 3, para. a CECAF Statutes.
[14]Art. 2, para. a IOFC Resolution.
[15]Art. 3, para. e CECAF Statutes. Art. 2, para. b IOFC Resolution.

support from such international funding agencies as the United Nations Development Programme.[16] The IPFC and GFCM Agreements also stress full utilization. The Mediterranean Council, for example, is responsible for formulating all oceanographical and technical aspects of the problems of development and proper utilization of the aquatic resources of the Mediterranean.[17] The research functions of both Councils are primarily instruments for achieving this.[18]

2.3 Implementation

Functions concerning full utilization are generally advisory in nature. Accordingly, they must be implemented by making recommendations to the member States. The Salmon Commission is an exception: its staff is directly involved in the realization of fishery development projects, while the Commission itself improves spawning grounds, constructs and maintains hatcheries, etc.[19] In these areas the Salmon Commission is limited by financial considerations, rather than by its terms of reference. However, the Commission can merely make a recommendation to its member States if the action proposed involves the removal of obstructions to the ascent of salmon. Here its authority is more limited.[20] The powers granted to other fisheries organizations for implementing their full utilization functions are similarly restricted to recommending certain measures to their member States or other international organizations. This latter action is a

[16]FAO, *Report of the third session of the Committee on Fisheries*, FAO Fisheries Reports No. 58, Rome 1968, p. 3.
[17]Art. IV, para. a GFCM Agreement.
[18]Art. IV, para. a IPFC Agreement.
[19]IPSFC, *Annual Report 1970*, New Westminster 1971, pp. 3–8.
[20]Art. III IPSFC Convention; for the recommendation to remove the obstructions at Hell's Gate, see *Treaties and other international agreements on oceanographic resources, fisheries, and wildlife to which the United States is a party*, by the Legislative Reference Service of the Library of Congress for the use of the Committee on Commerce of the United States Senate, Washington 1970, pp. 356–361.

special feature of the FAO-related fishery bodies, which are required to submit periodic reports to the FAO Director-General.[21] These reports usually contain a variety of recommendations in the area of full utilization. However, the Indo-Pacific and Mediterranean Councils have the authority to undertake, where appropriate, cooperative fishery development projects.[22] Consequently, in respect of full utilization they have powers beyond just the making of recommendations and they may act in a way similar to that of the Salmon Commission. However, neither Council has used this authority.[23]

2.4 Evaluation

It has been discussed that there is still considerable opportunity to expand marine fisheries and that one of the challenges to international fisheries organizations is to stimulate such expansion to the extent of its being both biologically possible and economically attractive.[24] Yet the terms of reference of most international fisheries organizations do not deal explicitly with full utilization. For most fisheries commissions functions concerning conservation and research are far more important. Moreover, those fisheries organizations with more direct responsibilities concerning full utilization have, with the exception of the Salmon Commission, no powers beyond the hortatory. As most of these organizations are part of the FAO structure, the single most important

[21]Art. 5 CECAF Statutes. Art. 5 IOFC Resolution. Art. 9 CARPAS Statutes. Art. IV, para. i IPFC Agreement. Art. IV, para. k GFCM Agreement.
[22]Art. IV, para. e IPFC and GFCM Agreements.
[23]F B Zenny, *Establishment, structure, functions and activities of international fisheries bodies – General Fisheries Council for the Mediterranean (GFCM);* FAO Fisheries Technical Paper No. 78, Rome 1968, p. 16. J E Carroz, *Establishment, structure, functions and activities of international fisheries bodies – Indo-Pacific Fisheries Council (IPFC),* FAO Fisheries Technical Paper No. 57, Rome 1965, p. 18.
[24]*Supra* p. 44.

instrument of international fisheries commissions for bringing about the full utilization of the sea's living resources is to make recommendations to FAO and its Department of Fisheries. Nevertheless, they have made an important contribution towards the expansion of marine fisheries and towards assisting developing countries in sharing equitably in this expansion. Thus, they are instrumental in overcoming one of the problems of the freedom of fishing in respect of full utilization.[25] However, the full utilization functions of international fisheries organizations can unquestionably be expanded. Such expansion should not make full utilization a legal obligation: biological and economic factors, rather than legal factors, must determine the extent to which the living resources of the seas are utilized. Yet fisheries commissions could be granted more explicit functions and powers in this area, particularly for the purpose of developing maricultural fisheries.

A related point is that international fisheries organizations show quite an artificial specialization. Commissions with primary responsibilities in respect of conservation have merely indirect functions with regard to full utilization, and commissions with primary responsibilities in the area of full utilization have merely indirect functions with regard to conservation. The result is that one group of international fisheries organizations is concerned with limiting marine fisheries to biologically acceptable levels, while a second group of fisheries commissions is involved in an effort to expand marine fisheries. This creates several problems, particularly if a full-utilization-oriented commission is successful, i.e., if catches expand to the maximum sustainable yield level. As its functions are largely limited to full utilization, it can not effectively cope with the resulting conservation problems. This appears to be a problem in the IOFC and

[25]*Supra* p. 43.

CECAF.[26] Even if another fisheries organization can assume responsibility for the conservation of the stocks in question, several problems may arise in coordinating the activities of the organizations concerned, particularly since their membership may not be identical. Thus, the functions of international fisheries organizations do not reflect the fact that full utilization and conservation are closely linked issues. The obvious conclusion is that their responsibilities in these two areas should be integrated. Fisheries organizations must be fully capable of dealing with both questions. This implies that the full utilization functions of conservation commissions and the conservation functions of full utilization commissions must be enhanced. Functions concerning full utilization could include at the minimum the authority to make recommendations to the member States with respect to fishery development projects and with regard to the necessary investigations. A more liberal approach could give a commission the authority to undertake its own development projects. The Salmon Commission sets here a precedent.

3. FUNCTIONS CONCERNING CONSERVATION[27]

3.1 Indirect Functions

Conservation is the major concern of international fisheries organizations. Most commissions have direct functions in this area, but a few are merely indirectly involved in conservation problems. This applies, first of all, to those fisheries organizations whose primary responsibilities deal with research. For example, although the International Council is concerned exclusively with scientific research, the results of its efforts

[26]FAO, *Report of the second session of the Indian Ocean Fishery Commission*, FAO Fisheries Reports No. 95, Rome 1970, p. 2. FAO, *Report of the first session of the FAO Fishery Committee for the Eastern Central Atlantic (CECAF)*, FAO Fisheries Reports No. 69, Rome 1969, p. 3.
[27]For a discussion of the extra-legal background of conservation functions, see *supra* pp. 45–54.

are used by the North-East Atlantic Commission as a basis for regulatory recommendations.[28] Therefore, the International Council has, like most research organizations, an indirect function with respect to conservation. Fisheries bodies that are primarily responsible for the full utilization of the sea's living resources often have such an indirect conservation function as well. The IOFC and CECAF, for example, may advise their member States with respect to the scientific base for conservation measures which these States might wish to adopt.[29] In addition, they may examine conservation problems.[30] Such functions imply that these organizations may discuss the conservation of the stocks for which they are responsible in general terms, but that they seem to lack the authority to adopt specific regulatory measures.[31]

3.2 Objectives of Conservation Functions

Pre-World War II fisheries conventions define the objectives of the conservation functions of fisheries commissions in rather general terms. The original IPHC Convention and the IPSFC Convention, for example, formulated their objectives as: '. . . the protection, preservation and extension . . .' of, respectively, the halibut and salmon fisheries of the Eastern Pacific.[32] After World War II, advances in marine science made it possible to define the objectives of conservation more precisely. The IWC Convention heralds this change: it refers to the objective of the Convention as the protection of whales, but it also points out that there is a relationship between the size of the stocks and the number of whales which can be taken without endangering this species. It is declared to be in the common interest to bring the stocks

[28]Art. 1 ICES Convention. Art. 11, para. 1 NEAFC Convention.
[29]Art. 3, para. b CECAF Statutes. Art. 2, para. a IOFC Resolution.
[30]Art. 2, para. c IOFC Resolution.
[31]*Supra* p. 111, p. 112.
[32]Preamble IPHC Convention. Preamble IPSFC Convention.

of whales up to their 'optimum level'.[33] However, it was the ICNAF Convention which for the first time unequivocally defined the objectives of conservation as the achievement of the maximum sustainable yield.[34] The proposals of this Commission had to be designed to keep the stocks of fish supporting international fisheries in the Convention area at a level permitting a maximum sustained catch.[35] Achieving the maximum sustainable yield is also the explicit objective of the Pacific Tuna Commission,[36] the North-Pacific Commission,[37] the Japan-Soviet Commission,[38] the Fur Seal Commission,[39] and the Atlantic Tuna Commission.[40] Since the revision of the IPHC Convention in 1953, the Halibut Commission, too, must design its regulatory proposals to reach this goal.[41] As a result, most international fisheries organizations with direct functions concerning conservation are required to maintain the stocks of fish for which they are responsible at a level which permits a maximum sustainable yield. Therefore, their objectives are fully consistent with those of the 1958 Fisheries Convention.[42] However, some of the most recently established fisheries organizations pursue more flexibly defined aims. The North-East Atlantic Commission is here the most important illustration: the Convention defines the objectives of NEAFC's regulatory recommendations as: '. . . to ensure the conservation of the fish stocks and the rational exploitation of the fisheries . . .'[43] The Black Sea Commission and the

[33]Preamble IWC Convention.
[34]Preamble ICNAF Convention.
[35]Art. VIII, para. 1 ICNAF Convention.
[36]Preamble IATTC Convention. Art. II, para. 5 IATTC Convention.
[37]Preamble INPFC Convention.
[38]Preamble Japan-Soviet Commission Convention.
[39]Preamble NPFSC Convention.
[40]Preamble ICCAT Convention. Art. VIII, para. 1(a) ICCAT Convention.
[41]Art. I, para. 1 IPHC Convention.
[42]Art. 2 1958 Fisheries Convention.
[43]Preamble NEAFC Convention. Art. 6, para. 1(b) NEAFC Convention.

Southeast Atlantic Commission have similar goals.[44] Consequently, the objectives of these fisheries organizations are not defined exclusively in terms of achieving the maximum sustainable yield of stocks of fish, but include other values as well. ICNAF has also been successful in enhancing the scope of its objectives: it must now achieve an 'optimum utilization' of the stocks.[45]

3.3 Conservation Methods

Fisheries organizations are authorized to employ a variety of methods and techniques[46] in order to bring about the conservation of those living resources for which they are responsible. In this respect there are essentially two alternatives: (1) some fisheries conventions list exhaustively the methods which the commission is allowed to use; and (2) other conventions give the commission freedom of choice in regard to the measures it may use to achieve its goal of conservation.

The IPHC Convention illustrates the first alternative. It lists all the methods which the Halibut Commission may consider in maintaining the stocks at the maximum sustainable yield level:[47] (1) to divide the Convention waters into areas; (2) to establish one or more open or closed seasons for each area; (3) to limit the size of the fish and the quantity of the catch to be taken from each area within any season during which fishing is allowed; (4) to regulate the incidental catch of halibut; (5) to prohibit the departure of more vessels if the vessels at sea suffice to catch the limits set for an area; (6) to fix the size and character of halibut fishing appliances; and (7) to close areas which are populated by small and immature halibut. That the IPHC has no other powers is clear

[44]Preamble ICSEAF Convention. Preamble Black Sea Commission Convention.
[45]Infra p. 182.
[46]For a general survey of such methods, see supra p. 50.
[47]Art. III, para. 2 IPHC Convention.

from the fact that in 1953 a revision of the Convention was necessary to give the Commission the authority to establish more than one open or closed season in the various areas into which the Convention waters could be divided.[48] Similarly restricted in the choice of conservation methods are the Whaling Commission[49] and, until recently, ICNAF.[50] At its 1968 annual meeting the United States introduced a proposal to amend the ICNAF Convention in this respect.[51] At its next annual meeting, ICNAF adopted a Protocol on this subject for presentation to the member States.[52] This Protocol entered into force on 15 December 1971; it authorizes the Northwest Atlantic Commission to make all appropriate proposals designed to achieve an optimum utilization of the stocks of fish which support international fisheries in the ICNAF area. As a result, the Northwest Atlantic Commission has now complete flexibility with respect to its objectives, as well as with respect to the methods it may use to achieve those objectives.

The ICSEAF Convention exemplifies the second alternative. After listing several conservation techniques available to the Southeast Atlantic Commission, it provides that th Commission may use: '. . . any other type of measure directly related to the conservation of all fish and other living resources in the Convention area'.[53] The Pacific Tuna Commission is also completely free in recommending conservation methods,[54] while the North Pacific Commission is authorized to recommend all 'necessary' conservation

---

[48]IPHC, *Regulation and investigation of the Pacific halibut fishery in 1953*, Seattle 1954, p. 8.
[49]Art. V, para. 1 IWC Convention.
[50]Art. VIII, para. 1 original ICNAF Convention.
[51]ICNAF, *Annual Proceedings for the year 1967–1968*, Dartmouth 1968, pp. 21–22.
[52]*Ibidem, 1968–1969*, Dartmouth 1969, p. 20.
[53]Art. VIII, para. 2(h) ICSEAF Convention.
[54]Art. II, para. 5 IATTC Convention.

measures.[55] The North-East Atlantic Commission is restricted to specific methods, but has the authority to request additional ones. The NEAFC Convention provides that the Commission may propose adding measures for regulating the total catch, the amount of fishing effort in a given period or any other type of conservation measure to those methods which the Commission may consider under Article 7, para. 1.[56] Such a proposal must be adopted by the Commission by a two-thirds majority vote and must be accepted by all member States in accordance with their constitutional procedures. At its eighth annual meeting the North-East Atlantic Commission adopted a resolution in which it proposed that it be given the authority to make recommendations for the regulation of the total catch and its allocation among the member States, and for the regulation of the amount of fishing effort and its allocation among the member States.[57] These proposals will be reviewed in greater detail in the section dealing with the functions of fisheries commissions in respect of allocation.[58]

3.4 Other Conditions

In adopting recommendations for conservation measures, international fisheries organizations must usually respect several conditions. Some of these are more or less general, but most differ from commission to commission. As far as general conditions are concerned, most international fisheries conventions require conservation measures to be designed to achieve the objectives of the convention[59] and to be based on the results of scientific evidence.[60] In regard to more specific

[55]Art. III, para. 1(c) (ii) INPFC Convention.
[56]Art. 7, para. 2 NEAFC Convention.
[57]NEAFC, *Report of the eighth meeting*, London 1970, pp. 11–12.
[58]*Infra* pp. 207–208.
[59]Art. VIII, para. 1 ICSEAF Convention. Art. VIII, para. 1(a) ICCAT Convention. Art. 7, para. 1 NEAFC Convention. Art. VIII, para. 1 ICNAF Convention. Art. V, para. 2(a) IWC Convention.
[60]*Infra* pp. 211–214.

conditions fisheries commissions can be separated into two categories: (1) commissions responsible for formulating completely new conservation measures; and (2) commissions responsible for amending the measures already laid down by the convention itself. The Halibut Commission, the Salmon Commission, the Pacific Tuna Commission, the Northwest Atlantic Commission, the North-East Atlantic Commission and the Atlantic Tuna Commission belong to the first category. The conventions establishing these organizations do not incorporate any conservation measures, but merely create the machinery for adopting such measures. The fisheries organizations in this group are not subject to any conditions other than the above two general requirements. Such flexibility is not a characteristic of the commissions in the second category, of which the Whaling Commission is the most important example.[61] The Annex to the original IWC Convention specified *ab initio* the regulations applicable to whaling operations. In carrying out its task to keep these regulations up-to-date,[62] the IWC is subject to several conditions: (1) amendments of the Annex may not involve restrictions on the number or nationality of factory ships or land stations; (2) they may not allocate specific quotas to any factory ship or land station, or to any group of factory ships or land stations; and (3) they must take into account the interests of the consumers of whale products and the whaling industry.[63] Consequently, the Whaling Commission has been, and continues to be, under rather severe constitutional limitations in respect of the measures it may propose to its member States for the conservation of whales.

There are other specific conditions which international fisheries organizations must observe when making proposals

[61]The North Pacific Commission is subject to similar conditions in respect of its allocation functions, *infra* p. 202.
[62]Art. V, para. 1 IWC Convention.
[63]Art. V, para. 2(c) and (d) IWC Convention.

concerning the conservation of the stocks for which they are responsible. The Salmon Commission, for example, is prohibited from adopting regulations which would suspend the requirements of the State of Washington and Canada regarding licences for salmon fishing.[64] The same Commission was also required to conduct scientific investigations during an initial period of eight years before making proposals concerning conservation.[65] Another example of a specific condition is that some commissions may only make recommendations with respect to the conservation of stocks subject to exploitation by more than one member State. The Northwest Atlantic Commission, for example, may recommend conservation measures for stocks which support 'international fisheries'.[66] The same applies to the North Pacific Commission: it is authorized to make conservation proposals, provided that the stock in question is being exploited by at least two of the three member States.[67] As such conditions are different for each commission, no attempt will be made to list them exhaustively.

3.5 Implementation

International fisheries organizations proceed essentially in two ways in carrying out their functions concerning conservation. If a commission has a permanent research staff, this staff is instrumental not only in discharging the commission's research functions, but in implementing its functions concerning conservation as well. For example, at each annual meeting the staff of the Halibut Commission presents its

[64]Art. IV IPSFC Convention; a requirement that all IPSFC regulations apply uniformly to all United States internal waters, to all Canadian internal waters and to all the territorial waters and waters of the high seas was dropped by a Protocol of 1956, Legislative Reference Service of the Library of Congress, *op. cit.*, note 20, p. 350 or *UNTS* vol. 290, p. 10.
[65]Protocol of Exchange, Legislative Reference Service of the Library of Congress, *op. cit.*, note 20, p. 348.
[66]Art. VIII, para. 1 ICNAF Convention.
[67]Art. III, para. 1(c) (ii) *iuncto* Art. III, para. 1(c) (i) INPFC Convention.

proposals for regulation to the Commission.[68] The Commission discusses these proposals with representatives of the industry and adopts them, with or without modification, as recommendations to the member States. The same procedure is followed in the other two commissions with a permanent research staff: the Salmon Commission[69] and the Pacific Tuna Commission.[70] International fisheries organizations without such a staff rely on a committee structure for formulating proposals which can be adopted as regulatory recommendations to their member States. Although each commission has its own procedures in this respect, it seems that in most cases the interaction between the plenary group and the committee structure is rather informally organized. However, there are a few arrangements that give subsidiary bodies a precisely defined role in the process by which a commission implements its functions concerning conservation. Such arrangements exist in the Northwest Atlantic Commission, the North-East Atlantic Commission and the Atlantic Tuna Commission.

It has been discussed in the previous Chapter that the two North Atlantic commissions have special panels or regional committees for the sub-areas into which the Convention areas have been divided, that representation on these panels is based upon participation in the fisheries of a sub-area and upon coastal proximity, and that these panels may take the initiative for regulatory proposals to the member States.[71] These subsidiary bodies are crucial elements in the implementation of the conservation functions of the three commissions. This is most clearly illustrated by Article VIII of the ICNAF Convention. The plenary group of ICNAF may not make regulatory proposals to the member States at its own

[68]IPHC, *Annual Report 1970*, Seattle 1971, pp. 8–9.
[69]IPSFC, *Annual Report 1970*, New Westminster 1971, p. 8.
[70]IATTC, *Annual Report for the year 1969*, La Jolla 1970, p. 8.
[71]*Supra* pp. 138–144 *passim.*

initiative, unless these proposals concern the Convention area as a whole and unless all area panels have been consulted.[72] However, if a regulatory proposal concerns a specific sub-area, the plenary group may only act on the basis of a recommendation of the panel for that area.[73] If one of the panels makes a recommendation to the plenary group, this group is required to study it.[74] Thereafter it must choose between two alternatives: (1) transmit the panel recommendation, with or without modifications, as a regulatory proposal to the member States; or (2) refer the recommendation back to the panel for reconsideration.[75] If the panel decides to reconfirm its recommendation and if the plenary group is still unable to adopt it as a regulatory proposal, the plenary group is then required to transmit the panel's recommendation to all member States for their consideration.[76]

Similar, but less detailed, arrangements exist in the North-East Atlantic Commission and the Atlantic Tuna Commission. A difference is that the NEAFC plenary group is not required to take certain formal actions with respect to the recommendations of its regional committees,[77] and is under no restrictions with regard to the proposals it may make at its own initiative. The ICCAT Convention follows an intermediate approach. The Atlantic Tuna Commission may make proposals to the member States which are not based on a recommendation of one of its panels, provided that at least two-thirds of its members approve such a proposal. If there is no panel for the sub-area or for the stock in question, the plenary group may make regulatory proposals by a simple majority.[78] A difference between the ICCAT Convention

[72]Art. VIII, para. 5 ICNAF Convention.
[73]Art. VIII, para. 1 ICNAF Convention.
[74]Art. VIII, para. 2 ICNAF Convention.
[75]*Ibidem.*
[76]Art. VIII, para. 3 and 4 ICNAF Convention.
[77]Art. 6, para. 3 NEAFC Convention.
[78]Art. VIII, para. 1(b) ICCAT Convention.

and the ICNAF-NEAFC arrangements is that in ICCAT panel representation is not explicitly based upon participation in the fisheries or upon coastal proximity. However, since the financial contributions to ICCAT increase with the number of panels on which a State is represented,[79] it likely that most ICCAT panels will also consist of States which have an interest in the fisheries of such panels.

The objective of the above arrangements is to give a certain degree of decision-making priority to those States directly affected by a specific decision. There are a few international fisheries conventions which achieve the same objective by their voting arrangements. If the North Pacific Commission, for example, makes a decision concerning a recommendation for conservation measures, only the national sections of those members which have a substantial exploitation of the stocks in question may cast their votes.[80] A similar provision is included in the NPFSC Convention.[81]

3.5.1 Decisions

As a general rule, international fisheries organizations do not have the power to make decisions concerning conservation that are directly binding on the member States or their fishermen. The Japan-Soviet Commission is one exception: it is authorized to determine the annual catch of certain species and to notify the member States of its decision.[82] Another exception is the Black Sea Commission. Usually, it may only make recommendations to its members, but it has the power to make binding decisions concerning the minimum size of certain species.[83] Thirdly, the Fur Seal Commission may determine the number of seals that may be taken at sea

[79] Art. X, para. 2 ICCAT Convention.
[80] Art. III, para. 1(c) (ii) INPFC Convention.
[81] Art. V, para. 4 NPFSC Convention.
[82] Art. IV, para. b Japan-Soviet Commission Convention.
[83] Art. 10 *iuncto* Art. 9, para. 2 Black Sea Commission Convention.

for scientific purposes.[84] However, the Salmon Commission undoubtedly offers the most important examples of conservation decisions which are directly binding. A 1956 amendment to the IPSFC Convention added a clause to Article VI providing that all regulations made by the Commission must be approved by the two member States '. . . with the exception of orders for the adjustment of closing or opening of fishing periods and areas in any fishing season and of emergency orders required to carry out the provisions of the Convention'.[85] The Salmon Commission has used this power for making directly binding emergency amendments to its regulations for the purpose of achieving an adequate escapement of salmon to the spawning grounds and for achieving an equal distribution of the catch between Canadian and United States fishermen participating in the salmon fishery.[86] With these few exceptions, international fisheries organizations have the authority of recommendation only.[87] As a result, almost all conservation measures do not become binding on member States and their fishermen until these States have explicitly accepted such measures. Here, acceptance requires positive action on the part of member States: they must complete their constitutional procedures and inform the commission in question of the outcome. In an attempt to simplify this procedure, some fisheries conventions have adopted a more refined system: recommendations automatically become binding within a certain period unless a member State undertakes positive action to avoid this.

The IWC Convention was the first international fisheries

[84]Art. V, para. 3 NPFSC Convention.
[85]Legislative Reference Service of the Library of Congress, *op. cit.*, note 20, p. 351 or *UNTS* vol. 290, p. 106.
[86]IPSFC, *Annual Report 1970*, New Westminster 1971, p. 7.
[87]Art. VIII, para. 1 ICSEAF Convention. Art. VIII, para. 1 ICCAT Convention. Art. 7, para. 1 NEAFC Convention. Art. III, para. 2 IPHC Convention. Art. VII INPFC Convention. Art. II, para. 5 IATTC Convention. Art. V, para. 3 IWC Convention.

agreement to incorporate this system.[88] Recommendations of the Whaling Commission for amending the Schedule to the Convention become binding ninety days after notification of the member States, unless there are member States that lodge an objection within that period. In that case the amendment does not become effective during an additional period of ninety days in which other States may object. After this second period, the recommendation enters into force for all States which have not lodged objections. Although the details differ from convention to convention, several other fisheries agreements contain similar arrangements.[89] The periods within which States may object to a recommendation range from two to six months, while a few conventions also provide that a recommendation will not become effective for any State if more than a certain number of States object. The ICCAT Convention is very detailed in this respect. If not more than one-fourth of its member States object, these objecting States must reaffirm their objections within an additional period of sixty days. After the expiration of this additional period, the recommendation becomes binding for all States except for those that have reaffirmed their objection. If more than one-fourth, but less than the majority of the ICCAT members object, the recommendation becomes effective for those States that have not lodged an objection. In this case, there is no additional period for reaffirmation. Finally, if more than the majority of member States object, the recommendation does not become effective at all.[90]

[88]Which technically is known as 'opting out'.
[89]Art. IX, para. 2 and 3 ICSEAF Convention. Art. VIII, para. 2 and 3 ICCAT Convention. Art. 10 Black Sea Commission Convention. Art. 8, para. 2 and 3 NEAFC Convention; a special Protocol relating to Entry into Force amended Art. VIII, para. 8 of the original ICNAF Convention to provide for a similar arrangement for the entry into force of ICNAF proposals, *ILM* 1966, p. 718; this amendment became effective on 19 December 1969, ICNAF, *Annual Proceedings for the year 1969–1970*, Dartmouth 1970, p. 19. Art. V, para. 3 IWC Convention.
[90]Art. VIII, para. 3 ICCAT Convention.

3.6 Evaluation

Conservation functions are undoubtedly the most important responsibilities of those international fisheries organizations that are involved in regulating marine fisheries. Most of these fisheries commissions are explicitly required to achieve the maximum sustainable yield of the stocks for which they are responsible. However, such a rigid approach to the objectives of the international regulation of marine fisheries is of questionable desirability in view of the increasing inter-relationship between the various problem areas of marine fisheries. It has already been suggested that full utilization functions and conservation functions must be integrated; this also applies to conservation and functions concerning allocation and economic efficiency. Solutions in the latter areas have become a prerequisite for action in respect of conservation.[91] As a result, defining the objectives of a fisheries commission exclusively in terms of achieving the maximum sustainable yield is no longer desirable: it negates the fact that conservation is but a part of a complex maze of problems. Consequently, the NEAFC Convention and the amended ICNAF Convention offer a much more constructive approach to the objectives of international fisheries commissions.

A second problem of existing arrangements concerns the conditions to which international fisheries bodies are subject in making recommendations for the purpose of conservation. In view of the rapid and often unpredictable changes in marine fisheries, it is undesirable to list in complete detail all conservation methods available to the commission. It is certainly possible to change such a list, but experience suggests that amending a fisheries convention is a very time-consuming matter,[92] even if it may be initiated by both the

[91] *Supra* p. 62.
[92] IPHC, *Regulation and investigation of the Pacific halibut fishery in 1953*, Seattle 1954, p. 8.

member States and by the commission itself. This is emphasized by the fact that the Northwest Atlantic Commission has proposed facilitating the procedures of the ICNAF Convention in respect of such amendments.[93] Moreover, no State is obligated to respect any conservation measures, unless it explicitly or tacitly accepts them. Therefore, there seems to be little reason for not giving fisheries commissions maximum flexibility with regard to the conservation methods they may consider. These observations are equally valid for other restrictions to which fisheries organizations are subject in recommending conservation measures. The general conditions that these measures must be designed to achieve the objectives of the convention and must be based on scientific evidence does not unduly limit the freedom of action of international fisheries commissions. This can not be said of some of the more specific restrictions. For example, the constitutional limitations imposed upon the Whaling Commission did certainly contribute to its failure in protecting the stocks of whales. However, it must be kept in mind that in most cases these conditions are part of the political compromises which enabled States to reach agreement on the fisheries convention in question. Without such conditions there might not have been a commission to begin with. Nevertheless, they should be avoided to every extent possible.

As far as the implementation of conservation functions is concerned, a major question concerns the relative advantages of an international research staff and a committee structure. Most implications of these alternatives involve the research functions of fisheries commissions,[94] but certain aspects are also relevant from the point of view of conservation. A first point is that a committee structure usually requires more

[93]ICNAF, *Annual Proceedings for the year 1969–1970*, Dartmouth 1970, p. 19.
[94]*Infra* pp. 214–216.

time for formulating draft conservation measures than a staff: a committee must be appointed, its terms of reference must be determined, a series of meetings must be scheduled and a report must be drafted. All these activities are time-consuming. A staff can generally respond more quickly if the commission needs certain regulatory proposals. Accordingly, the fact that most fisheries organizations rely on a committee structure may contribute to the delays they experience in adopting effective conservation measures. On the other hand, a committee structure may facilitate the acceptance of a regulatory recommendation by the member States. The reason is that all groups which influence the national decision concerning such acceptance can participate quite easily in the deliberations of the various committees. This involvement is more difficult to achieve if a commission relies on a staff. In this case the consultations with the fishing industry tend to take place after the commission has drafted its regulatory proposals, whereas a committee structure enables the fishing industry to participate from the beginning. The conclusion must be drawn that both alternatives have advantages and disadvantages and that the specific circumstances of a commission will determine which alternative is preferable.

Another relevant aspect of a committee structure concerns the relationship between the various committees and the plenary group, and more specifically the desirability of the ICNAF-NEAFC-ICCAT arrangements. The general purpose of these arrangements is to place the primary responsibility for formulating conservation measures in the hands of those States which are directly affected by such measures. This has the advantage of limiting the number of States participating in a certain decision, which may facilitate the process of reaching agreement. Another useful aspect of the ICNAF arrangement is that the plenary group is required to respond formally to the proposals of the subsidiary group.

This ensures that the plenary group will act promptly if the States directly interested in a specific fishery have reached agreement on regulatory measures with respect to that fishery. It has been mentioned that this positive aspect is not part of the NEAFC and ICCAT arrangements. However, the ICNAF arrangement also provides that the plenary group may only make regulatory recommendations to the member States if there is a draft proposal of one of its panels. This requirement is undesirable, since it forces the plenary group of ICNAF to remain ineffective as long as the States which have a direct interest in a fishery are unable or unwilling to agree on regulatory measures. Thus, while the ICNAF arrangement does not tolerate inaction of the plenary group, it does accept inaction on the panel level. It is fortunate that the ICCAT and NEAFC arrangements give more authority to the plenary group for initiating action at its own initiative.

The question of the effect of decisions of international fisheries bodies is predominantly political in nature and closely linked to the fundamental fact that the international community consists of sovereign States. Although there are a few exceptions,[95] international organizations generally lack the authority to make decisions that are directly binding on their member States. Therefore, it is not surprising that with a few minor exceptions, no international fisheries organization has such forcible powers. The fact that they can not make binding decisions is also related to the freedom of fishing on the high seas, which makes the establishment of, and membership in, international fisheries organizations a voluntary matter. Hence, it can hardly be expected that those States which agree to establish such an organization and which become members would also be willing to grant it the authority to make binding decisions. This would expose them to the risk of being forced to accept a certain conservation measure, whereas non-member States would be under no

[95]Most notably within the context of the European Economic Community.

obligation with regard to such a measure. Thus, unless dramatic changes occur in the nature of the international community and the freedom of fishing on the high seas, political realities will dictate that fisheries commissions operate on the basis of recommendations, rather than on the basis of binding decisions.

However, accepting this fundamental restriction makes it possible to seek improvements elsewhere. First of all, if fisheries commissions can not directly bind their member States, there is little justification for a minimalistic approach to the other aspects of their functions and powers concerning conservation. This applies in particular to the requirement that fisheries commissions must adopt conservation recommendations by a two-thirds majority vote or even by an unanimous vote. If these commissions could adopt conservation recommendations on the basis of a simple majority vote, they would be capable of acting more promptly without unduly infringing upon the prerogatives of the member States. Secondly, the fact that fisheries organizations can not make binding decisions does not preclude special arrangements for the purpose of avoiding unnecessary procedural delays and for the purpose of bringing pressure to bear on member States to accept their recommendations. These are precisely the dual goals of the provisions under which a conservation recommendation enters into force after a certain period of time for those States which have not lodged a formal objection. Such a mechanism serves the interests of timely action because it minimizes the risk that entry into force becomes entangled in the various national constitutional procedures required for explicit acceptance. It serves the interests of a wider acceptance of a recommendation because States are forced to declare publicly that they are unable or unwilling to accept a recommendation, rather than simply being able to remain silent. However, it is possible to improve on these arrangements. A first step would be to shorten the periods within which States may lodge objections. Since the fishing industry and other relevant national groups participate actively in most fisheries commissions, there is little need for extensive consultation with these groups once a commission has recommended certain conservation measures. Moreover, technological advances have drastically reduced the time required for communication among governments and international organizations. This suggests that it is quite realistic to limit to one or two months the period in which governments may object. Recommendations could enter into force after a short additional period in which other governments could lodge objections. Such an approach would assist in overcoming the delays experienced by most fisheries organizations regarding the entry into force of their recommendations. Another improvement would be to utilize more widely the ICCAT provision requiring States to reaffirm objections if only a few member States have initially taken such action. This contributes to a more uniform acceptance of a recommendation.

4. FUNCTIONS CONCERNING ECONOMIC EFFICIENCY[96]

4.1 Legal Provisions

Conservation measures inevitably have economic implications.[97] Therefore, it is by necessity and not by choice that international fisheries organizations must be able to deal with the economic aspects of marine fisheries. Nevertheless, most international fisheries commissions do not have any explicit functions concerning such economic matters. It has been mentioned[98] that the regulatory recommendations of the

[96]For a discussion of the extra-legal background of economic efficiency functions, see *supra* pp. 54–63.
[97]FAO, *The management of fishery resources*, Rome 1967, pp. 9–11.
[98]*Supra* p. 180.

majority of fisheries organizations must be designed to achieve the maximum sustainable yield of the stocks for which they are responsible, and that there are only a few commissions whose objectives allow them to take into account matters of economic efficiency. A first important example of such a commission is the North-East Atlantic Commission: its regulatory recommendations must ensure not only the conservation of the stocks, but the 'rational exploitation of the fisheries.'[99] The Southeast Atlantic Commission and the Black Sea Commission have similar goals.[100] Although even these provisions do not explicitly address themselves to the issue of economic efficiency, it may be assumed that the responsibility to ensure a rational exploitation also covers any measures designed to prevent overcapitalization. Since the amendment of the original ICNAF Convention,[101] the same applies to the Northwest Atlantic Commission. Its general task to make recommendations for the '. . . optimum utilization of the stocks of those species of fish which support international fisheries in the Convention Area . . .'[102] certainly authorizes the Commission to propose measures for reducing the overcapitalization of the fisheries in the Northwest Atlantic.

The extremely limited scope of the economic efficiency functions of all existing international fisheries organizations is also evident from the universal requirement that regulatory recommendations must be based on scientific, i.e., biological, evidence.[103] This requirement even limits the functions of

[99]Preamble NEAFC Convention. Art. 6, para. 1(b) NEAFC Convention.
[100]Preamble ICSEAF Convention. Preamble Black Sea Commission Convention.
[101]*Supra* p. 182.
[102]ICNAF, *Annual Proceedings for the year 1968–1969*, Dartmouth 1969, p. 20.
[103]Art. VIII, para. 1(a) ICCAT Convention. Art. V, para. 3 NPFSC Convention. Art. IV, para. a Japan-Soviet Commission Convention. Art. IV, para. 1 (b) INPFC Convention. Art. VIII, para. 1 ICNAF Convention. Art. V, para. 2(b) IWC Convention.

those commissions whose objectives allow them to be concerned with matters of economic efficiency. This is clearly demonstrated by the North-East Atlantic Commission. In objecting to the request of the Commission for additional powers regarding economic efficiency, the Polish delegate stated that such powers would require the Commission to include economic aspects in the criteria on which it bases its recommendations.[104] In his opinion, the Commission was prohibited from including such aspects since the NEAFC Convention requires the Commission to base its regulatory proposals on scientific findings.[105] However, several other nations did not accept this restrictive interpretation of the Convention in view of the fact that the wider objectives of the Convention could not be achieved on the basis of scientific criteria alone. Regardless of the merits of these viewpoints, this discussion makes clear some of the problems created in respect of economic efficiency functions by a requirement that regulatory proposals must be based on scientific findings. This is the reason why under the amended ICNAF Convention the area panels have the authority to make proposals to the plenary group '. . . upon the basis of scientific investigations, and economic and technical considerations . . .'[106] The Commission itself would base its recommendations to member States on the same criteria.

However, the above limitations have not prevented international fisheries organizations from discussing the economic aspects of their regulatory work. The Whaling Commission offers an excellent illustration here. Although it is required to take into account the interests of the consumers of whale products and the whaling industry,[107] the Commission declared in its Eighth Report that it was concerned with the

[104]NEAFC, *Report of the ninth meeting*, London 1971, p. 13.
[105]Art. 6, para. 1(d) NEAFC Convention.
[106]ICNAF, *Annual Proceedings for the year 1968–1969*, Dartmouth 1969, p. 20.
[107]Art. V, para. 2(d) IWC Convention.

conservation of the whale resources and not with the economic regulation of whaling.[108] Nonetheless, at its next meeting the Whaling Commission stressed the need to maintain the catch at such levels that the Antarctic whaling fleets could continue to operate,[109] which is clearly an economic consideration. In subsequent years the Commission requested FAO to study the economic aspects of whaling and to report back to the Commission.[110] ICNAF and NEAFC have also extensively discussed the economic problems of the fisheries for which they are responsible, particularly within the context of allocation questions.[111]

4.2 Evaluation

It will be clear from this analysis that the functions of international fisheries organizations in respect of the economic efficiency of marine fishing operations are minimal indeed. A few commissions have at best terms of reference broad enough to enable them to include these aspects in the objectives they seek to achieve in their regulatory proposals. And even these commissions may be required to base their recommendations on biological evidence. As a result, international fisheries commissions have in some cases aggravated the problems of overcapitalization, rather than contributed to their solution. This has occurred especially if a commission's work led to the adoption of an overall limit on the catch of a specific stock. As has been discussed,[112] overcapitalization may become particularly serious in a situation in which catches can no longer be expanded, either as the result of such an overall quota or as the result of the factual unavailability of more fish.

[108]IWC, *Eighth Report of the Commission*, London 1957, p. 5.
[109]*Ibidem, Ninth*, London 1958, p. 3.
[110]*Ibidem, Nineteenth*, London 1969, p. 17; these studies were discontinued in 1971, *ibidem, Twenty-first*, London 1971, p. 20.
[111]*Infra* p. p. 207–208.
[112]*Supra* p. 62.

However, there are a few mitigating circumstances regarding the inability of fisheries commissions to deal with questions of economic efficiency. First of all, overcapitalization is directly linked to the fact that the freedom of fishing on the high seas does not allow any restrictions or controls on access to high seas fisheries. Fisheries commissions have no choice but to accept this fundamental characteristic of the freedom of fishing. If they would attempt to limit or regulate the total effort applied by their member States to a specific fishery, such decision would in no way obligate non-member States, which as a result could freely reap the benefits of the self-imposed effort limitations of other nations. Consequently, problems of overcapitalization can not be solved simply by giving fisheries organizations certain functions and powers in this area. A final solution may require fundamental changes in the international law of marine fisheries – changes which directly concern the basic characteristics of the freedom of fishing. A second mitigating circumstance is that international fisheries organizations are trying to deal with the problems of economic efficiency in an indirect fashion. It has been suggested that a system of national quotas creates to a large extent the conditions required for solving the problems of overcapitalization.[113] The following section, which will discuss functions concerning allocation, will point out that international fisheries organizations are actively involved in efforts to work out national quota arrangements, not only for their own sake, but also in an attempt to contribute to a solution of the problems of overcapitalization.

The above considerations do not eliminate the desirability of granting fisheries commissions more explicit functions and powers with respect to economic efficiency. First of all, the objectives of their regulatory proposals should include the economic aspects of marine fisheries and should not be concerned solely with the biological condition of the stocks.

[113] *Supra* p. 68.

Secondly, such proposals should be based not only on biological information, but also on economic criteria. Essentially, the amendments made in the original ICNAF Convention incorporate these suggestions. They constitute a major step towards enabling ICNAF to cope more effectively with the overcapitalization of the fisheries for which it is responsible. The functions of other international fisheries organizations should be revised in a similar manner.

5. FUNCTIONS CONCERNING ALLOCATION[114]

5.1 Direct Functions

Few international fisheries organizations have explicit responsibilities concerning the allocation of the catch of marine fisheries: the Salmon Commission, the North Pacific Commission and the Japan-Soviet Commission are here the primary examples. The IPSFC Convention provides that the two Contracting States must share equally in the Fraser River salmon fisheries.[115] This equal distribution of the catch is motivated on the ground that it would require a joint effort of the two States to re-establish a depleted fishery.[116] The Salmon Commission must regulate the fisheries '. . . with a view to allowing, as nearly as may be practicable, an equal portion of the fish that may be caught each year to be taken by the fishermen of each Contracting Party'.[117] This responsibility is the major reason why the Salmon Commission usually meets several times during the fishing season: it adjusts its regulations in order to achieve the required equal distribution of the catch between Canadian and United

[114]For a discussion of the extra-legal background of allocation functions, see *supra* pp. 63–69.
[115]Art. VII IPSFC Convention.
[116]*Ibidem.*
[117]*Ibidem.*

States fishermen.[118] Such emergency amendments are directly binding.[119]

The INPFC Convention confers major allocation responsibilities upon the North Pacific Commission. Under the original Convention, Japan agreed to abstain from fishing in specific areas off the coasts of Canada and the United States for certain species which originated in these waters or in the rivers of the American continent.[120] Canada and the United States agreed to carry out the necessary conservation measures with respect to these stocks. In addition, Canada and Japan agreed to abstain from salmon fishing in a certain area of the Bering Sea, and the United States agreed to undertake a conservation programme.[121] The North Pacific Commission is responsible for determining annually: (1) whether or not stocks under abstention continue to qualify; and (2) whether or not new stocks must be placed under abstention.[122] The Convention specifies the criteria which the Commission must use in making this determination.[123] Essentially, these are: (1) scientific research must indicate that a more intensive exploitation of the stock will not result in a substantial increase in the catch which can be maintained year after year; (2) the stock must be subject to regulation by the States which are substantially engaged in its exploitation and this regulation must be designed to achieve the maximum sustainable yield; and (3) the stock must be subject to extensive scientific study to determine whether or not it is being fully utilized. There are a few restrictions regarding the applicability of these criteria, but generally they indicate under what conditions stocks must be added to, or removed from, abstention. It will be clear that these provisions on abstention directly affect the distribution of catches among

[118]IPSFC, *Annual Report 1970*, New Westminster 1971, pp. 5–8.
[119]*Supra* p. 189.
[120]Annex to the INPFC Convention.   [121]*Ibidem.*
[122]Art. III, para. 1(a) and (b) INPFC Convention.
[123]Art. IV INPFC Convention.

the three member States. Consequently, in administering the abstention clauses the North Pacific Commission has important functions concerning allocation. It should be mentioned here that the Commission has removed several stocks from abstention, but that no new stocks have been added.[124]

The Japan-Soviet Commission is a final example of a fisheries organization with explicit responsibilities concerning the allocation of the catch. If the Commission is required to determine the total annual catch of a stock of fish, it must also determine the distribution of the total catch between the two member States.[125] These provisions have resulted in often difficult negotiations concerning the allocation of the total allowable salmon catch between Japanese and Soviet fishermen.[126]

Other international fisheries commissions have recently requested, or even obtained, direct responsibilities with regard to allocation. At its eighth meeting, the North-East Atlantic Commission adopted a resolution in which it requested the authority to propose: (1) measures for the regulation of the amount of the total catch and its allocation among the member States; and (2) measures for the regulation of the total amount of fishing effort and its allocation among the member States.[127] It has been discussed that at the next annual meeting Poland raised a number of questions with regard to this proposal.[128] The Polish delegate took the view that allocation measures could not be considered part of the more general conservation functions of the Commission. Other member States considered this view a rather narrow

[124]INPFC, *Annual Report 1969*, Vancouver 1971, *passim*.

[125]Art. IV, para. b Japan-Soviet Commission Convention.

[126]D M Johnston, *The international law of marine fisheries. A framework for policy-oriented inquiries*, New Haven and London 1965, p. 395.

[127]NEAFC, *Report of the eighth meeting*, London 1970, p. 12.

[128]*Supra* p 198.

interpretation of NEAFC's functions and powers. It has also been discussed that since the entry into force of an amendment of the original ICNAF Convention, the Northwest Atlantic Commission has complete freedom in selecting the regulatory measures required for achieving its aims.[129] This development resulted in several ICNAF proposals for national quota arrangements. A first national quota system was proposed by the Commission after a special meeting in January and February 1972 with respect to certain herring stocks. At its 1972 annual meeting ICNAF reached agreement on national quotas for cod, American plaice, yellowtail flounder and silver and red hake stocks. Thus, ICNAF has made a most effective use of its new powers.

5.2 Indirect Functions

Although few international fisheries organizations have direct responsibilities in this respect, the terms of reference of many are formulated broadly enough to enable them to have certain indirect functions concerning allocation. An exception is the Whaling Commission. It is responsible for making recommendations to its member States for the purpose of protecting the stocks of whales, but these recommendations may not involve '. . . restrictions on the number or nationality of factory ships or land stations, nor allocate specific quotas to any factory ship or land station or group of factory ships or land stations'.[130] This clause effectively prohibits the Whaling Commission from having any direct or indirect functions concerning allocation. However, other commissions have been indirectly involved in allocation questions. For example, the efforts of the FAO-related fisheries commissions to improve the fishing operations of their member States have consequences for the allocation of the living resources of the sea, particularly since they concentrate on

[129] *Supra* p. 182.
[130] Art. V, para. 2(c) IWC Convention.

expanding the catches of developing States. The most common forms of indirect allocation functions are: (1) a commission deals with allocation issues as part of its other functions; and (2) a commission participates informally in reaching a separate international agreement on allocation.

The Pacific Tuna Commission offers an illustration of the first type of involvement in allocation problems. Although it is under no restrictions regarding the conservation methods it may propose to its member States,[131] it relies mainly on an overall quota for protecting the stocks of yellowfin tuna. The associated[132] overcapitalization of the yellowfin tuna fisheries has been particularly detrimental to those member States which operate with small, less efficient vessels. Mexico, for example, has experienced a relative decline of its catches as a result of these developments. In an attempt to correct this allocation problem, the Commission has included in its 1971 regulatory proposals a provision allowing vessels under 400 tons to catch 6,000 tons of yellowfin tuna after the closure of the fisheries to other vessels.[133] Consequently, the regulatory measures proposed by the IATTC are also concerned with the effects of such measures on the allocation of the catch. Secondly, both the Northwest Atlantic Commission and the North-East Atlantic Commission have dealt with allocation problems as part of their other functions. This is particularly evident from the discussions in these commissions concerning high seas salmon fisheries. On the basis of a Canadian proposal,[134] ICNAF has adopted resolutions requesting member States engaged in high seas salmon fisheries to limit their catches to the level of the preceding year.[135] The United

[131]Art. II, para. 5 IATTC Convention.   [132]*Supra* p. 62.
[133]IATTC, *Annual Report for the year 1971*, La Jolla 1972.
[134]ICNAF, *Annual Proceedings for the year 1967–1968*, Dartmouth 1968, p. 30.
[135]*Ibidem, 1967–1968*, Dartmouth 1968, p. 30. *Ibidem, 1969–1970*, Dartmouth 1970, p. 29. *Ibidem, 1970—1971*, Dartmouth 1972, p. 22; in 1969 ICNAF even proposed a total prohibition of all high seas salmon fisheries, *ibidem, 1969–1970*, Dartmouth 1970, p. 28.

Kingdom introduced similar proposals at the meetings of NEAFC.[136] Initially, NEAFC recommended a complete prohibition of high seas salmon fisheries, but when it became clear that the States affected by such a prohibition were not willing to accept the recommendation, it proposed merely to restrict these fisheries.[137] Apart from their conservation aspects, these proposals also change the allocation of salmon catches in favour of those nations in whose rivers salmon spawns, and to the detriment of States engaged in high seas salmon fisheries. A last example of a commission which deals with allocation problems as part of more general responsibilities is the Fur Seal Commission. The NPFSC Convention contains very detailed rules concerning the allocation of the catch.[138] As the convention prohibits pelagic sealing, only the United States and the USSR are able to harvest fur seals: they breed on islands subject to their sovereignty. In order to compensate Canada and Japan for the loss from the prohibition of pelagic sealing, the United States and the USSR are required to deliver a certain number of sealskins to these two countries. Consequently, Canada and Japan continue to share in the wealth of these resources even though they may not participate in their harvest. The Fur Seal Commission's responsibilities with respect to this sophisticated allocation arrangement are very limited. However, since an amendment of the Convention in 1963, the Commission must make a recommendation concerning the question of whether or not pelagic sealing can again be permitted.[139] This recommendation may have strong consequences in respect of allocation.

The second type of indirect involvement of fisheries commissions in matters of allocation – informal participation in

[136]NEAFC, *Report of the seventh meeting*, London 1969, pp. 19–21.
[137]*Ibidem, eighth*, London 1970, p. 23.
[138]Art. IX NPFSC Convention.
[139]Legislative Reference Service of the Library of Congress, *op. cit.*, note 20, p. 83 or *UNTS* vol. 494, p. 303.

reaching a separate agreement on national quotas – is a special feature of the ICSEAF Convention. The Southeast Atlantic Commission has the explicit authority to invite its member States to elaborate agreements on the allocation of the total catch quotas proposed by the Commission.[140] If the States in question reach agreement on the allocation of the catch, they must report the terms of such an agreement to the Commission, which, without prejudicing its binding force, may make recommendations on the matter. Thus, although such national quota arrangements are based on a separate international agreement, the Southeast Atlantic Commission may participate in its formulation. Other commissions have been involved in working out national quota schemes without any explicit authorization. This seems to apply even to the Whaling Commission.[141] Such an indirect involvement is strongly suggested by the fact that the negotiations among the Antarctic whaling countries for the 1962 national quota agreement[142] took place before and during the annual meetings of the Whaling Commission.[143] However, the role of the IWC in these negotiations was relatively insignificant. The North-East Atlantic Commission and the Northwest Atlantic Commission have been more active in this respect.[144] After preliminary discussions at the fifth and sixth annual meetings,[145] NEAFC received at its seventh meeting a report which recommended the adoption of national quotas in several fisheries in the North East Arctic.[146] Quotas were to be based on: (1) past catches; (2) dependence of coastal States; and (3) claims of new entrants. At its next meeting,

[140]Art. VIII, para. 3(a) ICSEAF Convention.
[141]Which is explicitly prohibited from making recommendations with respect to allocation, *supra* p. 204.
[142]*UNTS* vol. 486, p. 263.
[143]IWC, *Seventeenth Report of the Commission*, London 1967, p. 22.
[144]As has been discussed both Commissions have requested more direct powers concerning allocation problems, *supra* p. 203.
[145]NEAFC, *Report of the sixth meeting*, London 1968, p. 10.
[146]*Ibidem, seventh*, London 1969, pp. 22–23.

NEAFC requested the States concerned to develop such national quota agreements outside the Commission as long as it would lack the power to make recommendations concerning these matters.[147] As a result of these NEAFC activities, Denmark, Iceland, Norway and the USSR were able to reach agreement on national quotas for the Atlanto-Scandian herring fisheries.[148] Negotiations on other national quota agreements have made considerable progress. NEAFC modifies its regulations if the States participating in a fishery reach agreement on allocation.[149] It also urges other States to respect such an agreement, presumably by not entering the fishery to which it applies.[150] The Northwest Atlantic Commission has been involved in similar discussions since 1965.[151] A temporary working group on this subject[152] was converted into a Standing Committee on Regulatory Measures in 1967. Its terms of reference make it responsible for studying the scientific, economic and administrative aspects of a quota system. In its first report, the Committee took the view that: (1) overall quotas should be set on the basis of the maximum sustainable yield of the species concerned; (2) allocation of such overall quotas should be carried out primarily on the basis of the past performance of States; and (3) a small portion of the overall catch should be set aside for new entrants, for member States with developing fisheries, for coastal State preferences and for those member States whose fleets can not be diverted to other fisheries.[153] These preparatory activities paved the road for the national quota arrangements discussed in the previous section.[154]

[147] *Ibidem, eighth,* London 1970, p. 11.
[148] *Ibidem, ninth,* London 1971, p. 17.
[149] *Ibidem,* p. 14.
[150] *Ibidem,* p. 13.
[151] ICNAF, *Annual Proceedings for the year 1964–1965,* Dartmouth 1965, pp. 47–56.
[152] *Ibidem, 1966–1967,* Dartmouth 1968, pp. 48–84.
[153] *Ibidem, 1968–1969,* Dartmouth 1969, p. 24.
[154] *Supra* p. 204.

5.3 Evaluation

The living resources of the high seas are still principally allocated on the basis of free competition among those nations which fish for these resources. But many high seas fisheries continue to suffer from the problems associated with allocation through such free competition. As these problems have been discussed previously,[155] let it suffice here to say that this method of allocation is at the root of a great deal of political confrontation among fishing nations and leads in many cases to the overcapitalization of the fisheries. In its turn, this hinders action with regard to conservation. Therefore, it has become undesirable that fisheries commissions have no direct functions concerning questions of allocation. The fact that the Whaling Commission was forced to be a helpless bystander in matters of allocation has been a major cause for its failure with respect to conservation. The few fisheries organizations with direct allocation functions often owe such responsibilities to factors not necessarily related to the problems of allocation *per se:* the equal distribution clause of the IPSFC Convention is a result of the fact that the Commission was established for the purpose of rebuilding stocks which had been depleted earlier; the North Pacific Commission is involved in allocation on the basis of the rather unique provisions of the INPFC Convention on abstention; and the Japan-Soviet Commission is responsible for dividing up the allowable salmon catch because it was established after a 1955 dispute regarding this issue between its two member States. Moreover, membership in all these organizations is limited to two or three States, which simplifies considerably the implementation of responsibilities concerning allocation. The conclusion must be that the Northwest Atlantic Commission is the first multi-member international fisheries organization whose functions and

[155] *Supra* p. 65.

14

powers concerning allocation reflect the crucial importance of these problems.

This importance is further stressed by the extent to which several fisheries commissions have been indirectly involved in questions of allocation. It is fortunate that the terms of reference of most fisheries organizations are flexible enough to allow such indirect involvement. However, the questions raised by Poland in NEAFC demonstrate that in this respect the traditional emphasis on maximum sustainable yield and biological criteria may be a limiting factor. Here the same conclusion must be reached as in the evaluation of the economic efficiency functions: it is no longer possible to deal with the problems of marine fisheries on the basis of biological considerations alone. Regardless of such limitations, fisheries organizations have been quite successful as far as indirect allocation functions are concerned. It has been mentioned, for example, that the lack of objective criteria on which allocation can be based is a serious obstacle in reaching agreement on national quotas.[156] The work of ICNAF and NEAFC in defining such criteria has been instrumental in the development of general rules and principles to govern the allocation of the living resources of the seas.

However, all existing international fisheries organizations have one fundamental limitation in respect of allocation. It has been discussed[157] that the question of new entrants is one of the most serious problems in reaching agreement on the allocation of the catch and that this problem could be largely minimized by distinguishing between access to the fisheries and access to the wealth of the resources. The present concept of the freedom of fishing on the high seas assimilates these two forms of access: if a State wishes to share in the wealth of the living resources of the high seas, it has no

[156]*Supra* p. 67.
[157]*Supra* p. 66.

choice but to engage in fishing operations. The only existing arrangement which makes a distinction between the two kinds of access is the NPFSC Convention: Canada and Japan share in the wealth of the seal resources of the North Pacific without engaging in their harvest. As the existing fisheries commissions are essentially organizations of States participating in a certain fishery, it is doubtful that they will be capable of making substantial contributions towards developing a distinction between access to fisheries and access to wealth. Formulating this distinction requires the participation of all States, regardless of whether or not they fish for specific resources.

6. FUNCTIONS CONCERNING RESEARCH[158]

6.1 Legal Provisions

There are some international fisheries organizations that are exclusively involved in research with respect to the living resources of the sea. The prime example is the International Council. Its responsibilities are: (1) to promote and encourage research for the study of the sea and particularly of the living resources; (2) to draw up programmes and to organize investigations in agreement with the member States; and (3) to publish the results of these investigations.[159] Accordingly, it is the Council's function to coordinate the scientific investigations of the member States and to assist in the exchange and publication of the results. It has no direct responsibilities concerning such questions as conservation, full utilization, economic efficiency or allocation.[160] In the International Council research activities are an end in themselves. In this regard ICES differs from those fisheries com-

[158]For a discussion of the extra-legal background of research functions, see *supra* pp. 69–73.
[159]Art. 1 ICES Convention.
[160]But NEAFC relies on ICES for scientific advice, *supra* p. 156.

missions whose research functions are primarily designed to support other responsibilities.

As the development of new fisheries and the expansion of existing ones is dependent upon a detailed knowledge of the species involved, all commissions with full utilization functions have substantial responsibilities concerning research. The Indo-Pacific Council, for example, is required: (1) to formulate the scientific aspects of the problems of proper utilization; (2) to coordinate research programmes in fishing practices; (3) to assemble and publish relevant information; (4) to recommend research projects to its member States; (5) to undertake cooperative research projects; and (6) to propose measures for the standardization of scientific equipment.[161] The general objectives[162] of the Indo-Pacific Council imply that these research functions are largely instruments to bring about a fuller utilization of the resources for which it is responsible. This is also, but to a lesser extent, the case with CARPAS[163], the IOFC[164] and CECAF.[165] As far as conservation functions are concerned, most fisheries organizations are explicitly required to base their regulatory proposals on scientific, *i.e.*, biological, findings.[166] The 1958 Fisheries Convention also contains such a requirement.[167] Some fisheries conventions are not very detailed regarding the research functions of the commission they establish. The Halibut Commission, for example, is simply required to '. . . make such investigations

[161]Art. IV IPFC Agreement. Art. IV GFCM Agreement is almost identical.
[162]Preamble IPFC Agreement.
[163]Art. 2 CARPAS Statutes.
[164]Art. 2 IOFC Resolution.
[165]Art. 3 CECAF Statutes.
[166]Art. VIII, para. 1(a) ICCAT Convention. Art. V, para. 3 NPFSC Convention. Art. IV, para. a Japan-Soviet Commission Convention. Art. IV, para. 1(b) INPFC Convention. Art. VIII, para. 1 ICNAF Convention. Art. V, para. 2(b) IWC Convention.
[167]Art. 7 and Art. 10, para. 1 1958 Fisheries Convention.

as are necessary into the life history of the halibut in the Convention waters . . .',[168] while the IPSFC Convention is equally brief.[169] Other international fisheries agreements are more detailed. The Atlantic Tuna Commission, for instance, must study the populations of tuna and tuna-like fishes and especially the abundance, biometry and ecology of these species, the oceanography of their environment and the effects of natural and human factors upon their abundance. In addition, ICCAT must collect and analyze statistical data and study and appraise methods to ensure maintenance of the stocks at levels permitting the maximum sustainable yield.[170] The research responsibilities of other fisheries commissions are defined in a similar way.[171]

Most international fisheries organizations are subject to certain restrictions in respect of the scope of their research functions. Obviously, a fundamental restriction is that all research work must fall within the general terms of reference of the organization as far as area, species and general objectives are concerned. However, some commissions must respect additional conditions. ICCAT, for example, may study only such stocks of tunas as are not under investigation by other international fisheries organizations,[172] while ICNAF's research functions are limited to stocks that support international fisheries.[173] The North Pacific Commission is especially subject to such limitations. Its research work is largely restricted to studies that are required for the administration of the abstention provisions of the INPFC Convention. Except for abstention-oriented research, the Commission may organize studies for determining the need for

[168]Art. III, para. 1 IPHC Convention.
[169]Art. III IPSFC Convention.
[170]Art. IV ICCAT Convention.
[171]Art. V, para. 2 NPFSC Convention. Art. II IATTC Convention. Art. VI, para. 1 ICNAF Convention. Art. IV IWC Convention.
[172]Art. IV, para. 1 ICCAT Convention.
[173]Art. VI, para. 1 ICNAF Convention.

joint conservation measures, provided that: (1) it concerns stocks which are under exploitation by two or more of the member States; (2) these stocks are not covered by another conservation agreement between such States; and (3) one of the member States requests such studies.[174]

6.2 Implementation

Functions concerning research are inherently advisory in nature. In most cases their purpose is to make available a body of knowlege on which international fisheries organizations can base decisions with respect to the problems of marine fisheries. Fisheries commissions implement such advisory research functions in two ways: (1) they rely on internationally organized research; or (2) they rely on the investigations of the member States. The first alternative is essentially limited to those commissions which have a permanent research staff.[175] This staff collects basic information by conducting the necessary investigations and it reports to the commission on its evaluation of the results.[176] Consequently, these commissions implement their research functions internationally. Several international fisheries organizations have the authority to carry out their research functions in a similar manner, but have refrained from using it. The Indo-Pacific Council and the Mediterranean Council are the first examples. Under the terms of their respective Agreements, they may undertake cooperative research projects, which are funded and administered through FAO.[177] Accordingly, such projects would constitute internationally organized research. However, neither Council carried out any

[174]Art. III, para. 1 (c) (i) INPFC Convention.
[175]*Supra* p. 147.
[176]See IPHC, *Annual Report 1970*, Seattle 1971, pp. 14–18. IPSFC, *Annual Report 1970*, New Westminster 1971, pp. 23–27. IATTC, *Annual Report for the year 1969*, La Jolla 1970, pp. 15–39.
[177]Art. IV, para. e *iuncto* Art. VII, para. 4 IPFC and GFCM Agreements.

cooperative research programmes.[178] Other commissions that did not use their authority to implement research functions internationally are the North Pacific Commission and the Northwest Atlantic Commission. Both Commissions could have employed an international research staff,[179] but decided instead to rely on the investigations of the member States.[180] Their staffs do not conduct any scientific investigations, although they perform such research-oriented tasks as the compilation and publication of statistical data. The Whaling Commission, on the other hand, has used its authority[181] to organize independent research once: in 1960 it apppointed three scientists from non-Antarctic whaling countries to assess the condition of the stocks.[182] Their reports made a major contribution towards reducing the catch quotas for Antarctic pelagic whaling.[183] However, this authority has not been used for giving the IWC staff research or research oriented responsibilities. Its staff is purely administrative in character, since the compilation of statistical data is entrusted to the Bureau of International Whaling Statistics, a Norwegian organization.[184] Finally, the Southeast Atlantic Commission and the Atlantic Tuna Commission may possibly join this group: although they may conduct independent research to supplement the investigations of the member States, such research is conditional upon a special supplementary budget.[185]

The fact that several international fisheries organizations have refrained from implementing their research functions internationally implies that most fisheries commissions

[178]Zenny, *op. cit.*, note 23, p. 16. Carroz, *op. cit.*, note 23, p. 18.
[179]Art. II, para. 13 INPFC Convention. Art. III ICNAF Convention.
[180]*Supra* p. 146.
[181]Art. IV, para. 1 IWC Convention.
[182]IWC, *Twelfth Report of the Commission*, London 1961, p. 16.
[183]*Ibidem, Fifteenth*, London 1965, pp. 47–61.
[184]*Ibidem, Twenty-second*, London 1972, p. 20.
[185]Art. VI, para. 2 ICSEAF Convention. Art. IV, para. 1 ICCAT Convention.

follow the second alternative: they rely on the investigations of the member States. These member States are generally required to submit the necessary scientific information to the organization in question.[186] This information is then usually reviewed by an appropriate committee, which reports on its findings to the plenary group. These reports provide the plenary group with the scientific advice it needs for decisions with respect to conservation, full utilization, etc. Compared with the few commissions which have a permanent research staff, most fisheries bodies implement their research functions in a decentralized way. The only organization which combines the two basic alternatives is the North-East Atlantic Commission: it relies on the decentralized efforts of another international organization. The fact that the Commission must seek the scientific advice of the International Council[187] has resulted in an arrangement under which ICES reports to the Commission on those aspects of the scientific investigations of ICES member States which are of interest to the North-East Atlantic Commission.[188] Accordingly, NEAFC has neither a permanent research staff, nor an elaborate committee structure.

6.3 Evaluation

The research functions of international fisheries organizations reflect the fact that most commissions are still primarily concerned with conservation problems. Hence, the emphasis on scientific information and biological studies.[189] However, as has been pointed out, problems of economic efficiency and allocation have gained greatly in importance.[190] Because fisheries commissions must have access to studies concerning the economic, social and legal aspects of marine fisheries in

[186]Art. VI, para. 3 ICNAF Convention. Art. VII and Art. VIII, para. 3 IWC Convention.
[187]Art. 11 NEAFC Convention.
[188]Supra p. 156.
[189]Supra p. 70.
[190]Supra p. 62.

order to deal effectively with these new problem areas, it has become necessary to re-orient their research functions. These functions should cease to over-emphasize biological research and should enable international fisheries organizations to seek advice concerning all relevant aspects of marine fisheries. Fortunately, most fisheries commissions have a considerable degree of flexibility regarding the scope of their research work. Some commissions, however, are subject to undesirable restrictions. For example, it will often be necessary to initiate investigations with respect to stocks not yet subject to international fisheries.

As far as the implementation of research functions is concerned, a permanent international research staff has several advantages over a committee structure. First of all, such a staff ensures fully the objectivity of the scientific findings, which facilitates agreement on their regulatory implications. In a committee structure, on the other hand, scientific evidence may become an instrument to support national positions, rather than a neutral body of knowledge on which decisions can be based. This is caused largely by the fact that in a committee structure each member State not only collects the basic data, but also evaluates these data with a view to their regulatory implications. Such a national evaluation might avoid conclusions which would necessitate regulatory measures with detrimental consequences for the fisheries of the State in question. Conversely, internationally organized research provides a guarantee that scientific facts will not become the object of interest-oriented interpretations. A second point is that an international research staff can tailor its investigations quite precisely to the regulatory needs of a commission. The research institutions of member States, on the other hand, are usually involved in a variety of projects and are faced by often conflicting demands for the available facilities. As a result, such agencies might find it difficult to conduct the specific investigations required by an international fisheries organization or to complete them in time. Finally, to rely on the investigations of the member States is to assume that these States have the capability of conducting such investigations. This creates no problems for those commissions whose membership consists of the developed fishing nations of Western Europe and North America. However, the number of developing nations which are members of international fisheries organizations is increasing, and they generally lack the manpower and capital to conduct their own research work. Accordingly, if a commission depends on the research of its members, these nations have no choice but to accept the scientific findings of other States. Obviously, this does not enhance their willingness to adopt the decisions based upon such findings. The impartiality of the conclusions of an international research staff, however, can not be questioned by States without independent research capabilities. In addition, such an international staff can be used as a centre for training experts from the developing countries. These observations do not imply that a committee structure has nothing but disadvantages. One of its positive features is that it enables the organization to draw a great number of practising scientists into its work. This strengthens support for the organization's recommendations on the national level.

The conclusion must be that as far as the implementation of research functions is concerned, a permanent international research staff is preferable to a committee structure, particularly if the commission in question is concerned with controversial issues or if its membership includes developing nations. Therefore, it is regrettable that not more fisheries organizations have the authority to employ such a staff, or if they have this authority, have not used it more effectively. It has been discussed that in this respect the major obstacle is formed by financial limitations.[191] However, since the most

[191] *Supra* p. 72.

urgent need for internationally organized research exists with respect to the *interpretation* of basic data and not with respect to the *collection* of such data, it would be possible to make a financially realistic improvement in the research functions of a fisheries commission by authorizing it to employ a relatively small international staff which is solely responsible for evaluating the data collected by the member States. Such a staff should have expertise concerning all relevant aspects of marine fisheries and not only concerning marine biology. Member States should have the obligation of collecting the necessary basic information and making it available in agreed form to the commission for evaluation.

7. FUNCTIONS CONCERNING ENFORCEMENT[192]

7.1 Methods of Enforcement

If States accept the regulations proposed by a fisheries commission, their fishing vessels must comply with such regulations, which may lay down rules concerning closed seasons, closed areas, minimum fish sizes, minimum mesh sizes, etc. This raises the question of how these rules can be enforced. The term 'enforcement' refers here to all aspects of the process by which fishing vessels are compelled to respect international regulations. This process includes not only inspection at sea or in port, but also the prosecution and

[192]A W Koers, *The enforcement of fisheries agreements on the high seas: a comparative analysis of international State practice*, Law of the Sea Institute, University of Rhode Island, Occasional Paper No. 6, June 1970. A W Koers, *The enforcement of international fisheries agreements*, in *Netherlands Yearbook of International Law* 1970, pp. 1–31. J S Wiegand, *Seizures of United States fishing vessels. The status of the wet war*, San Diego Law Review 1969, pp. 428–446. A J Aglen, *Problems of enforcement of fisheries regulations*, in *The future of the sea's resources*, L M Alexander ed., Kingston, R I 1968, pp. 19–23. J E Carroz and A G Roche, *The international policing of high sea fisheries*, in *Canadian Yearbook of International Law* 1968, pp. 61–90. E C Surrency, *International inspection in pelagic whaling, ICLQ* 1964, pp. 666–671.

punishment of offences. Essentially, fisheries conventions adopt three methods of enforcement: (1) national enforcement; (2) mutual enforcement; and (3) international enforcement.

In the first approach the flag State of a fishing vessel is responsible for ensuring that such a vessel respects all applicable rules. The Convention on the High Seas of Geneva 1958 provides[193] that ships must sail under the flag of one State only, and that, save in exceptional cases expressly provided for in international treaties or in the articles of the Convention itself, ships are subject to the exclusive jurisdiction of that State on the high seas. Thus, unless fisheries conventions contain provisions to the contrary, enforcement of fisheries regulations on the high seas is the exclusive responsibility of the flag State. However, quite a few fisheries agreements make an exception to this general principle by creating a system of mutual enforcement. In this system fishery inspectors may board not only fishing vessels carrying their own flag, but also vessels under the flag of the other Contracting Parties.[194] A general condition of these arrangements is that inspectors may not board vessels while they are engaged in fishing operations. If an inspector discovers an infraction, he must usually draw up a report and submit this to the appropriate authorities. A few conventions go further and allow him to seize the offending vessel and arrest its crew. However, even in a system of mutual enforcement, the flag State remains exclusively responsible for the prosecution of infractions. This is also the case in international enforcement under which an international fisheries organization is

[193]Art. 6, para. 1 Convention on the High Seas of Geneva 1958, *UNTS* vol. 450, p. 86.
[194]NEAFC, *Report of the sixth meeting*, London 1968, Annex A. ICNAF, *Annual Proceedings for the year 1969–1970*, Dartmouth 1970, pp. 20–22. Art. VI, para. 2 NPFSC Convention. Art. VII, para. 2 Japan-Soviet Commission Convention. Art. II, para. 1 IPHC Convention. Art. X, para. 1(b) INPFC Convention.

responsible for enforcing its own regulations. In 1963 the Antarctic pelagic whaling countries signed an Agreement concerning an International Observer Scheme for Factory Ships Engaged in Pelagic Whaling in the Antarctic,[195] which provides for a system of international enforcement. Although this Agreement expired without entering into force, a revised, but similar, international enforcement arrangement was put into effect by Japan, Norway and the USSR in 1971.[196]

7.2 Functions of Fisheries Organizations

Some international fisheries organizations have the authority to make recommendations concerning the manner in which their regulations are enforced. The NEAFC Convention, for example, stipulates that the Commission may make recommendations for measures of national control in the territories of the member States and for measures of national and international control on the high seas.[197] After preliminary discussions,[198] NEAFC adopted a recommendation for a Scheme of Joint Enforcement at its fifth annual meeting;[199] it provides for mutual enforcement of the NEAFC regulations. Although a few States have lodged objections to its provisions regarding inspection of catch and gear below deck,[200] almost all NEAFC member States have gradually accepted the Scheme of Joint Enforcement and now participate in its implementation. The Northwest Atlantic Commission introduced an enforcement arrangement in 1970.[201] Under the original Convention, ICNAF did not have the authority to make proposals concerning methods of enforce-

[195]*ILM* 1964, p. 107.
[196]*Commercial Fisheries Review*, October 1971, p. 26.
[197]Art. 13, para. 3 NEAFC Convention.
[198]NEAFC, *Report of the fourth meeting*, London 1966, pp. 6–7.
[199]*Ibidem, fifth*, London 1968, pp. 79–81.
[200]*Ibidem, sixth*, London 1968, p. 7.
[201]ICNAF, *Annual Proceedings for the year 1969–1970*, Dartmouth 1970, p. 20.

ment. However, a Special Protocol relating to Measures of Control of 1965[202] amended Article VIII, para. 5 of the Convention for the purpose of giving the Commission the power to make recommendations for national and international measures of enforcement on the high seas. After the entry into force of this Protocol in 1969, ICNAF adopted in 1970 a recommendation for a Scheme of Joint International Enforcement, which is quite similar to the NEAFC arrangement. Finally, a third fisheries organization which has been instrumental in the adoption of enforcement arrangements is the Whaling Commission. In 1955 Norway proposed to make the Whaling Commission responsible for appointing inspectors to factory vessels engaged in Antarctic pelagic whaling. However, the Commission took the view that this proposal was *ultra vires* and that it could not act upon it until the IWC Convention was amended.[203] Such an amendment entered into force in 1959 and thus gave the Commission authority to make proposals concerning methods of inspection. Unfortunately, Norway and the Netherlands withdrew from the Commission in that year and, as a result, the Commission could merely request the United Kingdom to invite the nations concerned to a conference on this subject.[204] This and similar requests at subsequent meetings resulted in the aforementioned 1963 Agreement on an International Observer Scheme.

International fisheries organizations have functions not only in respect of the adoption of new enforcement arrangements, but they also assist in carrying out existing schemes. Such a function is an inherent feature of international enforcement. Under the 1963 International Observer Scheme,[205] the Whaling Commission must appoint inspectors

[202]*ILM* 1966, p. 719.
[203]IWC, *Seventh Report of the Commission*, London 1956, p. 12.
[204]*Ibidem, Eleventh*, London 1960, p. 6.
[205]*ILM* 1964, p. 107.

to the factory vessels of the Antarctic whaling countries who must be of a different nationality than the vessel on which they serve. These inspectors are paid by, and are responsible to, the Whaling Commission. They may freely inspect the operations of the factory vessels, but they are prohibited from interfering with such operations. Inspectors report any infractions to the Commission. Accordingly, this Scheme makes the Whaling Commission directly responsible for enforcing its own regulations. Although it did not enter into force, its basic characteristics can also be found in the international enforcement arrangement accepted by Japan, Norway and the USSR in 1971. Fisheries commissions are involved in implementing mutual enforcement schemes as well. A first function is based on provisions which require member States to report to the commission on their enforcement effort.[206] Several fisheries commissions have established special committees to review these reports.[207] Examples are here the Whaling Commission,[208] the Northwest Atlantic Commission[209] and the North-East Atlantic Commission.[210] Apart from such reporting procedures, arrangements for mutual enforcement may also give fisheries commissions certain other functions. In the NEAFC and ICNAF Schemes member States must, for example, inform the Commission of the names of their inspectors. These Commissions must also approve the form of the document of identity of inspectors, the form of their reports and the form of the identification mark which must be attached to nets used in violation of the applicable regulations. Finally, these Schemes require

[206]Art. IX, para. 1 ICCAT Convention. Art. 13, para. 2 NEAFC Convention. Art. VI, para. 4 Japan-Soviet Commission Convention. Art. IX, para. 2 and Art. X, para. 2 INPFC Convention. Art XII ICNAF Convention. Art. IX, para. 4 IWC Convention.
[207]Supra p. 143.
[208]IWC, *Twenty-second Report of the Commission*, London 1972, p. 149.
[209]ICNAF, *Annual Proceedings for the year 1970–1971*, Dartmouth 1971, p. 23.
[210]NEAFC, *Report of the ninth meeting*, London 1971, p. 14.

member States to submit provisional plans for inspection activities to the Commission. Both Commissions may make recommendations in order to coordinate such activities.

7.3 Evaluation

International fisheries organizations have undoubtedly made substantial contributions to the creation of more effective arrangements for enforcing international fisheries regulations. Therefore, they should have full authority to make recommendations concerning these issues. A provision such as Article IX, para. 3 of the ICCAT Convention, which makes the Contracting Parties, rather than the Commission, responsible for the adoption of enforcement arrangements is undesirable. If a commission has the necessary powers, it should utilize them effectively. There is no doubt that in this respect the Whaling Commission could have been more active. Although it had the authority to make recommendations on methods of inspection, it limited its role to inviting member States to draw up new enforcement arrangements at separate international conferences. The two North Atlantic Commissions have been more productive, even though they have restricted their efforts to creating schemes of mutual, rather than international, enforcement. However, there is little reason for taking the view that in all cases international enforcement is to be preferred over mutual enforcement.[211] A first problem of international enforcement is that the existing fisheries organizations are incapable of prosecuting offences, but must rely in this respect on member States. In addition, the effectiveness of mutual enforcement can be greatly enhanced by giving fisheries commissions substantial responsibilities concerning its implementation. First of all, not all international fisheries organizations seem to have made the fullest possible use of the provisions which require mem-

[211]Koers, *op. cit.*, note 192, in *Netherlands Yearbook of International Law*, p. 28.

ber States to report on their inspection efforts.[212] Here, stricter standards could be adopted. In addition, member States could be required to report not only regarding their inspection effort, but also with regard to the manner in which they have prosecuted those offending vessels that carry their flag. This would ensure that States apply similar standards in punishing offenders. Finally, one of the advantages of mutual enforcement over national enforcement is that it allows a more efficient use of the available inspectors. However, this advantage will fail to materialize if the inspection activities of the various States lack adequate coordination. Therefore, all mutual enforcement arrangements should follow the example of the NEAFC and ICNAF Schemes and make fisheries organizations responsible for coordinating the inspection programmes of member States.

8. FUNCTIONS CONCERNING INTRA-USE AND INTER-USE CONFLICTS[213]

8.1 Intra-Fisheries Conflicts

Several international fisheries conventions have been concluded in order to avoid conflicts among fishermen at sea and to prevent damage to fishing gear. One of the first modern fisheries agreements – the North Sea Fisheries Convention of 1882[214] – was concerned with these problems. This Convention was replaced by the Convention on Conduct of Fishing Operations in the North Atlantic, which was signed on 1

[212] Although the INPFC Convention contains such a provision, the annual reports of the North Pacific Commission do not refer to any discussion with respect to reports on enforcement.
[213] For a discussion of the extra-legal background of intra-use and inter-use conflict functions, see *supra* pp. 73-76.
[214] *United Nations legislative series, Laws and regulations on the régime of the high seas*, New York 1951, vol. I, p. 179.

15

June 1967 at London.[215] Like its predecessor, the 1967 Convention makes provision for the registration and marking of fishing vessels and gear and for rules that fishing vessels must observe in carrying out fishing operations. Intra-use conflicts among different forms of marine fisheries occur in particular between operations with mobile gear and operations with fixed gear. In order to prevent incidents,[216] agreements have been concluded which prohibit fishing with mobile gear in certain areas and/or in certain periods. One example is the Agreement relating to Fishing Operations in the Northeastern Pacific Ocean between the United States and the Soviet Union, which was originally signed on 14 December 1964 at Washington, DC.[217] Generally, international fisheries organizations have no direct functions under such agreements for the avoidance of intra-fisheries conflicts. The 1967 Convention on Conduct of Fishing Operations in the North Atlantic, for example, does not establish a commission to administer its provisions. However, this has not prevented fisheries organizations from being concerned with these problems. The Halibut Commission and the North Pacific Commission, for instance, have studied the effects of trawling operations on the halibut fisheries in the Gulf of Alaska and the Bering Sea. The INPFC established a Gulf of Alaska Groundfish Committee and a Sub-Committee on Bering Sea Groundfish to study this question.[218] As a result, the Commission has made considerable progress in defining the scope and extent of this intra-fisheries conflict.

[215]*ILM* 1967, p. 760. D W van Lynden, *The Convention on Conduct of Fishing Operations in the North Atlantic*, NTIR 1967, pp. 245–258. M Voelckel, *La Convention du 1er Juin 1967 sur l'exercice de la pêche en Atlantique Nord*, in *Annuaire Français de Droit International* 1967, pp. 647–672.

[216]*E.g.*, in September 1971 Soviet trawling operations caused serious damage to the fixed lobster pots of American fishermen off the coast of New England, *Ocean Science News* 1971, No. 47, p. 3.

[217]*UNTS* vol. 531, p. 213.

[218]INPFC, *Annual Report 1969*, Vancouver 1971, p. 10, p. 13.

8.2 Inter-Use Conflicts

The functions of international fisheries organizations concerning conflicts among different uses of the sea are as indirect as those concerning intra-fisheries conflicts. The only fisheries commission with considerable experience in this area is the Salmon Commission. Already in 1956 it expressed concern about changes in the natural condition of the Fraser River caused by the industrial and municipal development of the region.[219] The Commission stated that it was clearly not its responsibility to decide upon the course of such development, but that its function was to clarify the consequences of the various proposals on the salmon resources. Subsequently, the Salmon Commission has reviewed the effects on Fraser River salmon of such other uses of the river basin as: (1) hydro-electric dams; (2) waste disposal; (3) forest spraying; (4) mosquito control; (5) water supply diversions; (6) dredging; (7) logging; (8) road construction; and (9) seismic explorations.[220] In addition, the Commission attempts to develop artificial spawning methods which might enable salmon to remain an economically viable resource regardless of the deterioration of the Fraser River's natural conditions. Other fisheries organizations which study the effects of pollution on the living resources of the sea are the International Council and FAO. The FAO organized, for example, a Technical Conference on Marine Pollution and Its Effects on Living Resources and Fishing, which was held in Rome from 9–18 December 1970. This Conference adopted several recommendations primarily calling for an increased research effort.[221] It also recommended prohibiting the dumping of toxic wastes on fishing grounds.

[219]IPSFC, *Annual Report 1956*, New Westminster 1957, p. 5.
[220]*Ibidem, 1962*, New Westminster 1963, pp. 29–31.
[221]FAO, *Technical Conference on Marine Pollution and Its Effects on Living Resources and Fishing 1970. Conclusions and recommendations as approved.* Document FIR:MP/70/Rec., Rev. 1, Rome 1971, pp. 1–3.

8.3 Evaluation

With the intensification of the exploration and exploitation of the resources of the oceans, intra-use and inter-use conflicts will undoubtedly become more serious. Consequently, it is desirable that international fisheries organizations be given more explicit functions in this respect. As far as intra-fisheries conflicts are concerned, fisheries commissions could be empowered to make recommendations to their member States for measures designed to minimize such conflicts. In addition, if incidents were to occur, they could function as fact-finding bodies, which would greatly facilitate the settlement of damages. In respect of inter-use conflicts, the activities of the Salmon Commission might very well be indicative of the problems which other fisheries commissions will face in the future. The Salmon Commission is ahead of other organizations because it regulates fisheries in a river basin, rather than fisheries in the waters of the sea. Its involvement in inter-use conflicts points out that it is desirable to give fisheries organizations the authority to make clear the effects of other uses of the sea on fisheries, particularly those of marine pollution. Such a task would enable fisheries commissions to articulate the interests of marine fisheries in the process by which the world community defines the future rules and principles of the international law of the sea concerning inter-use conflicts.

Chapter V

Alternatives and Proposals: a Discussion

1. THE TWO BASIC ALTERNATIVES

It is evident from the preceding Chapters that in many respects international fisheries organizations are incapable of coping effectively with the problems of marine fisheries. Therefore, several suggestions have been made concerning improvements in their structure, functions and powers. However, it would be erroneous to assume that such improvements constitute a panacea for all problems. Many of the inadequacies of international fisheries organizations are directly related to the basic rules and principles of the international law of marine fisheries, the international law of the sea and, indeed, international law in general. Thus, a discussion of proposals with regard to future arrangements can not limit itself to the structure, functions and powers of fisheries organizations, but must necessarily involve all aspects of the international law of marine fisheries. Accordingly, this Chapter will discuss a wide range of suggestions and proposals concerning the future legal regime of marine fisheries in general.

Essentially, these suggestions and proposals fall into two broad categories:[1] (1) proposals to enhance the authority of

[1] J J Dykstra, *Remarks*, in *The United Nations and ocean management*, L M Alexander ed., Kingston, R I 1971, p. 51. P A Larkin, *Critique: fisheries management provisions in the Commission Report*, in *National policy recommendations*, L M Alexander ed., Kingston, R I 1970, pp. 297–305. D M Johnston, *The legal theory of fishery organization*, in *International rules and organization for the sea*, L M Alexander ed., Kingston, R I 1969, pp. 432–435. R G R Wall, *A European view*, in *International rules and organization for the sea*, L M Alexander ed.,

Continued on next page

coastal States; and (2) proposals to enhance the authority of international fisheries organizations. A third possibility would be to suggest that marine fisheries should not be regulated at all. It is, for example, possible to take the view that the financial costs of regulation are higher than the financial costs of non-regulation. In the absence of detailed figures concerning the costs of the international regulation of marine fisheries, this viewpoint can be illustrated by reference to national fisheries regulation. It has, for example, been estimated that the United States spends approximately $110 million annually for marine fisheries research and regulation, while the total value of the catch of United States fishermen is approximately $600 million annually.[2] These figures raise the question for the United States of whether or not the returns from marine fisheries justify the costs involved in regulation and research. The same question may be asked concerning international fisheries regulation. However, even if the answer would be that its financial benefits do not warrant its costs, there still remain compelling non-financial considerations to justify the international regulation of marine fisheries. Among these considerations is the need to avoid conflicts among nations and to maintain public order on the seas. Therefore, this third possibility of non-regulation will not be discussed further. As a result, the above two general categories represent the basic alternatives for improving the international law of marine fisheries. The

Continued from previous page
Kingston, R I 1969, p. 368. J A Crutchfield, Overcapitalization of the fishing effort, in The future of the sea's resources, L M Alexander ed., Kingston, R I 1968, p. 27. P M Dodyk, Comments on international law and fishery policy, Clearinghouse for Federal Scientific and Technical Information, Doc. PB 179 427, Springfield, Va. 1968, pp. 83–168. F T Christy, Jr., in A symposium on national interests in coastal waters, in Offshore boundaries and zones, L M Alexander ed., Columbus, Ohio 1967, p. 127.
[2] J L McHugh, Domestic wrangles and international tangles, Woodrow Wilson International Center for Scholars, Washington 1971, p. 192.

following discussion will not attempt to review all possible variations of these alternatives, but will concentrate on a few representative examples.

2. PROPOSALS TO ENHANCE THE AUTHORITY OF COASTAL STATES

2.1 Introduction

A fundamental problem of the international law of the sea is the absence of agreement within the international community with regard to the limits and scope of the rights of coastal States over the living resources of the sea.[3] As far as the limits are concerned, it is a well-discussed fact that the 1958 and 1960 Conferences on the Law of the Sea failed to reach agreement on the breadth of the territorial sea and exclusive fisheries zones.[4] Partly because of this failure, many coastal States have extended their exclusive fishery limits, either by unilateral action or on the basis of international agreement.[5]

[3]For a survey, see FAO, *Limits and status of the territorial sea, exclusive fishing zones, fishery conservation zones and the continental shelf*, FAO Legislative Series No. 8, Rome 1969; a more recent version is: FAO Fisheries Circular No. 127, Rome 1971. For the text of various national laws, see *United Nations legislative series, Laws and regulations on the regime of the territorial sea*, New York 1956.

[4]F V Garcia Amador, *The exploitation and conservation of the resources of the sea, A study of contemporary international law*, 2nd ed. 2nd enl. printing Leyden 1963, pp. 13–86. S Oda, *International control of sea resources*, Leyden 1963, pp. 35–44, pp. 98–111. W W Bishop, *The 1958 Geneva Convention on Fishing and Conservation of the Living Resources of the High Seas, Columbia Law Review* 1962, pp. 1206–1230. A H Dean, *The second Geneva Conference on the Law of the Seas, AJIL* 1960, pp. 751–789. A H Dean, *The Geneva Conference on the Law of the Sea: what was accomplished, AJIL* 1958, pp. 607–628.

[5]Recent examples of unilateral extensions can be found in legislation of Brazil, *ILM* 1971, p. 1224, of Canada, *ILM* 1971, p. 438 and of Iceland, Ministry for Foreign Affairs of Iceland, *Fisheries jurisdiction in Iceland*, Reykjavik 1972, *ILM* 1972, p. 643. An example of extension by international agreement is the European Fisheries Convention of London 1964, *ILM* 1964, p. 476.

Most coastal States now claim exclusive jurisdiction over the living resources of the sea in a zone which extends up to twelve miles from the baseline of the territorial sea. However, some States go considerably beyond such a limit. Several Latin American countries, for example, claim exclusive fishery zones that extend up to 200 miles from their shores.[6] The result is that there is not yet an uniformly accepted limit for the exclusive fisheries jurisdiction of coastal States, although there is a growing consensus with regard to the legality of the twelve mile zone. A second uncertainty with regard to the rights of coastal States concerns their scope. Article 2, para. 4 of the Convention on the Continental Shelf of Geneva 1958,[7] for example, includes sedentary species in the natural resources of the continental shelf over which coastal States have sovereign rights. Sedentary species are defined as: '... organisms which, at the harvestable stage either are immobile on or under the seabed or are unable to move except in constant physical contact with the seabed or the subsoil'. Apart from the fact that the Continental Shelf Convention does not demarcate the precise limits of the continental shelf,[8] the above definition of sedentary species leaves ample room for different interpretations. Its vagueness

[6] F V Garcia Amador, *Latin America and the law of the sea*, Law of the Sea Institute, University of Rhode Island, Occasional Paper No. 14, July 1972. *Case studies in regional management: Latin America*, in *The United Nations and ocean management*, L M Alexander ed., Kingston, R I 1971, pp. 333–369. J J Santa Pinter, *Latin American countries facing the problem of territorial waters*, San Diego Law Review 1971, pp. 606–621. F Thibaut, *L'Amérique latine et l'évolution du droit international de la mer*, RGDIP 1971, pp. 742–758. T Wolff, *Peruvian-United States relations over maritime fishing: 1945-1969*, Law of the Sea Institute, University of Rhode Island, Occasional Paper No. 4, March 1970. S A Bayitch, *Inter-american law of fisheries. An introduction with documents*, New York 1957.
[7] *UNTS* vol. 499, p. 312.
[8] Art. 1 Convention on the Continental Shelf of Geneva 1958; for more information, see B H Oxman, *The preparation of Article 1 of the Convention on the Continental Shelf*, Clearinghouse for Federal Scientific and Technical Information, Doc. PB 182 100, Springfield, Va. 1968.

led, for example, to a dispute between France and Brazil and between Japan and the United States concerning lobsters and crabs.[9] Thus, the scope of the exclusive fisheries jurisdiction of coastal States is almost as ambiguous as its limits. Nevertheless, as a generalization it can be said that a coastal State has exclusive rights over all living resources in its exclusive fishery zone and over the sedentary species of its continental shelf.

2.2 Extending the Exclusive Fishery Rights of Coastal States

Some proposals with respect to the international law of marine fisheries suggest the solving of some of its problems by extending the exclusive fishery rights of coastal States beyond their present limits. Most of these suggestions have been made within the context of the international debate concerning the law of the sea generally and concerning the legal regime for the exploration and exploitation of the mineral resources of the seabed and subsoil beyond limits of national jurisdiction specifically.[10] Although the various proposals differ greatly from each other, it is possible to discuss in general terms the effects of a significant extension of the exclusive rights of coastal States over the living resources of the sea on questions of full utilization, conservation, economic efficiency and allocation.

Several observers take the view that an extension of exclusive rights would reduce the productivity of the seas'

[9]L F E Goldie, *Sedentary fisheries and Article 2(4) of the Convention on the Continental Shelf. A plea for a separate regime*, *AJIL* 1969, pp. 86–97. L F E Goldie, *Sedentary fisheries and the North Sea continental shelf cases*, *AJIL* 1969, pp. 536–544. R Young, *Sedentary fisheries and the Convention on the Continental Shelf*, *AJIL* 1961, pp. 359–373. A Papandreou, *La situation juridique des pêcheries sédentaires en haute mer*, Athens 1958.
[10]The *Working Paper by the Delegations of Australia and New Zealand. Principles for a Fisheries Regime*, UN Doc. A/AC. 138/SC. II/L. 11, 11 August 1972, submitted to the UN Seabed Committee, envisages an extension of coastal State exclusive fishery limits.

living resources.[11] A number of considerations support this viewpoint. First of all, the statistics indicate that in the past coastal States have made a much smaller contribution to the expansion of marine fisheries than distant water fishing nations.[12] Peru is the only coastal fishing nation whose catches have increased at a rate comparable to those of distant water fishing States. Many coastal States lack the resources to undertake fishery development programmes. This refers not only to the financial aspects, but also to the capability of collecting the knowledge on which fisheries development depends.[13] Developing nations in particular do not have either of these resources. Another point is that coastal State fisheries tend to concentrate on a few species only. Distant water fishing nations, on the other hand, are less discriminating and often exploit species in which coastal States have no, or only a small, interest. Finally, the fishing capacity of distant water States not only exceeds that of most coastal fishing States, but is also much more mobile.[14] Consequently, distant water States can adapt their fisheries to natural changes in the abundance of species more easily than can coastal fishing States. Thus, an extension of the exclusive

[11] W M Chapman, *Some problems and prospects for the harvest of living marine resources to the year 2000*, paper at a meeting of experts at UNITAR, February 25–27, 1970, p. 56. M B Schaefer, *Some recent developments concerning fishing and the conservation of the living resources of the high seas*, San Diego Law Review 1970, p. 392. W T Burke, *Contemporary legal problems in ocean development*, in *Towards a better use of the ocean*, Stockholm, New York and London 1969, p. 65. *Panel reports of the Commission on Marine Science, Engineering and Resources*, vol. 3, *Marine resources and legal-political arrangements for their development*, Washington 1969, p. VIII–151. D L McKernan, *A developing policy for international fisheries*, in *The future of the sea's resources*, L M Alexander ed., Kingston, R I 1968, p. 149. W M Chapman, *Fishery resources in offshore waters*, in *Offshore boundaries and zones*, L M Alexander ed., Columbus, Ohio 1967, p. 104.
[12] *Supra* p. 35.
[13] W M Chapman, *The theory and practice of international fishery development-management*, San Diego Law Review 1970, p. 447. Commission on Marine Science, Engineering and Resources, *op. cit.*, note 11, p. VIII–150.
[14] *Supra* p. 35.

rights of coastal States may very well restrict distant water fisheries without resulting in a corresponding expansion of coastal State fisheries. Obviously, special arrangements could allow distant water fishing countries to continue to exploit stocks that are not exploited by the coastal State.[15] However, political considerations may make it very difficult to allow foreign fishing for any stock over which a coastal State has obtained exclusive jurisdiction: in most cases the major political impetus for an extension of exclusive rights stems from a desire to protect the national fishing industry by eliminating foreign competition.[16] Taking these considerations into account, the conclusion must be drawn that an extension of the exclusive rights of coastal States might very well have adverse effects from the viewpoint of full utilization, particularly since special arrangements to prevent such effects are apt to be politically unacceptable as conflicting with the very objectives of an extension of exclusive rights.

As far as conservation is concerned, it is possible to take the view that an extension of the exclusive rights of coastal States would have beneficial consequences since it would make coastal States, rather than international fisheries organizations, responsible for taking regulatory measures. Support for this view can, first of all, be found in the failure of several international commissions to adopt effective measures. Secondly, if coastal States were responsible for conservation, the procedures for working out regulations would have been simplified considerably: the complexities of international negotiations would have been replaced by the more efficient

[15]The Working Paper of Australia and New Zealand, *op. cit.*, note 10, provides, for example, that if the coastal State is unable to take 100 per cent of the allowable catch, it must permit the entry of foreign fishing.
[16]D L McKernan, *International fisheries arrangements beyond the twelve mile limit*, in *International rules and organization for the sea*, L M Alexander ed., Kingston, R I 1969, p. 258. The limited scope of the rights of foreign fishermen is also evident from D W Windley, *International practice regarding traditional fishing privileges of foreign fishermen in zones of extended maritime jurisdiction*, *AJIL* 1969, pp. 490–503.

procedures of national legislation.[17] Finally, if a coastal State has exclusive rights over a stock, it is in its self-interest to adopt conservation measures with respect to that stock.[18] However, there are also a number of considerations that cast doubt upon the ability of coastal States to be more effective in these matters than international fisheries commissions. In the first place, the past performance of many coastal States in respect of conservation is as poor as that of some international fisheries organizations.[19] There are situations in which coastal States do not depend upon the cooperation of other States in adopting effective conservation measures – a stock may be found primarily within its limits of exclusive jurisdiction or a high seas stock may be exploited by its fishermen only. Yet in these situations coastal States have been as ineffectual concerning conservation as international fisheries commissions. A survey of United States fisheries in the Middle Atlantic, for example, indicates clearly how stock after stock has been depleted, even though only United States fishermen were engaged in these fisheries.[20]

[17]H Kasahara, *International arrangements for fisheries*, in *The United Nations and ocean management*, L M Alexander ed., Kingston, R I 1971, p. 39. W L Sullivan, *A warning: the decline of international fisheries management looking particularly at the North Atlantic Ocean*, in *The United Nations and ocean management*, L M Alexander ed., Kingston, R I 1971, p. 48. Dodyk, *op. cit.*, note 1, p. 148. R I Jackson, *Some observations on the future growth of world fisheries and the nature of the conservation problem*, in *The future of the sea's resources*, L M Alexander ed., Kingston, R I 1968, p. 13.
[18]INPFC, *Annual Report 1968*, Vancouver 1970, p. 5. Commission on Marine Science, Engineering and Resources, *op. cit.*, note 11, p. VIII–150. Dodyk, *op. cit.*, note 1, p. 148.
[19]McHugh, *op. cit.*, note 2, p. 173. W L Sullivan, in *Management of international fisheries arrangements* (discussion), in *The United Nations and ocean management*, L M Alexander ed., Kingston, R I 1971, pp. 67–68. Chapman, *op. cit.*, note 11, 1970, p. 38. D L McKernan, in *Competing demands on the shelf* (discussion), in *International rules and organization for the sea*, L M Alexander ed., Kingston, R I 1969, p. 246.
[20]McHugh, *op. cit.*, note 2, *passim*. Commission on Marine Science, Engineering and Resources, *op. cit.*, note 11, p. VIII–150.

This makes obvious the oversimplification of associating overfishing exclusively with distant water fisheries; coastal States have overfished as well.

A second point is that there will always be species which migrate across the boundaries of the areas in which coastal States have exclusive rights, even if these areas are very large.[21] This applies not only to the lateral limits with neighbouring States, but also to the seaward limits. Some species of tuna, for example, migrate across the Pacific Ocean.[22] Moreover, many fishing fleets are equally mobile. Thus, an extension of exclusive rights does not eliminate the fact that in many fisheries coastal States can not adopt effective conservation measures unless they cooperate with other States.[23] Such cooperation is also imperative because the condition of the stocks over which a coastal State has exclusive rights is affected by factors originating beyond the limits of the area to which such rights apply. Pollution is here a prime example. No coastal State can protect the living resources over which it has exclusive rights against the dangers of pollution without cooperating with other nations.

The conclusion must be that extending exclusive rights merely transfers the problems of conservation from the

[21]Statement D L McKernan, United States representative to the UN Seabed Committee, Provisional Summary Records 31st Meeting, Subcommittee II, UN Seabed Committee, UN Doc. A/AC. 138/SC. II/SR. 31, 3 April 1972, p. 3. J L Kask, *Marine Science Commission recommendations on international fisheries organization*, in *National policy recommendations*, L M Alexander ed., Kingston, R I 1970, p. 288. R G R Wall, in *Competing demands on the shelf* (discussion), in *International rules and organization for the sea*, L M Alexander ed., Kingston, R I 1969, p. 248. M B Schaefer, in *The future development of world fisheries* (panel), in *The future of the sea's resources*, L M Alexander ed., Kingston, R I 1968, p. 127. Chapman, *op. cit.*, note 11, 1967, p. 96.
[22]J L Kask, *Tuna – a world resource*, Law of the Sea Institute, University of Rhode Island, Occasional Paper No. 2, May 1969, p. 22.
[23]W T Burke, *Some thoughts on fisheries and a new conference on the law of the sea*, Law of the Sea Institute, University of Rhode Island, Occasional Paper No. 9, March 1971, pp. 15–16. Burke, *op. cit.*, note 11, p. 65.

international arena to the national arena, and that this does not necessarily lead to more effective action. In addition, the conflicts provoked by such an extension may have an adverse effect on international cooperation, although such cooperation will remain a necessity in respect of conservation. Therefore, there is little assurance that an extension of exclusive rights will have a positive effect on the conservation of the living resources of the sea.

If coastal States were to obtain exclusive rights over most of the stocks off their shores, they would be capable of limiting the fishing effort applied to these stocks. This would enable them to increase the efficiency of fishing operations and to prevent overcapitalization. At the same time, they would not be forced to undertake such economic rationalization, but would be free to set their own priorities on the basis of considerations relating to employment, protein needs, etc. Thus, an extension of exclusive rights could make a substantial contribution towards solving the problems of economic efficiency since it would enable, but not force, coastal States to rationalize their fisheries economically. A few coastal fishing States already carry out programmes to improve the efficiency of their fishing operations. Canada, for example, has introduced measures to control access to the Pacific salmon fisheries.[24] On the other hand, the fishing operations of coastal States are generally less efficient than those of distant water fishing nations.[25] Since it eliminates competition with other States, an extension of exclusive rights does not seem to provide coastal States with the incentive to become more efficient. In addition, the domestic regulation of marine fisheries offers even more dramatic

[24] W C Herrington, *Canadian license control for salmon*, Law of the Sea Institute, University of Rhode Island 1970. See also the Canadian proposal to the UN Seabed Committee, UN Doc. A/AC. 138/SC. II/L. 8, 27 July 1972.

[25] J H Wedin, *Impact of distant water on coastal fisheries*, in *The future of the sea's resources*, L M Alexander ed., Kingston, R I 1968, pp. 16–17.

examples of legalized inefficiencies than the international regulation.[26] Thus, although an extension of exclusive fishery rights may create the conditions under which coastal States are in a position to rationalize their fisheries economically, it remains, nevertheless, very doubtful that they will use this opportunity effectively.[27] Moreover, there is no *a priori* reason why international arrangements can not solve these problems.[28]

Extension of exclusive rights has its most fundamental implications in respect of allocation: it alters the allocation of the living resources of the sea in favour of coastal States and to the disadvantage of distant water fishing States. This explains why the major political momentum in favour of an extension of exclusive fishery limits is to be found in the desire of coastal States to increase, or protect, their share in the catches of marine fisheries. Coastal States consider such an extension a solution to the problems created by distant water fisheries off their coasts. These distant water fisheries may overfish stocks which have been traditionally exploited by the fishermen of a coastal State.[29] They may also pre-empt the fishery development opportunities of coastal States by bringing stocks under full exploitation before these States are capable of participating in their harvest. This latter

---

[26]Dodyk, *op. cit.*, note 1, p. 37. R W Johnson, *State and federal laws which retard high seas fishing development*, in supplement *Transactions of the Second Annual Marine Technology Society Conference and Exhibit*, June 27–29, 1966.

[27]Burke, *op. cit.*, note 11, p. 66. Kask, *op. cit.*, note 21, p. 289. Chapman, *op. cit.*, note 11, 1967, p. 104.

[28]*Infra* p. 253; more realistically, *supra* p. 68.

[29]FAO, *Report of the first session of the FAO Fishery Committee for the Eastern Central Atlantic (CECAF)*, FAO Fisheries Reports No. 69, Rome 1969, p. 2. McKernan, *op. cit.*, note 16, p. 259. W C Herrington, *The future of the Geneva Convention on Fishing and the Conservation of the Living Resources of the Sea*, in *The future of the sea's resources*, L M Alexander ed., Kingston, R I 1968, p. 63.

aspect is of particular concern to developing nations.[30] An extension of exclusive rights would certainly be a major step towards solving these allocation problems of coastal States. However, for the same reason such action would be unacceptable to distant water fishing countries, which may have a long history of exploiting certain stocks of fish over which coastal States would then obtain exclusive rights. As a result, an extension of exclusive rights will in all probability create an intensive political confrontation.[31] It may also conflict with the vested rights of other nations.[32] Moreover, it is questionable that such an extension will result in a more equitable allocation of the living resources of the sea. States with a long coastline would benefit the most, whereas States with a short coastline and land-locked States would suffer. As some of the most developed States[33] have very long coastlines, it is, for example, doubtful that the developing nations as a group will benefit from an extension of exclusive fishery rights.[34]

Another relevant consideration is that in most cases the wish of coastal States to expand, or protect, their share in the allocation of the living resources of the sea refers to particular fisheries and not to all stocks off their coasts. Salmon is an

[30]FAO, *Report of the consultation on the conservation of fishery resources and the control of fishing in Africa*, FAO Fisheries Reports No. 101, vol. 1, Rome 1971, p. 1, p. 24. Commission on Marine Science, Engineering and Resources, *op. cit.*, note 11, p. VIII–68.
[31]Schaefer, *op. cit.*, note 11, p. 392. Commission on Marine Science, Engineering and Resources, *op. cit.*, note 11, pp. VIII 55–56. Dodyk, *op. cit.*, note 1, pp. 150–151.
[32]L F E Goldie, *The oceans' resources and international law. Possible developments in regional fisheries management, Columbia Journal of Transnational Law* 1969, pp. 25–28. R W Johnson, in *A symposium on the Geneva Conventions and the need for future modifications*, in *Offshore boundaries and zones*, L. M Alexander ed., Columbus, Ohio 1967, p. 272.
[33]*E.g.*, Australia, Canada, France, New Zealand, South Africa, the United Kingdom, the United States, and the USSR.
[34]Burke, *op. cit.*, note 11, p. 67.

example of such a specific case.[35] Coastal States are required to make considerable investments in this species. First of all, it is often necessary to take special steps in order to ensure that salmon is able to reach its spawning grounds. Secondly, since it is quite easy to catch most of the salmon returning from sea, coastal States must severely restrict the catches of their own fishermen for the purpose of ensuring an adequate escapement to the spawning grounds. Finally, coastal States must take into account the need to maintain certain ecological characteristics essential to this species. This may make the industrial and municipal development of the river basin in question more costly. These considerations explain why many coastal States take the view that the allocation of salmon catches should be made more favourable to them. Extending their exclusive rights would be a possibility of accomplishing this. However, such an extension would apply to all resources and not only to salmon. Therefore, it would give more to the coastal State than is required to meet its demands in respect of the specific problems of salmon. In addition, it would be necessary to grant a coastal State jurisdiction over a very large area of the sea, if salmon migrate over long distances. Consequently, an extension of exclusive rights may very well not solve the specific allocation problems of coastal States, even though in many respects it is the most drastic alternative.

There are two opposing schools of thought concerning the question of the effects of an extension of exclusive fishery rights on such other uses of the high seas as navigation, mineral exploitation, etc. These are: (1) an extension of fishery rights would prevent similar action with regard to the other uses of the high seas;[36] and (2) such an extension would lead to similar claims in respect of other activities on

[35]Statement D L McKernan, *op. cit.*, note 21, p. 4.
[36]Dodyk, *op. cit.*, note 1, p. 127.

the high seas.[37] It is difficult to speculate with regard to the likelihood of either alternative. A great deal will depend upon the manner in which the rights of coastal States would be extended. If this were done on the basis of international negotiations and by international agreement, the first alternative appears to be somewhat more probable than if coastal States were to extend their exclusive fishery rights by unilateral action. A great deal will also depend upon the precise scope and formulation of the extension of exclusive rights. However, one of the most striking features of post-World War II developments in the international law of the sea is the degree by which coastal States have unilaterally extended their jurisdiction over the waters of the high seas.[38] Therefore, past experience does not give much credibility to the view that an extension of fishery jurisdiction is the best way to avoid similar extensions in respect of other activities on the high seas.

In conclusion it can be said that extending the exclusive fishery rights of coastal States will fail to solve many problems of marine fisheries. It would indeed create the conditions necessary for improving the efficiency of fishing operations; it would also eliminate most allocation problems of coastal States. However, even in respect of these two problem areas extension of exclusive rights may very well not produce favourable results: coastal States may not utilize the opportunity for economic rationalization, and extension of exclusive rights may not solve a coastal State's *specific* allocation problems. In addition, it will in all probability have adverse effects on the full utilization of the sea's living resources, while it will not necessarily contribute to more effective arrangements with regard to conservation. Even more important is that such action will result in serious

[37]Commission on Marine Science, Engineering and Resources, *op. cit.*, note 11, p. VIII–151. Dodyk, *op. cit.*, note 1, p. 147.
[38]Dodyk, *op. cit.*, note 1, pp. 145–146.

political friction and confrontation among fishing nations. This will make it even more difficult to come to effective international cooperation, a matter of necessity even if coastal States obtain exclusive rights over large areas of the sea. As fish will continue to migrate across boundary lines and as their condition will continue to depend upon factors originating outside the area of exclusive jurisdiction, it is an illusion to think that extending the exclusive rights of coastal States will eliminate the frustrations of international cooperation in respect of marine fisheries.[39] It will most likely have the opposite effect. The only two forces that seem to support this particular proposal with respect to the international law of marine fisheries are its relative simplicity[40] and the fact that it can be implemented by unilateral action. Other possibilities are more complex and require international agreement.

2.3 Extending the Regulatory Jurisdiction of Coastal States

Some proposals with respect to the international law of marine fisheries do not envisage the extension of exclusive rights, but would merely grant coastal States additional powers in respect of the regulation of marine fisheries.[41] This additional regulatory authority is usually designed to bring about the conservation of the living resources in areas of the high seas adjacent to the exclusive fishery zones of coastal States. Such proposals are not a radical departure from

[39]Burke, *op. cit.*, note 23, p. 16. H Kasahara, in *Management of international fisheries arrangements* (discussion), in *The United Nations and ocean management*, L M Alexander ed., Kingston, R I 1971, p. 63. Burke, *op. cit.*, note 11, p. 65.

[40]Burke, *op. cit.*, note 23, p. 14.

[41]This aspect is stressed in *Management of the Living Resources of the Sea. Working Paper Submitted by the Delegation of Canada* to the UN Seabed Committee, UN Doc. A/AC.138/SC.II/L.8, 27 July 1972.

existing practice. In the Truman Proclamation of 1945,[42] for example, the United States asserted the right to adopt conservation measures in areas of the high seas adjacent to its coast if such areas were fished by its nationals alone. Foreigners who would subsequently enter these fisheries would be required to comply with the United States conservation measures. The 1958 Fisheries Convention gives coastal States a similar right:[43] they may impose non-discriminatory conservation measures on all fishermen in areas of the high seas adjacent to their coasts, provided that scientific evidence supports the need for such measures and provided that the States engaged in the fisheries have failed to reach agreement on appropriate conservation measures. Several proposals have been made recommending either a wider international acceptance of these rights of coastal States or an enhancement of their scope.[44]

Such an extension of non-discriminatory regulatory powers would, first of all, avoid the adverse effects on full utilization of an extension of exclusive fishery rights. Extending the regulatory jurisdiction of coastal States in matters of conservation does not prevent foreign fishermen from fishing for those stocks which they have traditionally exploited, provided that they respect the regulations of the coastal State. This eliminates the possibility of foreign

[42]E W Allen, *The fishery proclamation of 1945, AJIL* 1951, pp. 177–178; see also Commission on Marine Science, Engineering and Resources, *op. cit.*, note 11, pp. VIII 150–151.

[43]Art. 7 1958 Fisheries Convention; see also the Resolution on Cooperation in Conservation Measures adopted by the 1958 Conference, *UNTS* vol. 450, p. 60.

[44]Extension of coastal State regulatory authority is envisaged by the following proposals to the UN Seabed Committee: *The Union of Soviet Socialist Republics: Draft Article on Fishing*, UN Doc. A/AC.138/SC. II/L.6, 18 July 1972. The Canadian proposal, *op. cit.*, note 41. *United States Revised Draft Fisheries Article*, UN Doc. A/AC.138/SC.II/L.9, 4 August 1972. *Proposal for a Régime of Fisheries on the High Seas Submitted by Japan*, UN Doc. A/AC.138/SC.II/L.12, 14 August 1972.

fishermen being excluded from fisheries in which the fishermen of the coastal State have little interest. Secondly, the basic rationale for extending the regulatory jurisdiction of coastal States lies in the notion that replacing the uncertainties and inefficiencies of international arrangements with the coercive powers of the coastal State will result in more effective action in respect of conservation.[45] This may indeed be the case, particularly if the authority of coastal States to adopt unilateral conservation measures is conditional upon an inability of achieving international agreement. This requirement is included in most proposals in this category.[46] On the other hand, in adopting conservation measures under extended regulatory powers, the same problems may arise as in adopting conservation measures under extended exclusive rights: the past record of coastal States is as poor as that of international organizations, while the migratory characteristics of fish and their sensitivity to pollution will make it difficult for coastal States to act effectively unless they cooperate with other States.[47] An indication of the problems involved in acting unilaterally is that no coastal State has used the authority granted to it by Article VII of the 1958 Fisheries Convention.[48] Thirdly, an extension of regulatory jurisdiction does not contribute materially towards solving the problems of economic efficiency, unless it were to authorize coastal States to regulate access to the fisheries. However, in this case coastal States would obtain additional exclusive rights, rather than additional regulatory powers. Extending regulatory authority

[45]INPFC, *Annual Report 1968*, Vancouver 1970, p. 5. Dodyk, *op. cit.*, note 1, p. 140. W C Herrington, *The Convention on Fisheries and Conservation of Living Resources: accomplishments of the 1958 Geneva conference*, in *Offshore boundaries and zones*, L M Alexander ed., Columbus, Ohio 1967, p. 32.

[46]Art. 7, para. 1 1958 Fisheries Convention. It is also part of some of the proposals submitted to the UN Seabed Committee, see note 44.

[47]*Supra* p. 24, p. 26.

[48]Dodyk, *op. cit.*, note 1, p. 137.

has also little effect on allocation. Therefore, such action would undoubtedly be more acceptable to distant water fishing States than an extension of exclusive rights.[49] However, for the same reason it would most probably not satisfy the demands of coastal States in respect of allocation.

The conclusion must be that extending the regulatory jurisdiction of coastal States could indeed be useful from the point of view of conservation, particularly if it is used as an alternative method for adopting conservation measures if international cooperation should fail. Its limited scope will reduce the risks of serious political friction among fishing nations and, like an extension of exclusive rights, it can be implemented by unilateral action. This suggests its usefulness as a preliminary step towards a more definitive, internationally agreed upon solution. On the other hand, extending the regulatory jurisdiction of coastal States is merely a very partial answer to the problems of marine fisheries. It has little effect on questions of economic efficiency and allocation, which in many ways have become more important than conservation problems.[50] Therefore, extending the regulatory jurisdiction of coastal States may be an useful intermediate step, but would not be a real solution to the problems of marine fisheries.

2.4 Coastal State Preferential Rights

There is a third category of proposals which, if implemented, would enhance the authority of coastal States. It is rather difficult to discuss these suggestions in general terms, particularly since their most important common characteristic is that they are designed to solve specific problems of

[49]*Ibidem*, p. 142.
[50]J A Crutchfield, in *International fisheries regimes* (panel), in *National policy recommendations*, L M Alexander ed., Kingston, R I 1970, p. 347. D L McKernan, *International fishery regimes – current and future*, in *National policy recommendations*, L M Alexander ed., Kingston, R I 1970, p. 342.

coastal States. Consequently, their scope is intimately linked to the particular issues with which they are concerned. However, the proposals in this category have in common that their major purpose is to meet the allocation demands of coastal States by giving these States certain preferences over other nations.[51] To illustrate these proposals and to exemplify their differences, the following two suggestions will be discussed:[52] (1) an extension of the exclusive rights of coastal States subject to a right of innocent fishing; and (2) internationally agreed coastal State preferential rights in high seas fisheries.

The first proposal would give foreign fishermen a right of innocent fishing for those stocks which are subject to the extended exclusive rights of a coastal State, but which are not, or not fully, exploited by the coastal State's fishermen.[53] In principle, foreign fishermen would be allowed to catch that portion of the maximum sustainable yield of a stock not taken by the fishermen of the coastal State.[54] Coastal States could not prohibit such foreign fishing, but if they could impose a levy, it would be in their self-interest to allow foreign fishermen to catch their share. This right of innocent fishing would eliminate the possible adverse effects on full utilization of an extension of exclusive rights,[55] while the overall approach could be an improvement from the viewpoint of conservation, especially if the coastal State were made responsible for adopting effective conservation measures.

[51]Most of the proposals submitted to the UN Seabed Committee provide for coastal State preferential rights over high seas resources off their shores, see *e.g.*, Soviet proposal, *op. cit.*, note 44; Canadian proposal, *op. cit.*, note 41; United States proposal, *op. cit.*, note 44; and Japanese proposal, *op. cit.*, note 44. See also note 58.
[52]Schaefer, *op. cit.*, note 11, p. 400.
[53]Dodyk, *op. cit.*, note 1, pp. 129–137.
[54]*Ibidem*, p. 130.
[55]*Ibidem*, p. 136. Commission on Marine Science, Engineering and Resources, *op. cit.*, note 11, p. VIII–68.

Moreover, an extension of coastal State exclusive rights subject to a right of innocent fishing by foreign fishermen would most likely result in some kind of agreement on the allocation of catches among the States concerned. This could be an important step towards solving the problems of economic efficiency.[56] Having a fixed and agreed share in the total catch, all fishing nations could rationalize their fisheries economically, should they desire this. Presumably, such an allocation agreement would also solve most of the specific allocation problems of coastal States. However, since it might restrict distant water fisheries, any extension of exclusive rights will encounter opposition from distant water fishing States, even if it is subject to a right of innocent fishing. Thus, the implementation of this proposal will also provoke disputes and conflicts. A second problem is that it is a complicated arrangement, which, in addition, depends to some extent upon international agreements. One difficulty is that the fishing capacity of coastal States fluctuates, making it necessary to work out special arrangements with respect to the effects of changes in the fisheries of coastal States on the rights of distant water fishing States. These arrangements must give distant water fisheries a certain degree of protection against increases in the fishing capacity of coastal States, since these fisheries would cease to be economically viable if they were required to move out as soon as a coastal State is able to catch whatever the distant water fisheries were catching.[57]

The second approach – internationally agreed preferential rights – would give coastal States certain preferences in the allocation of high seas fisheries, particularly over distant

[56]Commission on Marine Science, Engineering and Resources, *op. cit.*, note 11, p. VIII–62, p. VIII–150.

[57]Most proposals to the UN Seabed Committee provide for a certain period in which foreign fishing must be phased out; see note 44.

water fishing States.[58] Such preferences would be based on an international agreement among the States concerned. Coastal State preferential rights already apply to some high seas fisheries.[59] The 1958 Fisheries Convention recognizes the 'special interest' of coastal States in maintaining the productivity of the living resources in areas of the high seas adjacent to their coast.[60] However, the Convention does not give coastal States any explicit preferential rights regarding the allocation of the catch. The 1958 Conference on the Law of the Sea adopted merely a Resolution on Special Situations relating to Coastal Fisheries,[61] which recommends that preferential treatment be given to a coastal State '. . . whose people are overwhelmingly dependent upon coastal fisheries for their livelihood and economic development.' The Conference was unable to reach agreement on legal provisions implementing this non-binding principle.[62] However, there are a few other international conventions that grant such preferential rights to coastal States.[63] The United

[58]This is essentially the approach of the proposals advanced in the UN Seabed Committee. Generally, coastal States would have the right to reserve to themselves such portion of the allowable catch as they can harvest. The United States proposal would give this right to all coastal States, the Soviet proposal would give it to developing States only, while the Japanese proposal would give developing States preferential rights based upon their fishing capacity and developed States a right to reserve a portion of the catch in order to protect their small scale coastal fisheries, see note 44.

[59]D Nguyen Quoc, *La revendication des droits préférentiels de pêche en haute mer*, in *Annuaire Français de Droit International* 1960, pp. 77–110.

[60]Art. 6, para. 1 1958 Fisheries Convention.

[61]*UNTS* vol. 450, p. 62.

[62]Schaefer, *op. cit.*, note 11, p. 383. H G Anderson, in *The Geneva Conventions – ten years later* (panel), in *International rules and organization*, L M Alexander ed., Kingston, R I 1969, pp. 76–77. W M Chapman, *The United States fish industry and the 1958 and 1960 United Nations conferences on the law of the sea*, in *International rules and organization for the sea*, L M Alexander ed., Kingston, R I 1969, p. 52. Garcia Amador, *op. cit.*, note 4, pp. 199–200.

[63]More often coastal States have extended their rights by unilateral action.

States, for example, has concluded fisheries agreements under which its fishermen enjoy preferences in certain high seas fisheries off its coast.[64] An illustration is the Agreement on Certain Fishery Problems on the High Seas in the Western Areas of the Middle Atlantic between the United States and the USSR, which was originally signed on 25 November 1967 at Moscow and which has been extended annually.[65] Article 2, para. b of the Agreement limits in effect the expansion of Soviet fisheries in this area, which amounts to a preferential right of United States fishermen. The abstention clauses of the INPFC Convention, which favour United States fishermen, can also be considered examples of United States preferential rights.

These few examples emphasize one of the most important advantages of internationally agreed preferential rights: their flexibility. They are designed to cope with specific allocation problems of coastal States and to eliminate these problems undogmatically and with a minimum of damage to the interests of distant water fishing States.[66] Preferential rights may give a coastal State a preferential share in the catch of those species which have been fished traditionally by its fishermen;[67] they may give a coastal State certain exclusive rights over a specific stock; they may impose limits on the growth of foreign fishing in certain areas off its shores; they may give a coastal State the authority to regulate access to certain fisheries, provided that it allows foreign fishermen to catch an agreed share; etc.[68] Moreover, preferential rights may be made subject to a variety of conditions. It can be

[64]Schaefer, op. cit., note 11, pp. 401–402. Commission on Marine Science, Engineering and Resources, op. cit., note 11, pp. VIII 143–148. McKernan, op. cit., note 16, p. 256. Wedin, op. cit., note 25, p. 15.
[65]ILM 1968, p. 144.
[66]Dodyk, op. cit., note 1, p. 154. McKernan, op. cit., note 50, p. 344.
[67]See e.g., the proposals under discussion in the UN Seabed Committee, note 44.
[68]Commission on Marine Science, Engineering and Resources, op. cit., note 11, pp. VIII 68–69. Dodyk, op. cit., note 1, pp. 154–157.

provided, for example, that coastal States lose their preferential rights if their fishermen do not utilize such rights effectively.[69] A coastal State can also be required to carry out scientific investigations and to adopt all necessary conservation measures. However, this flexibility illustrates a serious weakness of preferential rights as well: it reflects the absence of an international consensus with regard to their scope and acceptability.[70] This lack of general consensus makes it even more difficult for the States engaged in a fishery to reach agreement on coastal State preferential rights. Another problem is that if these States succeed in reaching such an agreement, other States are neither bound by it, nor otherwise required to respect its provisions. Thus, all preferential rights arrangements are exposed to the risk that non-party States may decide to enter the fishery to which they apply.

3. PROPOSALS TO ENHANCE THE AUTHORITY OF INTERNATIONAL FISHERIES ORGANIZATIONS

3.1 Introduction

A number of proposals with respect to the international law of marine fisheries envisage enhancing the authority of international fisheries organizations, rather than of coastal States. Such proposals range from suggestions to establish a single, global organization for carrying out the exploration and exploitation of all marine resources to suggestions for making modest improvements in existing regional commissions. The fact that the preceding two Chapters dealing with the structure, functions and powers of these existing fisheries bodies suggest ways in which they can be made

[69]Commission on Marine Science, Engineering and Resources, *op. cit.*, note 11, p. VIII–68. Dodyk, *op. cit.*, note 1, p. 154.
[70]But the work of the UN Seabed Committee could contribute to such consensus.

more effective does not eliminate the need to review more radical alternatives. However, proposals to establish a single, global organization for *all* ocean resources will be discussed solely with regard to their implications concerning the international law of marine fisheries and not with regard to their implications concerning the international law of the sea as a whole.

3.2 A Comprehensive International Fisheries Organization

Suggestions have been made to establish a comprehensive international fisheries organization with full authority over all living resources of the sea.[71] Some of these proposals support the idea of vesting such authority in the United Nations or in an United Nations agency. Presumably, Chapter IX of the Charter, which makes the United Nations responsible for improving the economic and social status of man and nations, could provide a legal basis for such action.[72] What are the advantages of such a comprehensive international fisheries organization?

In respect of full utilization a comprehensive fisheries organization would be capable of taking effective action for the expansion of marine fisheries. It would have at its

[71]Commission on Marine Science, Engineering and Resources, *op. cit.*, note 11, pp. VIII 152–153. E M Borgese, *The ocean regime: a suggested statute for the peaceful uses of the high seas and the seabed beyond the limits of national jurisdiction*, Center for the Study of Democratic Institutions, Occasional Paper No. 1, Santa Barbara 1968. Dodyk, *op. cit.*, note 1, pp. 87–99. F T Christy, Jr., *The distribution of the sea's wealth in fisheries*, in *Offshore boundaries and zones*, L M Alexander ed., Columbus, Ohio 1967, pp. 119–120. Commission to Study the Organization of Peace, *New dimensions for the United Nations: the problems of the next decade*, New York 1966. F T Christy, Jr. and A Scott, *The common wealth in ocean fisheries. Some problems of growth and economic allocation*, Baltimore 1965, pp. 239–240.

[72]C Q Christol, *The social complex of world fisheries: law in support of world needs*, in *The future of the fishing industry of the United States*, Seattle 1968, pp. 305–310.

disposal the means to carry out the necessary investigations for making available the knowledge on which fishery development depends and it would be able to undertake such development on the basis of the most modern technology in existence.[73] In addition, a comprehensive organization would in all probability pre-empt a further extension of the exclusive rights of coastal States, and therefore, would make it possible to avoid the detrimental effects that such an extension would have on full utilization.[74] As far as conservation is concerned, a comprehensive international organization would have the capability to prevent overfishing, regardless of whether marine fisheries are carried out by the organization itself or by States. It could conduct the necessary investigations, adopt effective conservation measures and enforce such regulations *vis-à-vis* its own fishing vessels or any vessels operating under its control.[75] In addition, since such an organization would operate on the basis of economic rationality, and since in most fisheries the maximum economic yield occurs at a catch level lower than the maximum sustainable yield,[76] a comprehensive organization would eliminate most conservation problems in achieving its economic goals. This already suggests that the major advantages of this type of organization are to be found in respect of the economic efficiency of marine fisheries. Its full authority over all living resources of the sea would obviate a most fundamental obstacle to economic rationalization: the fact that under the concept of freedom of fishing on the

[73]Commission on Marine Science, Engineering and Resources, *op. cit.*, note 11, p. VIII–152. Christy, *op. cit.*, note 71, p. 119.
[74]Burke, *op. cit.*, note 11, p. 69. Commission on Marine Science, Engineering and Resources, *op. cit.*, note 11, p. VIII–152. Dodyk. *op. cit.*, note 1, p. 92.
[75]Kask, *op. cit.*, note 21, p. 289. Burke, *op. cit.*, note 11, p. 68. Commission on Marine Science, Engineering and Resources, *op. cit.*, note 11, p. VIII–152. Dodyk, *op. cit.*, note 1, p. 90.
[76]*Supra* p. 55.

high seas, all States may freely enter marine fisheries.[77] A comprehensive international organization could regulate access to high seas fisheries for the purpose of achieving the maximum economic yield.[78] To that end, it could buy the capital and labour required for marine fisheries in the cheapest markets and sell the products of such fisheries in the dearest markets. Alternatively, it could auction off rights to engage in high seas fishing to the highest bidder, which could be either a State, or a private group.[79] Essentially, this organization could operate as a private entrepreneur: its profits would constitute the economic yield of marine fisheries. Finally, as far as allocation is concerned, an inherent feature of a comprehensive international fisheries organization is that it would be based on a distinction between access to the fisheries and access to the wealth of the living resources of the sea.[80] Access to the fisheries would be limited, either to the vessels of the organization or to the vessels of the highest bidders. Thus, only selected States would have direct access to the fisheries. However, if they are members, all nations would share in the revenues derived by the organization from marine fisheries. In this way, all States would continue to have access to the wealth of the sea's living resources.[81] Thus, a comprehensive international fisheries organization

[77] *Supra* p. 18.
[78] Kask, *op. cit.*, note 21, p. 289. Burke, *op. cit.*, note 11, p. 68. Commission on Marine Science, Engineering and Resources, *op. cit.*, note 11, p. VIII–152. Christy, *op. cit.*, note 71, pp. 118–120.
[79] Commission on Marine Science, Engineering and Resources, *op. cit.*, note 11, p. VIII–152. Dodyk, *op. cit.*, note 1, pp. 87–88. F T Christy, Jr., in *The future development of world fisheries* (panel), in *The future of the sea's resources*, L M Alexander ed., Kingston, R I 1968, p. 138; a third possibility would be to make the organization responsible for issuing licenses without bidding, Christy, *op. cit.*, note 71, pp. 116–117.
[80] Dodyk, *op. cit.*, note 1, p. 94. Christy, *op. cit.*, note 71, p. 120.
[81] F T Christy, Jr., *Fisheries and the new conventions on the law of the sea*, San Diego Law Review 1970, p. 467. Christy, *op. cit.*, note 71, p. 111. FAO, *The management of fishery resources*, Rome 1967, p. 25. Johnson, *op. cit.*, note 32, p. 271.

would continue to respect a notion which also underlies the freedom of fishing on the high seas: that the living resources of the high seas are a common resource of all nations.

On the other hand, the establishment of a comprehensive international fisheries organization would present substantial difficulties. Although it may be capable of effective action in respect of full utilization, such an organization would more than likely limit the catches of marine fisheries to the level of maximum economic yield, rather than to that of the maximum sustainable yield. As maximum economic yield catches occur in most fisheries at lower levels than maximum sustainable yield catches, this would result in utilizing the living resources of the sea below their full biological potential. It would depend on the protein needs of the world and on the productivity of other food sources whether or not this would be acceptable.[82] A comprehensive international fisheries organization may also prove to be a very inefficient mechanism for taking action regarding conservation problems. As these problems occur within the context of particular fisheries, it seems logical to make the nations participating in these fisheries responsible for adopting the necessary conservation measures, rather than a single, global organization in which all nations of the world would participate. As far as economic efficiency is concerned, it has been discussed that a maximization of the economic yield may very well be a less desirable objective of the international regulation of marine fisheries than the achievement of a maximum sustainable yield.[83] Let it suffice to say that, compared with maximum sustainable yield, maximum economic yield: (1) may reduce the food production from the sea; (2) may reduce employment opportunities; (3) requires much more information; and (4) is not as widely accepted. Indeed, the conclusion was drawn that it would be preferable to continue to em-

[82] Supra p. 30.
[83] Supra pp. 57-61.

phasize maximum sustainable yield as the objective of international fisheries regulation and to accommodate the problems of economic efficiency within this framework.[84] This conclusion, which would undermine the advantages of a comprehensive organization in respect of economic efficiency, would negate the principal justification for such an organization.[85] A comprehensive international fisheries organization may also have undesirable effects on allocation. If it were to buy manpower and capital in the cheapest markets and sell the products in the dearest markets, the result may very well be that developing nations will be forced to accept the role of catching the fish to be consumed by developed nations. If, on the other hand, the organization were to auction off rights to fish to the highest bidders, it might even occur that the developed nations would not only be the principal consumers of fish, but would also do the fishing. The fact remains that these States can afford to bid higher than developing nations, largely because their markets can more easily absorb higher prices. Thus, a comprehensive international organization could lead to a situation in which nations with the most urgent nutritional problems would indeed have access to the revenues produced by marine fisheries, but not to the fishery products required for feeding their people. This would be a most undesirable allocation of the living resources of the sea.[86]

It would be possible to avoid most of these disadvantages by making special arrangements. For example, a comprehensive international organization could be made res-

[84]*Supra* p. 60.
[85]Chapman, *op. cit.*, note 11, 1970, p. 34. Burke, *op. cit.*, note 11, p. 70. *J* A Crutchfield, *National quotas for the North Atlantic fisheries: an exercise in second best*, in *International rules and organization for the sea*, L M Alexander ed., Kingston, R I 1969, p. 270. Commission on Marine Science, Engineering and Resources, *op. cit.*, note 11, p. VIII–153.
[86]Schaefer, *op. cit.*, note 11, p. 389. Commission on Marine Science, Engineering and Resources, *op. cit.*, note 11, p. VIII–153.

ponsible for achieving the maximum sustainable, rather than the maximum economic yield and for catching this sustainable yield as efficiently as possible. However, such special arrangements would add to the complexity of a structure that is inherently already extremely complex. It is here that the most fundamental problems of a comprehensive international fisheries organization arise. First of all, such an organization would be very costly. Obviously, these expenses would reduce any profits it may generate – it has even been suggested that for this reason it would produce no profit at all.[87] Taking into account that existing fisheries organizations require funding as well, it, nevertheless, seems probable that the extreme complexity of a comprehensive international fisheries organization would substantially increase the cost of international fisheries regulation. Secondly, the functions and powers of a comprehensive international fisheries organization would constitute a radical departure from the functions and powers of the existing fisheries organizations. The wisdom of such a radical departure is very questionable: the organization would be required to function within an extra-legal context which would be largely unforeseeable at the time of its creation and, as it would have a virtual monopoly, the price of the organization's failure could be disaster.[88] This also explains why States will be extremely reluctant to create such an organization.[89] In view of the

[87]Burke, *op. cit.*, note 11, p. 71. Chapman, *op. cit.*, note 11, 1970, p. 34. Commission on Marine Science, Engineering and Resources, *op. cit.*, note 11, p. VIII–153. Chapman, *op. cit.*, note 11, 1967, p. 103.

[88]Commission on Marine Science, Engineering and Resources, *op. cit.*, note 11, p. VIII–152.

[89]Chapman, *op. cit.*, note 11, 1970, p. 34. INPFC, *Annual Report 1968*, Vancouver 1970, p. 4. Schaefer, *op. cit.*, note 11, p. 406. Commission on Marine Science, Engineering and Resources, *op. cit.*, note 11, p. VIII–153. Dodyk, *op. cit.*, note 1, p. 96. T A Fulham, in *The future development of world fisheries* (panel), in *The future of the sea's resources*, L M Alexander ed., Kingston, R I 1968, p. 131. H Kasahara, *Future regime for high seas fisheries*, in *The future of the sea's resources*, L M Alexander ed., Kingston, R I 1968, p. 134.

17

difficulties of obtaining their acceptance of minor improvements in the existing international fisheries commissions, the establishment of a comprehensive international fisheries organization must be deemed beyond the realities of the present international community of sovereign States. Thus, proposals for this type of organization appear to be at best a blueprint for a remote future, although not necessarily a blueprint for utopia.

3.3 A Global Conservation Organization

It would be possible to establish a global international organization which would lack the full authority over all living resources of the sea of a comprehensive international fisheries organization but which would be responsible for their conservation.[90] Its membership would consist not only of States participating in specific fisheries, but would be open to all nations of the world – reflecting the view that since the living resources of the high seas belong to all nations of the world, effective action in respect of conservation is a matter which does not concern fishing nations only. The essential function of a global conservation organization would be to give substance to a world community interest in preventing the overfishing of the living resources of the sea.[91] What could be the functions and advantages of such an organization ?

First of all, a global conservation organization would probably improve the quality of the scientific advice without which it is impossible to deal effectively with conservation problems. Since membership could consist of all nations of the world, the deliberations in the global conservation organization would subject the scientific investigations of fishing nations to the scrutiny of other nations, regardless of whether or not these nations have any interest in the fisheries with which the investigations are concerned. This could

[90]Dodyk, *op. cit.*, note 1, pp. 99–109.
[91]*Supra* pp. 53–54.

have a beneficial effect on the objectivity of the regulatory conclusions derived from such investigations.[92] In order to enhance the effectiveness of the organization in this respect, it could have a relatively small, internationally recruited staff of scientists whose main responsibility would be to examine objectively the research programmes of States and other international fisheries organizations. Secondly, on the basis of these scientific activities, a global conservation organization could assist in bringing about effective action with respect to conservation.[93] It could draft model conservation conventions and recommend their adoption to the nations participating in the fisheries with which these conventions would be concerned. It could point out shortcomings in existing arrangements and suggest ways in which they could be corrected. It could also bring to the attention of nations participating in specific fisheries that catch levels are exceeding the maximum sustainable yield of the stocks in question.[94] And if the organization had authority beyond adopting resolutions and recommendations, it could have the power to prescribe overall catch quotas that fishing nations would be required to respect. By using such functions and powers, a global conservation organization could undoubtedly make a substantial contribution towards more effective international cooperation with respect to the conservation of the living resources of the sea.

Essentially, the organization could act to enforce the substantive provisions of the 1958 Fisheries Convention concerning the obligation of fishing States to adopt conservation measures. To achieve this the organization would use its political influence, which could very well produce better

[92]H Kasahara, *International arrangements for fisheries*, in *The United Nations and ocean management*, L M Alexander ed., Kingston, R I 1971, p. 42.
[93]In a sense COFI performs already such a role, *supra* p. 106.
[94]Commission on Marine Science, Engineering and Resources, *op. cit.*, note 11, p. VIII–67. Dodyk, *op. cit.*, note 1, p. 101.

results than the system of compulsory arbitration contained in the Convention itself. Replacing compulsory arbitration with political persuasion as a means of enforcing the obligations of States in the area of conservation would also eliminate a major reason why the 1958 Fisheries Convention failed to be ratified by several States.[95] Another advantage of a global conservation organization is that it would not make the existing regional fisheries commissions obsolete.[96] These commissions could function within its overall global framework by continuing to be the arenas in which the nations participating in a particular fishery try to reach agreement with respect to conservation measures. However, in contrast to the existing situation, the activities of regional commissions would be subject to the scrutiny of the global conservation organization. This could make regional bodies accountable for not preventing the overfishing of the stocks for which they are responsible. In addition, a global fisheries organization could assist in solving a serious problem of the existing commissions: the voluntary nature of membership.[97] If a State participates in certain fisheries, but has not joined the commission which is responsible for such fisheries, a global conservation organization would be in a much better position to bring pressure to bear on such a State than the regional commission, particularly if the State in question were a member of the global organization.[98] A final advantage of a global conservation organization is that its limited scope and functions would make it more acceptable to States than a comprehensive organization, as discussed in the previous

[95]*Supra* p. 118.
[96]A Pardo, *The place of fisheries in a future regime for the ocean*, in *Report of the sixth session of the Committee on Fisheries*, FAO Fisheries Reports No. 103, Rome 1971, p. 37. Johnston, *op. cit.*, note 1, pp. 433–434. D M Johnston, *New uses of international law in the North Pacific*, WLR 1967, *passim*.
[97]*Supra* p. 124.
[98]Dodyk, *op. cit.*, note 1, pp. 102–103.

section. Yet it could very well be the first step in the direction of more ambitious international fisheries organizations.

However, there are several considerations which make a global conservation organization less desirable. Some of these considerations stem from difficulties similar to those associated with an extension of the regulatory authority of coastal States in matters of conservation. Like the extension of coastal State regulatory authority, a global conservation organization does not address itself to some of the most serious problems of marine fisheries: the economic efficiency of fishing operations and the allocation of the catch. If existing fisheries commissions are incapable of taking action in respect of conservation, it is often because States can not reach agreement on questions of overcapitalization and allocation. A global conservation organization would be of little use in solving these problems. It may also have some of the disadvantages of a comprehensive international fisheries organization: a global conservation organization may increase the costs of international fisheries regulation and it may result in complex arrangements. However, its limited scope and functions suggest that these two aspects will carry considerably less weight than for a comprehensive fisheries organization.[99] A global conservation organization could also have its own problems. It may be difficult to bring the existing fisheries commissions within its framework and to coordinate its activities with the work of these existing bodies, particularly since membership may differ. This also raises questions concerning the scope of the supervisory functions of the global organization and more specifically concerning its authority if a regional body fails to adopt effective conservation measures. Here the essential question is whether or not a global conservation organization would have powers beyond the hortatory. Undoubtedly, its effectiveness would be greatly increased if it could take

[99] *Ibidem*, p. 107.

binding decisions, rather than mere recommendations. However, the fact that apart from a few minor exceptions, none of the existing *regional* bodies has such powers[100] makes it extremely unlikely that States will grant the power of binding decision to a *global* organization. Here again, a basic problem is that no State is obliged to join the global conservation organization. Therefore, the States which do join are not willing to commit themselves in advance with regard to the decisions of the organization. Consequently, a global conservation organization will most probably be required to achieve its objectives through political persuasion rather than through binding decisions. This and the fact that such an organization will not be capable of acting effectively against overfishing by non-member States may seriously reduce its effectiveness.

It is obvious from the above that the establishment of a global conservation organization would not solve all problems of marine fisheries. However, it will in all probability result in more effective action in respect of conservation, since the organization could make fishing nations, either individually or jointly, accountable to the world community. In addition, its creation will not impede the process of finding solutions to the problems of allocation and economic efficiency. The organization may even have a beneficial effect in these areas, since the necessity of dealing effectively with conservation may very well induce fishing nations to reach agreement regarding questions of allocation and economic efficiency. Therefore, the advantages of a global conservation organization seem to outweigh its disadvantages, particularly since most of these disadvantages stem from practical problems, rather than from inherent deficiencies.[101]

---

[100]*Supra* p. 188.
[101]None of the proposals submitted to the UN Seabed Committee refers to the creation of a global conservation organization, see note 44.

3.4 Multinational Public Fishing Enterprises

The distinction between multinational *private* enterprises and intergovernmental international organizations is sufficiently clear and needs no special clarification here. However, it may be quite difficult to distinguish between intergovernmental international organizations and multinational *public* enterprises: both are organizations of States and both perform sometimes similar functions. The major differences seem to be: (1) a multinational public enterprise performs an economic task; (2) a multinational public enterprise requires a long range investment of capital; and (3) a multinational public enterprise performs operational functions and has direct powers of action.[102] As some intergovernmental international organizations also have economic tasks or require long range investments, it is the combination of these factors, rather than a single element, which makes it possible to separate multinational public enterprises from intergovernmental international organizations.

It has been suggested that some of the problems of marine fisheries could be solved by establishing multinational public fishing enterprises:[103] companies established and funded by States for the purpose of making a profit by engaging in marine fisheries. In some respects such multinational public fishing enterprises could closely resemble the comprehensive international fisheries organization discussed above, especially if such a comprehensive organization were to achieve its goals by operating its own fishing fleet. However, a multinational public fishing enterprise would not have full authority over

[102]C Fligler, *Multinational public enterprises*, International Bank for Reconstruction and Development, Washington 1967. W G Friedman and G Kamanoff, *Joint international business ventures*, New York 1961.
[103]Goldie, *op. cit.*, note 32, pp. 47–51. Johnston, *op. cit.*, note 1, pp. 434–435; an analogy would be the International Telecommunications Satellite Consortium which operates the space segment of a global communications satellite system through its managing arm, the Communications Satellite Corporation.

all living resources of the sea and it would lack the regulatory functions of the comprehensive fisheries organization. In addition, States would participate in a multinational fishing enterprise as commercial entrepreneurs, rather than in their capacity as sovereigns. This latter capacity would predominate in a comprehensive international fisheries organization.

The establishment of a multinational public fishing enterprise could offer a number of advantages. For example, if an extension of coastal State exclusive fishery rights were to have extremely detrimental effects on certain distant water fisheries, the resulting political conflicts could be minimized if the States concerned established a multinational public fishing enterprise for the purpose of operating the fisheries in question. Such a minimization of conflict could also be achieved through the mechanism of a multinational *private* enterprise in which foreign and coastal State fishermen would invest jointly, provided that the coastal State would allow this private enterprise to exploit the stocks subject to its exclusive rights.[104] But if private interests were unable or unwilling to set up a multinational fishing company, governments could take the initiative and create a public enterprise, which could, of course, use private fishing vessels for carrying out the actual fishing operations. This example points out that multinational public fishing enterprises can indeed contribute towards accommodating conflicts between fishing nations.[105] However, their very objectives and functions place them in the category of the regulated, rather than in that of the regulators. Multinational fishing enterprises – public and private alike – do not seem capable of regulating marine fisheries in order to solve problems of full utilization, conservation, economic efficiency, allocation, etc. Thus,

---

[104]Art. II, para. 2 of the Brazilian Decree-Law Regulating Fishing in Territorial Sea allows foreign participation in the fisheries in the zone between 100 and 200 miles from the Brazilian coast, *ILM* 1971, p. 1226.
[105]Johnston, *op. cit.*, note 1, p. 435.

although a multinational public fishing enterprise may be useful from the point of view of conflict amelioration, it appears not to be a substitute for a regulatory intergovernmental fisheries organization.

3.5 New Area and Species Organizations

A number of proposals envisage the establishment of international fisheries organizations which would be similar to the existing fisheries commissions, but whose scope would be much broader. It is not possible to discuss all these suggestions in detail, but the following three will be reviewed briefly: (1) proposals to establish a global tuna organization; (2) proposals to establish a single organization for the North Pacific Ocean fisheries; and (3) proposals to vest full authority over all whale stocks in an international organization.

Tunas are highly migratory – certain species even cross the Pacific Ocean. The fishing fleet is equally mobile – many vessels move from one ocean to the other.[106] Thus, the resource and the fishery are truly global in scope, which produces a rather sharp contrast with the fact that not one, but several organizations are concerned with tuna research and regulation: FAO, the Pacific Tuna Commission, the Indo-Pacific Council, the Atlantic Tuna Commission, the Indian Ocean Commission and the Southeast Atlantic Commission. This organizational fragmentation creates several problems. First of all, the fact that tuna cross the boundary lines between the areas of competence of the various commissions calls for close cooperation among these organizations in respect of scientific research. Secondly, the migratory character of the fish and of the fleets causes the regulations of one commission to affect other tuna organizations. If, for example, the Pacific Tuna Commission were to restrict catches, additional tuna vessels would then move

[106]*Supra* p. 35.

from the Pacific Ocean to areas for which the Atlantic Tuna Commission is responsible. These problems explain proposals to establish a single, global tuna organization.[107] Obviously, such an organization would solve the problems of coordination and cooperation among the existing tuna commissions. This could indeed make an important contribution towards a more effective regulation of tuna fisheries, particularly if its terms of reference allowed the global tuna organization to base its regulations not only on biological, but also on economic criteria. A single tuna organization would be in a much better position to prevent the over-capitalization of the tuna fisheries than all existing organizations together. Moreover, since a global tuna organization could combine the financial resources of many States, it would be easier to overcome the financial obstacles associated with the creation of a truly international research staff.[108] On the other hand, one of the problems of a global tuna organization could be that its large membership could frustrate the decision-making process. However, special arrangements that give a certain decision-making priority to States directly affected by a decision, could eliminate this problem to a large extent.[109] Therefore, the creation of a global tuna organization would probably have a beneficial effect on the regulation of world tuna fisheries.

Several international fisheries organizations are concerned with the fisheries of the North Pacific Ocean. These are: the Salmon Commission, the Halibut Commission, the North Pacific Commission, the Japan-Soviet Commission and the Japan-Korea Commission. The number of States participating in these fisheries is not very large, the principal fishing nations being: Canada, Japan, the Republic of Korea, the United States and the USSR. This is the background

[107]Kask, *op. cit.*, note 22, Appendix I.
[108]*Supra* p. 72.
[109]See *e.g.*, the ICNAF, NEAFC and ICCAT arrangements, *supra* pp. 186–188.

of suggestions that a single organization be made responsible for all fisheries in the North Pacific.[110] Such an organization would solve the problems of coordinating the work of the existing North Pacific fisheries commissions. Moreover, its creation could have a positive effect on the acceptability of regulatory decisions, especially since a single North Pacific organization would increase the latitude for trade offs and political compromise among the nations fishing in that area. Presumably, such an organization would also solve the problems[111] arising from the fact that the Republic of Korea and the USSR do not belong to the North Pacific Commission – the most important North Pacific organization. But since these States have not joined an existing commission, they may also not join a new organization, thus greatly reducing its effectiveness. In addition, most fishery problems of the North Pacific are concerned with specific areas and specific stocks. The existing organizations, fragmented as they are, may be capable of dealing more effectively with these specific problems than a single North Pacific organization. Therefore, replacing the existing North Pacific fisheries commissions with a new organization is not an absolute guarantee of a more efficient regulatory process. The most important positive aspect of such a single North Pacific fisheries organization appears to be that its creation would reflect an increased willingness on the part of the States in question to enhance the scope of international cooperation in respect of the fisheries of the North Pacific.

Finally, it has been proposed that full authority over all stocks of whales be given to an international organization,[112]

[110] J A Crutchfield, *Management of the North Pacific fisheries: economic objectives and issues*, WLR 1967, p. 297, p. 306. Johnston, *op. cit.*, note 96, pp. 108–114. Kasahara, *op. cit.*, note 17, pp. 41–43.

[111] *E.g.*, INPFC, *Annual Report 1970*, Vancouver 1972, p. 3, p. 5.

[112] Kasahara, *op. cit.*, note 89, p. 134. F T Christy, Jr., and D B Brooks, *Shared resources of the world community*, in Commission to Study the Organization of Peace, *New dimensions for the United Nations*, New York 1966, p. 151.

which could be the Whaling Commission or an United Nations agency. This organization's primary responsibility would be to rebuild the stocks to a higher level of abundance. To accomplish this it could suspend all whaling operations. When the stocks had recovered sufficiently, the organization could function as the comprehensive international fisheries organization discussed above. It could, for example, hire a whaling fleet in the cheapest market and sell the whale products in the dearest market. It could also closely resemble a multinational public fishing enterprise, except that it would have certain regulatory functions. This resemblance to proposals discussed previously makes it unnecessary to discuss the advantages and disadvantages of a comprehensive whaling organization in detail. The most important aspect of this proposal is that if not only whaling nations, but also non-whaling nations would become members, the organization would give substance to a principle which could become a central element in the future international law of marine fisheries: if fishing States abuse the rights of the world community by not taking effective action in respect of conservation, organizations of fishing countries lose control over the resources to an organization in which all nations are represented.

3.6 Improvements in Existing Fisheries Organizations

The suggestions made in Chapter III and IV concerning improvements in the structure, functions and powers of existing fisheries commissions are also designed to enhance the authority of international organizations in respect of marine fisheries.[113] These suggestions will not be repeated

[113]See also Commission on Marine Science, Engineering and Resources, *op. cit.*, note 11, pp. VIII 66–67. Dodyk, *op. cit.*, note 1, pp. 110–125. W T Burke, *Aspects of internal decision-making processes in intergovernmental fishery commissions, WLR* 1967, pp. 174–178. The fishery proposals submitted to the UN Seabed Committee generally fail to make such suggestions; instead, they rely on enhancing the coastal State's authority, see note 44 and 58.

here, but within the context of this Chapter a few general observations are in order. Improving existing fisheries organizations has very fundamental advantages over creating new organizations. First of all, the fact that these organizations already exist implies that they themselves can take the initiative for making desirable improvements in their own structure, functions and powers. The discussion of the previous two Chapters shows that several fisheries commissions have been quite active in this respect. The Northwest Atlantic Commission, for example, has made proposals for changes in its terms of reference that seem to have increased the effectiveness of the Commission greatly. Such proposals involve existing international fisheries commissions in the process of building the fisheries organizations of the future.[114] This has a second advantage: the expertise of existing organizations in respect of the problems of marine fisheries enables them to suggest improvements which are both needed and practical.[115] This minimizes the risk that ideas are implemented which may be sound in theory, but which will not survive the test of reality. Thirdly, proposals to improve existing organizations may be more readily acceptable to States than suggestions which require the creation of new organizations. The fact that the first type of proposal may be made by the organization itself and will usually reflect concrete problems also adds to their acceptability. Finally, improvements in existing fisheries organizations will remain desirable even if new organizations were established. As has been mentioned, a global conservation organization, for example, would increase, rather than obviate, the need for the existing fisheries bodies.[116]

However, there are also fundamental limitations to

---

[114]But see Dodyk, *op. cit.*, note 1, p. 124.
[115]Chapman, *op. cit.*, note 13, p. 452. Burke, *op. cit.*, note 11, p. 72. Chapman, *op. cit.*, note 11, 1967, p. 105.
[116]*Supra* p. 260.

improvements in existing organizations and to the contributions which these organizations can make in this respect. First of all, it has been discussed that many problems of marine fisheries can not be solved unless changes are made in the international law of marine fisheries itself, rather than in international fisheries organizations.[117] This applies in particular to the concept of freedom of fishing on the high seas. To the extent that the problems of marine fisheries stem from the characteristics of this concept, improving existing organizations may very well be an exercise in futility. A second restriction is based on the fact that the established international fisheries organizations are primarily organizations of States which participate in specific fisheries. Consequently, their usefulness as catalysts in the formulation of more general world community prescriptions regarding marine fisheries may be very limited. It has been said, for example, that the development of a distinction between access to fisheries and access to wealth requires the participation of all nations, rather than of fishing nations only.[118] Nevertheless, improving existing fisheries organizations appears to be one of the most realistic and desirable approaches towards solving the problems of marine fisheries.[119] Among the most urgently needed improvements is the creation of regional commissions for ocean areas not yet covered by such bodies.

[117]*Supra* p. 53, p. 62, p. 69.
[118]*Supra* p. 69.
[119]Kasahara, *op. cit.*, note 17, pp. 38–39. A Laing, in *International fisheries regimes* (panel), in *National policy recommendations*, L M Alexander ed., Kingston, R I 1970, p. 325. Burke, *op. cit.*, note 11, p. 72. Crutchfield, *op. cit.*, note 85, p. 275. Goldie, *op. cit.*, note 32, p. 18. Dodyk, *op. cit.*, note 1, p. 110. W T Burke, *Law and the new technologies*, in *Offshore boundaries and zones*, L M Alexander ed., Columbus, Ohio 1967, p. 223.

4. THE CHOICE BETWEEN THE TWO BASIC ALTERNATIVES

4.1 Introduction

It is fortunate that the two basic alternatives for improving the international law of marine fisheries are incompatible only if they are taken in their most extreme form. Extending the exclusive rights of coastal States over very large areas of the sea is clearly irreconcilable with giving full authority over all living resources of the sea to a comprehensive international fisheries organization. However, less extreme forms of either alternative can be combined. For example, coastal States could extend their exclusive rights up to a certain limit, while full authority over the living resources beyond such a limit could be vested in an international organization; extended exclusive rights or internationally agreed coastal State preferential rights could be made subject to the authority of a newly established global conservation organization; and existing fishery organizations could be made responsible for formulating recommendations concerning coastal State preferential rights. The same compatibility exists within each of the two alternatives. Extension of exclusive rights in a relatively small area could be combined with coastal State preferential rights beyond the limits of that area; and, as has been mentioned, a global conservation organization would merely increase the need to improve existing fisheries commissions. This compatibility means that it is not necessary to make absolute choices: it is possible to use elements from almost all suggestions, except from the two most extreme forms at the same time. Practical considerations relating to the specific problems of marine fisheries and more general considerations relating to the development of the international community determine the desirability of using a particular element for improving the international law of marine fisheries.

4.2 Practical Considerations

As most practical considerations have already been discussed in the previous sections, it will be attempted here to substantiate the elements that provide the basis for the proposals of the following Chapter. Generally, the most convincing reasons for enhancing the authority of coastal States exist in respect of allocation. In many cases coastal State fishermen depend for their livelihood on coastal fisheries, while tradition, available equipment and market structures may limit their choice to a few species. Moreover, as has been discussed in regard to salmon,[120] coastal States are sometimes required to make considerable investments in certain stocks. Developing coastal States, finally, may wish to restrict the expansion of fisheries in waters off their shores until they are capable of participating in these fisheries. They may also wish to share in the wealth of the stocks without engaging in fishing operations.

An extension of exclusive rights would solve most of these allocation-oriented problems of coastal States. However, as discussed above,[121] such action: (1) may fail to solve specific aspects of these allocation problems; (2) may very well have adverse effects from the point of view of full utilization; (3) does not eliminate the need for international action in respect of conservation; (4) does not necessarily result in more efficient fishing operations; (5) will create a maximum of political conflict; (6) may violate the vested rights of other nations; (7) may not result in a more equitable allocation of the living resources of the sea; and (8) will most likely lead to similar extensions of jurisdiction in respect of other activities on the high seas. As extending the regulatory authority of coastal States will fail to deal adequately with their allocation problems, the other alternative for coping with these questions – preferential rights – seems to be the

[120]*Supra* p. 241.
[121]*Supra* pp. 233–243.

best solution. Such preferential rights can: (1) solve the specific allocation problems of coastal States; (2) avoid adverse effects on the full utilization of the sea's living resources; (3) minimize the risk of political conflicts among fishing nations; (4) find support in a certain history in international practice; and (5) reduce the likelihood of more extensive claims with respect to other uses of the high seas.[122] Although some of these advantages would also apply to unilaterally claimed coastal State preferences, they apply particularly to internationally agreed preferential rights. This would make it necessary to formulate general principles under which States can more easily reach agreement on such rights. These principles would be concerned with conditions justifying preferential rights and with their scope. In addition, they could provide for arrangements under which other States would be required to respect a preferential rights agreement among certain fishing nations.

If preferential rights should solve the allocation problems of coastal States in a way acceptable to distant water fishing States, a most important obstacle to more effective international action regarding the other problems of marine fisheries would have been eliminated. Such other problems could best be solved by enhancing the authority of international organizations, rather than of coastal States. This refers particularly to the creation of a global conservation organization and to improvements in the existing international fisheries organizations. It has been postulated that if fishing nations do not take effective action to ensure the conservation of the resources they exploit, this would be considered an abuse of the rights of the world community. A global conservation organization could be an entity capable of giving substance to this principle, either by political pressure or by binding decisions, while the existing fisheries organizations could continue to be the main instruments through

[22]*Supra* pp. 248–251.

18

which fishing States discharge their responsibilities with respect to conservation. In addition, since economic efficiency is primarily a concern of fishing nations, these existing commissions could also continue to have the responsibility of working out solutions in regard to this matter. However, as mentioned earlier, changes in the international law of marine fisheries itself may be required before organizations of fishing States can act effectively with respect to overcapitalization. Finally, these organizations can also be transformed into the arenas in which nations negotiate coastal State preferential rights. Such an enhancement of the authority of international fisheries organizations is essentially evolutionary in nature, which is stressed by the fact that it corresponds with proposals advanced by some of the existing commissions.[123]

In conclusion, considerations relating to the practical problems of marine fisheries suggest the desirability of improving the international law of marine fisheries on the basis of these three elements: (1) coastal State preferential rights; (2) a global conservation organization; and (3) improvements in the existing fisheries organizations. However, this does not imply that other elements and proposals are devoid of any practical relevance. Extension of coastal State regulatory authority may very well be the only way in which a certain stock can be protected; and a multinational public fishing enterprise may be the best solution in a specific situation. However, the above three elements generally appear to be the most desirable structural components of the future international law of marine fisheries.

4.3 General Considerations

The choice between enhancing the authority of coastal States or of international organizations can also be approached

[123]*E.g.*, proposals of ICNAF and NEAFC, *supra* p. 182, pp. 203–204.

as one facet of a more fundamental dilemma.[124] In other areas, too, the international community has come to a juncture where it must choose between entrusting its future to States or to international institutions.[125] This is an extremely difficult and complex decision. First of all, it must be made regardless of the fact that the ultimate outcome of either alternative is unforeseeable. On the other hand, the importance of this consideration is diminished by the fact that the process of choosing between the two alternatives is a gradual and evolutionary one. The international community is not now required to make an absolute decision, but can gain experience with certain aspects of either alternative before making more fundamental commitments. A second problem is that the process of choosing is inherently distorted. As the international community is still primarily a community of States, the ultimate choice between the two alternatives will be largely the outcome of State decisions. Consequently, there is this basic contradiction: international institutions will be strengthened only if States are prepared to question their own viability as the final structural elements of the world community. This leads to a third problem. In the past choices between the two alternatives were made by States on the basis of necessity, rather than on the basis of desirability and free choice. States have demonstrated over and over again that they are willing to yield authority to international institutions only if this becomes unavoidable.[126] However, the dangers of this attitude have increased dramatically: scientific and technological progress has advanced to a point where irreparable harm may have been inflicted upon the resources of this planet before States become convinced of the neces-

[124]W Friedmann, *The future of the oceans*, New York 1971, p. 114.
[125]Protection of the global environment is another area.
[126]Chapman, *op. cit.*, note 11, 1970, p. 35. Crutchfield, *op. cit.*, note 85, p. 273.

sity to act collectively. The history of international fisheries commissions is an unfortunate illustration of this point.

If, then, there is reason for the international community to move gradually in the direction of further internationalization by enhancing the authority of international institutions, international fisheries organizations appear to be good objects for such action. First of all, they represent a tradition of international cooperation, which provides a useful platform for further development. Secondly, as has been suggested in the previous sections, considerations relating to the specific problems of marine fisheries also support the desirability of enhancing the authority of fisheries organizations. Thirdly, although fishery problems may be quite important, they do not command the political weight of other international questions, particularly those associated with questions of national security. Therefore, it will be more acceptable to States to yield certain prerogatives to an intertional fisheries commission than to an organization concerned with such political questions. However, most important of these general considerations in favour of enhancing the authority of international fisheries organizations is the fact that such action would reaffirm the idea that the living resources of the high seas belong to all nations. The freedom of fishing on the high seas, which has expressed this concept during the last three centuries, appears no longer to serve the needs of the present world. However, this does not necessarily also apply to the underlying idea that the fish stocks of the high seas are a common resource of the world–in fact this idea has been reasserted frequently.[127]

[127]This is particularly evident from the *Declaration of Principles Governing the Sea-Bed and the Ocean Floor, and the Sub-Soil thereof, beyond the Limits of National Jurisdiction* which was adopted by the United Nations General Assembly on 17 December 1970, even though this Declaration is not directly concerned with the sea's living resources, UNGA Res. 2749 (XXV) UN Doc. A/C.1/544.

One way in which the international community can preserve and strengthen this idea is by enhancing the authority of international fisheries organizations – even if this means abolishing the freedom of fishing on the high seas.

Chapter VI

The Future International Law of Marine Fisheries: a Proposal

1. INTRODUCTION

The general conclusion of the preceding Chapter was that the most desirable structural elements of the future international law of marine fisheries are: (1) a global conservation organization; (2) improved regional fisheries commissions; and (3) coastal State preferential rights.[1] This Chapter will attempt to develop these three elements into a proposal for a future international legal regime that will be capable of coping more effectively with the problems of marine fisheries than the present system. The preceding Chapter clearly demonstrates that virtually all suggestions and proposals with respect to future legal arrangements for marine fisheries have both advantages and disadvantages. It must also be kept in mind that any future regime must cope not only with the existing problems of marine fisheries, but also with future problems that can not yet be anticipated. Therefore, the following ideas merely represent a subjective and partial approach to the future international law of marine fisheries and to future international fisheries organizations. They are certainly not intended to be an utopian blueprint specifying the ideal solution for all present and future problems. The sole purpose of this Chapter is to outline the conceptual framework of one possible approach to the development of more adequate international legal arrangements for marine fisheries. If the following sections discuss certain aspects in detail, they merely try to illustrate a broader idea, without suggesting that such details are the unique and best solution. These observations imply that the

[1] *Supra* p. 274.

term 'the future international law of marine fisheries' refers not only to the ultimate outcome of the process of changing existing arrangements, but also to the process itself. The term will be used in a dynamic, rather than in a static sense. Finally, these proposals are not dictated solely by considerations of political acceptability,[2] although such considerations were certainly influential. Therefore, the following is essentially an idealized approach to the future international law of marine fisheries and to future international fisheries organizations.

2. THE TWO FUNDAMENTAL DISTINCTIONS

It appears that most problems of marine fisheries could be accommodated in a legal regime based on two fundamental distinctions. First of all, in order to recognize differences in the fishing activities of nations, future legal arrangements could make a distinction among: (1) coastal State fisheries; (2) distant water State fisheries; and (3) common fisheries. Secondly, in order to recognize differences in the condition of stocks of fish, future legal arrangements could make a distinction among: (1) biologically under-exploited stocks; (2) biologically fully exploited stocks; and (3) biologically over-exploited stocks. These two fundamental distinctions are interrelated: coastal State fisheries, for example, may be concerned with an under-exploited stock or with an over-exploited stock, while a fully exploited stock may be subject to coastal State fisheries, to distant water State fisheries or to common fisheries. Obviously, this interrelationship between the two fundamental distinctions results in nine combinations, each of which represents a different legal situation. In essence, it is proposed in this

[2]It has been said that the political desirabilities of today are the political necessities of tomorrow, D M Johnston, *The legal theory of fishery organization*, in *International rules and organization for the sea*, L M Alexander ed., Kingston, R I 1969, p. 431.

Chapter that the rules and principles of the future international law of marine fisheries and the powers and functions of future international fisheries organizations be adapted to the specific characteristics of each legal situation: rules applying to a coastal State fishery for fully exploited stocks should differ from rules applying to a common fishery for under-exploited stocks, etc.

The rules and principles of the existing international law of marine fisheries already reflect to some extent the differences among the various legal situations. For example, the functions and powers of existing fisheries commissions in respect of conservation can be considered as part of a legal distinction between under-exploited stocks and fully exploited stocks;[3] the various claims of coastal States concerning exclusive fishery limits or concerning additional regulatory powers can be viewed as attempts to define a special regime for coastal State fisheries;[4] the functions of FAO-related fisheries bodies in respect of full utilization represent special rules and principles for under-exploited species;[5] agreements on national quotas are particularly concerned with fully exploited stocks;[6] etc. This points out that adapting the existing international law of marine fisheries to the above nine legal situations does not imply radical changes, but rather a gradual transformation. It also indicates that if the proposed regimes appear to be complex, such complexity is part of existing arrangements as well, although in a less explicit form. In addition, since not all nine combinations of the above two basic distinctions are of concern to the international law of marine fisheries,[7] it is possible to limit

[3] *Supra* pp. 178–196.
[4] *Supra* pp. 231–233.
[5] *Supra* pp. 173–175.
[6] *Supra* p. 204.
[7] The condition of the stocks exploited in coastal State fisheries or distant water State fisheries would be the concern of the *national* fisheries regulation of the State in question.

the discussion of future arrangements to the following five basic situations: (1) coastal State fisheries; (2) distant water State fisheries; (3) common fisheries for under-exploited stocks; (4) common fisheries for fully exploited stocks; and (5) over-exploited stocks. The implications of these five situations will be examined, first of all, from the point of view of the substantive rules and principles of the future international law of marine fisheries and, secondly, from the point of view of the structure, functions and powers of future international fisheries organizations.

3. SUBSTANTIVE ASPECTS

3.1 Coastal State Fisheries

It has been discussed that the limits and scope of the exclusive rights of coastal States over the living resources of the sea are a matter of considerable ambiguity, but that generally coastal States have exclusive rights over all living resources within a twelve mile exclusive fishery zone and over those species which are included in the resources of their continental shelf.[8] It has also been suggested that an extension of the exclusive rights of coastal States beyond present limits is undesirable and that it is preferable to solve the allocation problems of coastal States by internationally agreed coastal State preferential rights.[9] Therefore, the future international law of marine fisheries could develop a special legal regime for coastal State fisheries, which would be defined as fisheries for stocks over which a coastal State has either exclusive rights or preferential rights.

Accepting coastal State preferential rights over certain high seas stocks would greatly facilitate international agreement with respect to a restrictive definition of coastal

[8] *Supra* p. 233.
[9] *Supra* pp. 272–273.

State exclusive fishery rights. The existing international law of marine fisheries offers a coastal State that wishes to solve a specific high seas allocation problem little choice except to extend its exclusive rights. If preferential rights over high seas stocks would give coastal States an alternative, the future international law of marine fisheries could resist any further expansion of the limits and scope of coastal State exclusive fishery rights. Obviously, the vested rights of coastal States must be respected, but it appears that restricting coastal State exclusive rights to a twelve mile exclusive fishery zone and to a specific number of continental shelf living resources meets this criterion in almost all cases. The future international law of marine fisheries could define coastal State exclusive rights not only as narrowly as possible, but also as precisely as possible. As far as the twelve mile exclusive fishery zone is concerned, this could present no special legal problems, provided that a political agreement could be reached. However, it might be difficult to work out a precise legal definition of continental shelf living resources; existing definitions, for example, have caused considerable confusion.[10] One possible solution would be to list exhaustively all species considered part of the continental shelf living resources. Finally, in order to resist the expansion of coastal State exclusive fishery rights, the future international law of marine fisheries could link exclusive rights and preferential rights in an arrangement which would deny preferential rights to those coastal States having extended their exclusive rights beyond generally accepted limits. Such an arrangement would also minimize the risk of coastal States attempting to extend their exclusive rights solely for the purpose of improving their bargaining position in negotiations on preferential rights.

In the future international law of marine fisheries, coastal State preferential rights could have the following three basic

[10] *Supra* p. 232.

283

characteristics: (1) they would give a coastal State certain preferences over other nations in the high seas fisheries off its shores; (2) they would be based on an international agreement among the States involved; and (3) a coastal State would enjoy its preferential rights as an agent of the world community since these rights would refer to high seas resources. In working out these basic characteristics, the future international law of marine fisheries could follow a split-level approach: general principles could be formulated on a world community level, while the detailed implementation could take place on a regional level. A world community level implies participation of all States, whereas on a regional level participation is limited largely to States engaged in specific fisheries.

A first set of general world community principles would be concerned with the criteria for establishing justification for coastal State preferential rights, as well as with the procedures for granting these rights.[11] As far as the first aspect is concerned, these criteria could, for instance, take into consideration: (1) the past record of coastal States in the exploitation of certain stocks; (2) the special needs – economic, nutritional or otherwise – of coastal States; (3) the dependence of coastal State fishermen upon particular species; (4) the past record of coastal States in respect of conservation; and (5) the proximity of stocks to the coastal State, their migratory patterns and their ecological relation-

[11]Such principles are under review in the UN Seabed Committee; the most detailed proposals are: *The Union of Soviet Socialist Republics: Draft Article on Fishing*, UN Doc. A/AC.138/SC.II/L.6, 18 July 1972. *Management of the Living Resources of the Sea. Working Paper Submitted by the Delegation of Canada*, UN Doc. A/AC.138/SC.II/L.8, 27 July 1972. *United States Revised Draft Fisheries Article*, A/AC. 138/SC.II/L.9, 4 August 1972. *Working Paper by the Delegations of Australia and New Zealand. Principles for a Fisheries Regime*, UN Doc. A/AC.138/SC.II/L.11, 11 August 1972. *Proposals for a Regime of Fisheries on the High Seas Submitted by Japan*, UN Doc. A/AC.138/SC.II /L.12, 14 August 1972.

ship with the land. In the case of developing coastal States, these considerations could also include a potential interest in specific stocks. Coastal State preferential rights would be justified only if these or similar world community criteria were met. Consequently, in contrast to exclusive rights, preferential rights would be restricted to specific and well-defined situations. For example, if a coastal State has a long history of fully exploiting a certain species, if it has taken effective measures to ensure its conservation and if the species is found in waters of the high seas adjacent to its coasts, the general world community principles would probably justify coastal State preferential rights over this species. Certain elements of these world community principles already exist or are in a formative stage; they can be found in Article 6 of the 1958 Fisheries Convention,[12] in the 1958 Resolution on Special Situations Relating to Coastal Fisheries[13] and in the preferential treatment given to coastal States under the ICNAF and NEAFC national quota arrangements.[14] However, basically these principles are still non-existent. As far as the procedural aspects of general world community principles would be concerned, they could make international negotiations compulsory if a coastal State would have a *prima facie* case for preferential rights. They could also provide for arrangements if these negotiations were to fail. In this case there would be essentially two alternatives: (1) compulsory arbitration,[15] or (2) certain political steps. The negative experience with compulsory arbitration in the 1958 Fisheries Convention[16] and the political nature of the failure to reach agreement on preferential rights strongly suggest that the second alternative

[12]With respect to conservation.
[13]With respect to allocation.
[14]*Supra* pp. 207–208.
[15]The 1958 Fisheries Convention follows this alternative if negotiations on conservation measures fail.
[16]*Supra* p. 118.

would be more realistic. Accordingly, the general principles could provide that States could bring the failure of international negotiations to the attention of an appropriate international fisheries organization, which would discuss the general criteria for preferential rights in view of their applicability to the dispute in question.

A second set of general world community principles would be concerned with the use of preferential rights by the coastal State.[17] These principles could, for example, require a coastal State to: (1) use its preferential rights in such a manner as not to affect adversely the degree of utilization of the stocks to which they apply; (2) take effective measures in respect of the conservation of the stocks concerned; (3) carry out all necessary scientific investigations; and (4) minimize interference with other activities on the high seas, including the fishing operations of other States. Certain elements of these principles can also be found in the 1958 Fisheries Convention: the Convention stipulates, for example, that a coastal State, in adopting unilateral conservation measures for high seas stocks, must base such measures on scientific findings.[18] Principles concerning the use of preferential rights could also be complemented by certain procedural conditions. A coastal State could, for example, be required to submit periodic reports to international fisheries organizations regarding its preferential right fisheries.[19] This would enable other nations to examine the regulatory practices of that State.

The detailed implementation of these two sets of general world community principles could be the responsibility of the States participating in specific fisheries.[20] This refers particularly to the negotiations required for reaching the

[17]The UN Seabed Committee also reviews such principles, see note 11.
[18]Art. 7, para. 2(b) 1958 Fisheries Convention.
[19]*Infra* p. 310.
[20]On the interaction between levels of decision-making, see Johnston, *op. cit.*, note 2, pp. 433–434.

international agreement on which coastal State preferential rights would be based. These negotiations would be guided and influenced by the general world community principles, but the participants would be limited to States having a direct interest in the fisheries to which the preferential rights would apply. Opening these negotiations to other nations would serve no purpose but to make reaching agreement much more difficult. The directly interested States would have maximum flexibility in negotiating preferential rights: any arrangement capable of accommodating the conflicting interests of the coastal State and of the nations fishing off its shores would be acceptable, provided that it respected the world community principles. A few examples of such arrangements have been discussed in the preceding Chapter.[21] They could also solve the special allocation problems of developing States by stipulating that a developed distant water fishing State pay certain fees to a developing coastal State for fisheries in waters off the coast of that developing State as long as the developing State does not participate in these fisheries.[22] This would enable developing nations to share in the wealth of their offshore resources even though they might be incapable of harvesting them. Such an arrangement would also enable a developing State to decide whether it prefers to develop its own fishing fleet or to buy the fishery products it needs with revenues from its preferential rights. Generally, any preferential rights agreement would be re-negotiated periodically: since coastal State preferential rights would be justified under specific conditions only, it would be necessary to determine from time to time whether or not these conditions still prevailed.[23] If the States in

[21] *Supra* p. 250.
[22] Such an arrangement already exists informally in the 200-mile exclusive fishery zone of Ecuador; it is also part of the Brazilian legislation concerning a 200 mile fishery zone, *ILM* 1971, p. 1226.
[23] The INPFC determines whether or not stocks continue to qualify for abstention, *supra* p. 202.

question disagreed with respect to the continued existence of these conditions, the matter could be brought to the attention of an international fisheries organization. However, since a decision concerning the continued validity of preferential rights would have a stronger juridical basis than the decision concerning their original acceptance, this appears to be an instance where political mechanisms could be fruitfully complemented by legal arrangements. The original preferential rights agreement could, for example, require that disputes concerning its continued validity be settled by compulsory arbitration. World community principles concerning the *use* of preferential rights could also be implemented regionally among the States directly interested in a specific fishery. The agreement under which a coastal State obtains certain preferential rights could, for example, contain rules concerning this matter. These rules could require coastal States to regulate preferential right fisheries in a certain manner or to maintain a certain catch level, etc. They could also require a coastal State to submit periodic reports on its preferential right fisheries, either to an organization of the States which originally negotiated such rights or to a fisheries organization open to all nations of the world.[24] This procedure could give substance to the principle that a coastal State would enjoy its preferential rights as an agent of the world community.

Salmon can be used as an illustration of coastal State preferential rights. It has been mentioned[25] that most coastal States have a long history of exploiting this species, that they are often required to make certain investments to ensure its productivity, but that legal arrangements do not fully solve the allocation problems which result for coastal States from high seas salmon fisheries. It has also been

[24]In the INPFC Canada and Japan report to the Commission concerning their fisheries for stocks subject to abstention by Japan, *supra* p. 202.
[25]*Supra* p. 241.

288

discussed that an extension of coastal State exclusive rights may very well fail to solve these problems. However, it is likely that the aforementioned world community principles would establish justification for some kind of coastal State preferential rights over salmon.[26] Thus, a coastal State could call for negotiations among all States participating in fisheries for salmon originating in its rivers. If these negotiations failed, the coastal State could then bring the matter to the attention of an appropriate international fisheries organization that would discuss the applicability of the world community criteria to the situation in question. If the negotiations were successful, the coastal State would obtain internationally agreed preferential rights over salmon spawning in its rivers. These rights would most probably result in restrictions on high seas salmon fisheries. The coastal State, on the other hand, could be required to make certain payments for its preferential rights. Such payments would reflect the fact that salmon is as much a high seas resource as a coastal State resource. Initially, these payments could be used by the States which agreed to limit their high seas salmon fisheries for indemnifying the segments of their fishing industry affected by that decision; later they could be used for such a generally acceptable purpose as fisheries research. If preferential rights enabled the coastal State to regulate access to salmon fisheries, it could undertake a programme to rationalize its fishing operations economically. The savings achieved by such a programme could very well exceed whatever a coastal State would be required to pay for its preferential rights. Thus, this arrangement would not necessarily add to the costs of salmon fisheries.

Preferential rights could also be used for accommodating the conflicts resulting from the claims of several Latin

[26]With the exception of the Japanese proposal, most proposals submitted to the UN Seabed Committee provide for such preferential rights, see note 11.

American countries in regard to their exclusive fishery limits.[27] Peru and the United States, for example, could negotiate an arrangement that would give Peru exclusive access to all anchovy stocks off its coast. Peru could also obtain certain rights which would allow it to share in the wealth of, rather than in the fisheries for, other stocks. The United States could, for instance, have a right to fish for tunas in waters presently claimed by Peru as part of a 200 mile exclusive fishery zone, provided that it made certain payments to Peru. If such preferential rights were to protect the fishing interests of Peru, they could result in lessening Peruvian insistence on very wide exclusive fishery limits. This could be a major reason for the United States to accept an arrangement as outlined above.

3.1.1 Coastal State Fisheries and Economic Resource Zones

Coastal State preferential rights as discussed above could result in very complex arrangements: they require difficult international negotiations, involve a large number of States, do not result in an uniform regime, must be re-negotiated periodically and, above all, can be implemented only if there is agreement among the States concerned. The nature of decision-making in the international community, on the other hand, suggests the desirability of solutions that avoid such complexity to every possible extent. An economic resource zone[28] extending up to 200 miles from the coast would certainly better serve the cause of simplicity. In this zone the coastal State could acquire additional rights over all marine resources, subject to certain obligations to

[27] Supra p. 232.
[28] The Latin American countries in particular are advocating the creation of such zones, see e.g., the Declaration of Montevideo on the Law of the Sea, ILM 1970, p. 1081, and the Declaration of Santo Domingo of 9 June 1972, ILM 1972, p. 892. The Working Paper submitted by the delegations of Australia and New Zealand to the UN Seabed Committee also provides for such a zone, see note 11.

the international community. These obligations could refer to coastal State responsibilities in respect of conservation, but they could also require a coastal State to allow foreign fishing for stocks which it does not exploit fully. Depending upon the scope of such obligations, economic resource zones would amount to an extension of coastal State exclusive rights or to geographically defined coastal State preferential rights. For reasons stated previously, the first type of economic resource zone appears to be undesirable.[29] The second approach to economic resource zones might indeed avoid some of the complexity of internationally agreed preferential rights without having the negative implications of an extension of exclusive rights. Even more important – particularly from the viewpoint of coastal States – is that in contrast to such preferential rights, economic resource zones do not depend solely upon the success of international negotiations: such zones could be created by unilateral action as well.

Regardless of these questions, internationally agreed preferential rights and economic resource zones in which coastal States would have substantial obligations towards the international community would be compatible to a large degree. If, for example, general world community principles were to justify coastal State preferential rights over virtually all stocks in a certain area, it would undeniably serve the cause of legal clarity and preciseness to provide for some geographical delimitation of these rights; this could make them indistinguishable from the rights of coastal States in an economic resource zone. The most important difference between the two alternatives seems to be that, compared with economic resource zones, internationally agreed preferential rights are inherently better instruments for giving substance to the idea that coastal States would enjoy their additional rights as agents of the world community.

[29] *Supra* pp. 272-273.

Economic resource zones could easily become just one more example of an unilateral extension of the rights of coastal States over the living resources of the sea. However, this does not negate the fact that both approaches towards solving the allocation problems of coastal States may very well produce nearly identical results.

3.2 Distant Water State Fisheries

The future international law of marine fisheries could also create a special legal regime for distant water State fisheries, which could be defined as fisheries for stocks over which a distant water fishing State has preferential rights. In contrast to coastal State fisheries, distant water State fisheries would never be based on exclusive rights, since only coastal States would enjoy exclusive rights over the sea's living resources. Distant water fishing State preferential rights could have characteristics identical to those of coastal State preferential rights: (1) they would give a distant water fishing State a certain preference over other nations in specific high seas fisheries; (2) they would be based on an international agreement; and (3) a distant water fishing State would enjoy these rights as an agent of the world community, since they would refer to high seas resources.

On a world community level, general principles could be formulated which would set forth the criteria establishing justification for distant water fishing State preferential rights. Generally, these principles would take into account factors similar to those for coastal State preferential rights. Relevant considerations could be: (1) the extent to which a distant water fishing State would have been responsible for the development of certain fisheries; (2) its dependence – economic, nutritional or otherwise – on such fisheries; and (3) its activities in respect of conservation. These general world community principles would reflect the fact that distant water fisheries are much more flexible than coastal fisheries.[30] Therefore, the criteria for distant water fishing State preferential rights would be considerably more restrictive than those for coastal State preferential rights. The general world community principles would also be concerned with certain procedural aspects: they could, for example, make international negotiations mandatory if a distant water fishing State would have a *prima facie* case for preferential rights. A second set of general world community principles could provide for certain guidelines that distant water fishing States would be required to respect in their use of preferential rights. Like coastal States, they could be required to report on their preferential right fisheries to appropriate international fisheries organizations.[31]

The actual implementation of these general world community principles could again be the responsibility of the States participating in a specific fishery. An international agreement among these States would provide the legal basis for distant water fishing State preferential rights, while these States could also ensure that distant water fishing States respect world community principles concerning the use of preferential rights. It is on this regional level that distant water fishing State preferential rights would have one of their most important advantages: they would increase the latitude for trade offs in negotiations concerning preferential rights in general. In most cases these negotiations would take place between coastal States, on the one hand, and distant water fishing States, on the other. If the future international law of marine fisheries were to provide for preferential rights of both coastal and distant water fishing States, it would considerably enhance the opportunities for compromise between these two categories of States.

[30] *Supra* p. 35.
[31] *Infra* p. 310.

3.3 Common Fisheries

3.3.1 Introduction

Apart from coastal State and distant water State fisheries, the future international law of marine fisheries could have a third component: a special legal regime for common fisheries. Negatively, common fisheries could be defined as fisheries for stocks over which no State has exclusive or preferential rights. Positively, common fisheries could be defined as fisheries for stocks which the world community has set aside for common use. For reasons discussed previously,[32] the future international law of marine fisheries should attempt to bring a maximum number of stocks under the regime of common fisheries: if this were not accomplished, enhancing the authority of fisheries organizations would, for example, have no real significance. The future international law of marine fisheries could ensure in several ways that a substantial number of stocks be reserved for common fisheries. First of all, a major reason for accepting coastal State *preferential* rights is that they would make it possible to restrict coastal State *exclusive* rights. Secondly, coastal State and distant water fishing State preferential rights would be governed by the criteria specified in world community principles. Thus, such preferential rights would be acceptable in specific situations only, while essentially the burden of proof would be on the coastal State or the distant water fishing State. In addition, since these principles would be formulated and developed on a world community level, *i.e.*, with the participation of all nations of the world, they would reflect the interests of all nations, rather than of coastal States and distant water fishing States.

It is with respect to common fisheries that the condition of a stock would become a decisive element of future international arrangements. The condition of a stock subject to

[32] *Supra* pp. 242-243.

coastal State or distant water fishing State preferential rights would concern such legal arrangements merely indirectly: the immediate responsibility for regulating the fisheries in view of the condition of the stock would be entrusted to the State with the preferential rights. However, with regard to common fisheries, the future international law of marine fisheries itself would be required to provide for rules and mechanisms designed to bring about such regulation. It must be stressed here that the condition of a stock would be defined in biological, rather than economic, terms.[33] Thus, a stock would be considered fully exploited if catches had reached the level of the maximum sustainable yield and not if fishing produced a maximum economic yield. If the maximum sustainable yield of a stock would differ from year to year, the future international law of marine fisheries could consider a stock fully exploited if average catches were equal to the average maximum sustainable yield. Economic problems would be accommodated within this overall framework.

3.3.2 Common Fisheries for Under-Exploited Stocks

Although conservation would not be a concern to the future legal regime of common fisheries for under-exploited stocks, it would be necessary to carry out investigations for the purpose of determining the maximum sustainable yield of these stocks; it would also be necessary to monitor catch levels. Problems of economic efficiency would not manifest themselves in their most serious form in these fisheries since additional amounts of fishing effort applied to under-exploited stocks result in an increase in production. This opportunity to expand catches also limits the political confrontation among States with respect to allocation. Thus, the most important problem of the future legal regime of

[33]See the discussion concerning maximum sustainable yield *versus* maximum economic yield, *supra* pp. 57-60.

common fisheries for under-exploited stocks is to bring about a fuller utilization of these resources. One *caveat* is here in order: in improving the utilization of under-exploited stocks, the future international law of marine fisheries should not lead to a misallocation of manpower and capital. Consequently, it should not induce, much less force, States to apply additional manpower and capital to marine fisheries, if such manpower and capital could have been employed more fruitfully in other applications.[34] In improving catches of under-exploited stocks, the future international law of marine fisheries would ensure that developing States could actively participate in the expansion of these fisheries. A last point is that the future regime of common fisheries for under-exploited stocks could give substance to the notion that fishing States would be agents of the world community since they would exploit a high seas resource.

Taking these considerations into account, the future international law of marine fisheries could leave the freedom of fishing on the high seas essentially uncompromised in its application to common fisheries for under-exploited stocks. This refers particularly to the most fundamental characteristic of the freedom of fishing: the fact that all States have free and unrestricted access to the living resources of the high seas. Open access would ensure that all States wishing to develop certain under-exploited stocks be capable of doing so without any restrictions. However, an exception to open access could be made if a State would wish to utilize certain under-exploited species for maricultural fisheries. In this case open access could form an impediment to full utilization, since no State would develop such fisheries because other nations could reap the benefits from its efforts. A first possibility of overcoming this problem would be to grant such internationally agreed preferential

[34]However, in most cases it will be rather difficult to make accurate comparisons.

rights to the State in question as it would require for initiating its maricultural operations. Another possibility would be that the interested States establish a multinational public fishing enterprise to exploit these maricultural fisheries.[35] The future international law of marine fisheries could provide that no State be allowed to exploit the stocks concerned unless it participated in this multinational public fishing enterprise.

In the future international law of marine fisheries, technical assistance and other international aid programmes could be effective instruments for ensuring that developing States participate actively in the expansion of marine fisheries.[36] In this respect, the main problems would be financial in nature. Future arrangements could find additional sources of revenues for such international assistance programmes in the form of levies imposed upon marine fisheries. The fact that a stock is under-exploited might indicate that its exploitation is commercially not very attractive. To impose a levy on the fisheries for such a stock would make these fisheries even less attractive, implying that the levy would be an impediment to full utilization. Therefore, the future international law of marine fisheries would find the additional revenues not in levies on fisheries for under-exploited stocks, but in levies on fisheries for fully exploited stocks.[37] Among other things, these levies could be used for fishery development projects in developing countries, provided that under-exploited and economically attractive stocks were available for such projects. If this were not the case, developing countries could probably use the available funds more productively in land-based applications.

There are several ways in which the future international law of marine fisheries could give substance to the principle

[35]*Supra* pp. 263-265.
[36]*Supra* p. 44.
[37]*Infra* p. 301.

that States participating in common fisheries for under-exploited stocks would be agents of the world community. One possibility would be to impose levies upon these fisheries and to use the revenues for the benefit of all nations. However, as said earlier, such levies would be undesirable from the point of view of full utilization. Therefore, the future international law of marine fisheries would merely require States engaged in common fisheries for under-exploited stocks to report on these fisheries to appropriate international fisheries organizations. This would also assist greatly in solving another problem of future arrangements: how to decide that a certain stock has ceased to be under-exploited. As will be discussed,[38] the future legal regime of common fisheries for fully exploited stocks would provide for an international group of neutral experts who would determine when the total catch of a stock has reached the maximum sustainable yield level. However, in order to make such a determination, these experts would need a variety of data concerning both the fisheries and the stocks. Therefore, States participating in common fisheries for under-exploited stocks would be required to make available any information specified by this group of experts. This could imply that these States would be required to under-take certain investigations.

3.3.3 Common Fisheries for Fully Exploited Stocks

It is with respect to common fisheries for fully exploited stocks that the problems of marine fisheries would manifest themselves most urgently.[39] As exploitation has reached the maximum sustainable yield level, it would be impossible to expand catches without jeopardizing the stocks in question. This limit on the available catch would lead to friction among fishing States concerning its allocation, unless they

[38]*Infra* p. 300.
[39]See generally Chapter I.

could agree on national quotas. However, it would be difficult to reach such an agreement as long as non-party States could freely enter the fisheries. Consequently, fishing nations would probably continue to allocate catches on the basis of free competition, which could result in overcapitalization problems. These problems would also be difficult to solve if new States were able to participate in these fisheries without any restrictions. In its turn, the inability to cope with overcapitalization problems would be a most serious obstacle towards dealing effectively with questions of conservation. Thus, fishing nations would continue to be very reluctant to accept any restrictions since other nations could reap the benefits from such action by entering the fisheries in question. Finally, free access to fully exploited stocks would not serve the interests of full utilization, simply because these stocks would already be fully utilized.

Considering these observations, the future legal regime of common fisheries for fully exploited stocks would have no choice other than to eliminate the most fundamental characteristic of the present freedom of fishing, *i.e.*, the fact that all nations of the world have free and unrestricted access to the fisheries for the living resources of the high seas. This would remove the single most important impediment to agreement among fishing nations on matters of allocation, overcapitalization and conservation, while it would have no detrimental consequences from the viewpoint of full utilization. However, the supreme *raison d'être* for the present principle of open access to high seas fisheries is that it permits all nations of the world to share in the wealth of the living resources of the sea by allowing them to engage in their harvest. As it would eliminate open access to certain fisheries, the future international law of marine fisheries would require special arrangements if it is to uphold the idea that the living resources of the high seas belong to all nations of the world. To accomplish this, it could make a distinction between access to the fisheries and access to the wealth of the resources.[40] Consequently, the three crucial problems of the future legal regime of common fisheries for fully exploited stocks are: (1) to work out rules and principles concerning the closure of access to common fisheries for fully exploited stocks; (2) to work out arrangements that would allow all nations of the world to share in the wealth of these fully exploited stocks; and (3) to give substance to the notion that States participating in common fisheries for fully exploited stocks are agents of the world community.

The rules and principles regarding the closure of access would, first of all, be concerned with the manner of determining that a stock has reached the point of full exploitation. It has been mentioned that States participating in common fisheries for under-exploited stocks would be required to provide data concerning their fisheries to an international group of neutral experts.[41] This group would decide when the total catch of a specific stock reaches the level of the maximum sustainable yield. Such a procedure would ensure the impartiality of the decision that stocks are subject to full exploitation. This impartiality is important since as a result of the determination by the group of experts,[42] access to the fisheries for the stock in question would be closed. Closure could be accomplished in several ways, but the most realistic method would be to limit access to those States which had participated in the fisheries during a certain base period.[43] Closing access to common fisheries on the basis of past performance would protect the efforts and investments of those countries which have developed these fisheries; it would also entrust the fisheries to those States which have the

[40]*Supra* p. 69.
[41]*Supra* p. 298.
[42]Under existing arrangements this decision is made by the fishing nations themselves.
[43]The ICNAF and NEAFC national quota arrangements are also largely based on this criterion.

equipment, market and knowledge to exploit the stocks concerned fully and rationally. However, rights of access to common fisheries for fully exploited stocks would be transferable: other States could acquire a right of access to these fisheries from the States which obtained such rights originally. Transferability would be in the interest of full utilization since it would enable other States to expand their catches by acquiring a right of access from a State that would no longer use its right. Transferability would also make it possible to give rights of access to common fisheries a financial value, which could have several advantages. It would, for example, make it easier for an efficient fishing nation to buy rights of access from a less efficient nation, since this less efficient nation could use the revenues from such a sale for the purpose of indemnifying those segments of its fishing industry which would be required to cease operations. A financially valuable right of access would also constitute an incentive for adopting effective regulations,[44] since a right of access to a well-regulated common fishery would have a higher financial value than a right of access to common fisheries for depleted stocks. However, this transferability of rights of access to common fisheries should not allow a specific nation to acquire a complete monopoly in world fisheries, since this could lead to undesirable practices. Therefore, future arrangements could limit the share of a nation in marine fisheries to a certain maximum.

The future international law of marine fisheries could require that States with a right of access to common fisheries pay levies that would be used for the benefit of the other nations of the world. This would ensure that States not having the right to participate in particular common fisheries

[44]This consideration is valid not only for governments, but also for the fishing industry: if fishermen were to have a financially valuable right of access to certain fisheries, it would be in their self-interest to protect the stocks.

share in the wealth of the resources exploited in these fisheries. Thus, future arrangements for common fisheries would distribute the wealth of fully exploited stocks in two alternative ways: (1) by giving States a right of access to the fisheries for these stocks; or (2) by giving States a right of access to the revenues generated by such fisheries. Such future arrangements could take several approaches towards determining the levies to be paid by nations with a right of access to common fisheries, but the following four principles could provide general guidelines. First of all, all nations of the world should participate in the process of specifying the amounts to be paid. If fishing nations only were responsible for setting levies, the arrangement could very well not result in an equitable sharing of the wealth of the living resources of the sea. Secondly, levies should be determined in such a way that access to common fisheries would be approximately of equal subjective value to nations as access to the revenues generated by these fisheries. However, this principle should not result in levies which are so high that no State would be willing to take the risks involved in marine fishing operations. Therefore, average financial returns from marine fisheries should exceed by a sufficient margin average financial returns from sharing in the revenues from levies. A third principle could be derived from the fact that an exclusive right of access to common fisheries would enable nations to rationalize their fishing operations economically. Thus, nations and fishermen would be able to derive a profit from marine fisheries, whereas existing legal regimes waste this profit potential in overcapitalization.[45] Consequently, the profitability of a certain fishery could be used as a basis for determining the levies, even if the nations concerned were to decide not to rationalize their fisheries. In this case States would in effect prefer to subsidize marine fisheries by paying the levies from general tax revenues. A last principle that

[45] *Supra* pp. 56-62

could govern these financial arrangements for common fisheries for fully exploited stocks would make the levies proportionate to the share of a State in the total world catch and to its *per capita* national income. If, for example, levies were set as a percentage of the value of a State's catch, this percentage could be made higher for States with a large share in the total world catch or with a high *per capita* national income. Such an arrangement would place the heaviest burden on rich nations with large scale marine fisheries.

It would be essential that all nations of the world also participate in the process of determining the *use* of the revenues from the above levy system. A certain portion could be set aside for financing the international group of experts discussed above. This would make the group financially independent from the national budgets of States, which would contribute to its efficient functioning.[46] Revenues could also be used for such generally acceptable purposes as the funding of international research projects or the financing of internationally organized fishery development programmes. However, a substantial part of the revenues could be used for re-distribution to States. As has been mentioned,[47] the future international law of marine fisheries would enable developing States to participate actively in the development of marine fisheries by making available to them revenues from the levies imposed upon fisheries for fully exploited stocks. To accomplish this, such revenues could be re-distributed under a formula which would base the share of a nation upon a reverse relationship with its share in the total world catch and its *per capita* national income. If, on the other hand, the future international law of marine fisheries were indeed to make the levies paid by a State proportionate to the share of that State in the total world catch and its

[46]*Supra* p. 72
[47]*Supra* p. 297

per capita national income, the result would be that the richest nations with the largest fisheries would pay the highest levies, while the poorest nations with the smallest fisheries would receive most of the revenues. If a country were to use its income from this arrangement for fishery development projects, it could expand fisheries for stocks subject to its exclusive or preferential rights, or it could enter common fisheries for under-exploited stocks. However, it could only enter common fisheries for fully exploited stocks if it acquired a right of access to these fisheries from one of the States with such a right. Rising labour costs, for example, could make a particular common fishery economically unattractive for a developed State, in which case a developing State with lower labour costs could buy the right to enter the fisheries in question. If income from the levy system could not be used in one of the above applications, nations could use it for other purposes.

The third area of concern to the future legal regime of common fisheries for fully exploited stocks would be to give substance to the concept that States participating in these fisheries are the agents of the world community. The above financial arrangements would already reflect this concept since they would require fishing States to pay for exploiting the living resources of the high seas. The agent status of fishing nations would also be evident from the fact that not only fishing nations, but all nations of the world would participate in the formulation and administration of these financial arrangements. This would also apply to general principles with respect to the closure of fisheries for fully exploited stocks and the transferability of the resulting rights of access to these fisheries. The world community could, for example, express its interest in full utilization by requiring fishing States to make a right of access available to other nations if they had not used this right during a certain period. Another important consequence of the agent status would be that fishing nations would be accountable to the world community for the regulation of the fisheries in which they would participate.[48] This accountability would extend in particular to the obligation of fishing nations to ensure the conservation of fully exploited stocks. Problems with respect to allocation and economic efficiency would largely be matters of concern to fishing nations only, although an inability to deal with these questions would not justify ineffectiveness in respect of conservation. To enforce this accountability, fishing nations could be required to report to the appropriate international fisheries organizations on their participation in common fisheries for fully exploited stocks and on regulatory measures applicable to these fisheries.

3.4 Over-Exploited Stocks

The future international law of marine fisheries could consider exploitation of high seas stocks beyond the level of their maximum sustainable yield an abuse of the rights of the world community. Consequently, it would revise the rights of the States responsible for such overfishing.[49] This would refer to coastal State preferential rights, to distant water fishing State preferential rights and to rights of access to common fisheries for fully exploited stocks. Coastal State exclusive rights could be an exception, if the overfished stock spent its whole life cycle within the coastal State's exclusive limits. If this were not the case, overfishing by a coastal State within its exclusive fishery limits could also be considered an abuse of the rights of the world community. The most important concern of the future legal regime for over-exploited stocks would be to compel

[48]It appears that this aspect of accountability has been relatively neglected in the fishery proposals to the UN Seabed Committee, see note 11.
[49]It has, for example, been suggested that full authority over all stocks of whales be vested in a special international organization, *supra* pp. 267-268.

nations to discontinue overfishing and to ensure that these stocks would be rebuilt to their former level of abundance. In order to ensure its impartiality, the decision that certain stocks are over-exploited would also be entrusted to the international group of neutral experts discussed above.[50] The fact that future arrangements would make it mandatory for fishing States to report on stocks and catches would provide this group with the necessary information, particularly if it could specify the kind of data to be made available.

If the group of experts decided that catches exceeded the maximum sustainable yield of a stock, the State, or States, engaged in the fisheries concerned should be required to reduce the catch to a level which in the opinion of the group of experts would enable the stock to recover. In addition, fishing nations could be required to report frequently to appropriate international fisheries organizations on their compliance with the decisions of the group of experts. If States did not comply, fisheries organizations could take further action. In the case of coastal State or distant water fishing State preferential rights, this action could be a refusal to re-negotiate such rights. This refusal would find support in general world community principles requiring States to ensure the conservation of the stocks over which they would have preferential rights.[51] In the case of common fisheries for fully exploited stocks, action would have to be taken on a world community level;[52] it could include a boycott of the fishery products of the offending States. However, since most States have already accepted in principle that catches should not exceed the maximum sustainable yield,[53] future arrangements could in all probability

[50]*Supra* p. 300.   *Infra* p. 312.
[51]*Supra* p. 286.
[52]Regional organizations would be ineffective here since they would consist of the fishing nations themselves.
[53]*Supra* p. 51.

306

rely on political pressure alone, provided that the impartiality of the determination of over-exploitation is unassailable.

4. ORGANIZATIONAL ASPECTS

4.1 Introduction

International fisheries organizations will be essential elements of the future international law of marine fisheries: they are indispensable not only for administering its rules and principles, but also for the formulation of these rules and principles.[54] Future international fisheries organizations would operate on a global and on a regional level. Global fisheries organizations would be those organizations whose membership would be open to all nations of the world. Regional fisheries organizations, on the other hand, would limit membership to States participating in certain fisheries, usually the fisheries of a particular ocean area. In this respect future regional organizations would resemble the existing regional fisheries commissions.

4.2 A World Marine Fisheries Organization[55]

4.2.1 Functions and Powers

The future international law of marine fisheries as outlined above would rest upon several general world community principles. These principles would, *inter alia*, be concerned with: (1) the conditions and procedures for granting coastal State or distant water fishing State preferential rights; (2) the conditions and procedures to be respected by States in their use of such preferential rights; (3) the conditions governing the closure of access to common fisheries for fully exploited stocks and the transferability of rights of access to

[54]The same applies to the existing fisheries organizations.
[55]A draft Convention for the Establishment of a World Marine Fisheries Organization is contained in Appendix I.

these fisheries; (4) the levies to be imposed upon common fisheries for fully exploited stocks and their re-distribution; and (5) the conditions and procedures to be respected by States in regulating common fisheries for fully exploited stocks. The formulation and administration of these world community principles would require the establishment of a World Marine Fisheries Organization whose membership would be open to all nations of the world. Its fundamental function would be to represent the interests of all nations of the world in the living resources of the high seas.[56]

A first aspect of this general function would concern full utilization: the World Marine Fisheries Organization could assist in bringing about the fullest desirable use of the sea's living resources. Such a task would have implications for the conditions governing coastal State and distant water fishing State preferential rights.[57] The Organization could ensure that these conditions require a full utilization of the stocks to which the rights refer; they could, for example, require a State which no longer uses its preferential rights to transfer these rights to States expressing an interest in carrying out the fisheries to which the rights apply. In order to administer such a principle, coastal States and distant water fishing States would be required to report to the Organization on their preferential right fisheries. Similar arrangements would apply to States with a right of access to common fisheries for fully exploited stocks. These States, too, could be prohibited from keeping such a right if they no longer used it and if other States were interested in expanding their catches. States with a right of access to common fisheries would also be required to report to the World Marine Fisheries Organization, either directly or through a regional organization. Another full utilization function of the Organization would

---

[56]COFI is the only existing organization with such a function, even though its membership is also largely composed of fishing States.
[57]Supra p. 286, p. 293.

be to assist developing nations in expanding their participation in common fisheries for under-exploited stocks and in improving fisheries for stocks over which these nations would have preferential or exclusive rights.[58] An important instrument for accomplishing this would be the levy system of common fisheries for fully exploited stocks. The Organization could ensure that the revenues from this system would indeed be used for the benefit of developing nations. This responsibility could extend not only to the process of formulating and administering principles governing the redistribution of revenues, but could also include the practical application of the available funds to specific fishery development projects.[59]

The most important functions of the World Marine Fisheries Organization would be concerned with conservation.[60] It has been discussed that in the future international law of marine fisheries, overfishing would be considered an abuse of the rights of the world community.[61] The Organization could be responsible for enforcing this principle *vis-à-vis* coastal States and distant water fishing States for their preferential right fisheries and *vis-à-vis* other States for their participation in common fisheries for fully exploited stocks. An exception could be made for fisheries based upon coastal State exclusive rights, but, as has been mentioned above, the world community interests would have to prevail even in these fisheries if the species in question spent most of their life cycle beyond the exclusive limits of the coastal State.[62] In carrying out this general conservation function, the Organization would be responsible for formulating general

[58]Duplication of effort with existing organizations could be avoided by limiting the role of the Organization to non-operational tasks, *infra* p. 317.
[59]But see note 58.
[60]See the discussion of proposals for a global conservation organization, *supra* pp. 258-262.
[61]*Supra* p. 305.
[62]*Ibidem.*

principles requiring States to implement effective conservation measures. These principles would deal not only with the substance of such measures, but also with the procedures for adopting them:[63] in the case of coastal State or distant water fishing State preferential right fisheries, the State in question would be required to take all necessary conservation measures; in the case of common fisheries for fully exploited stocks, this would be a joint responsibility of all States participating in these fisheries. The Organization could also be responsible for administering these principles. For this purpose, States would be required to report to the Organization concerning the adoption and application of conservation measures. They would report directly on their preferential right fisheries, but could report through a regional fisheries organization on common fisheries for fully exploited stocks. Depending upon its powers,[64] the Organization could point out shortcomings in existing arrangements and suggest improvements;[65] it could call the attention of nations to the fact that catches are reaching the level of the maximum sustainable yield of a stock; it could declare that certain fisheries are over-exploited; it could call for a boycott of the fishery products of a State, or States, which had refused to adopt effective conservation measures; or it could promulgate binding catch limits and other conservation measures.

The major responsibility of the Organization in respect of economic efficiency would be to work out principles regarding the closure of access to common fisheries for fully exploited stocks. Thus, the Organization's functions would be to create the conditions under which States could rationalize their fishing operations economically.[66] Although this should

[63]In this respect the 1958 Fisheries Convention would provide useful guidelines.
[64]*Infra* pp. 313-314.
[65]COFI already performs this function.
[66]*Supra* p. 62

not result in making economic rationalization compulsory, the Organization could offer certain incentives to States for taking such action. The levies imposed upon common fisheries for fully exploited stocks could be used for this purpose. States participating in these fisheries would have a choice between paying the levies from special taxes imposed upon the fishing industry or from general tax revenues. Political factors could make the first alternative more attractive, in which case the fishing industry could pay its taxes more easily if it operated profitably as a result of an economic rationalization programme. Thus, domestic political considerations could very well make an international levy system an incentive for improving the profitability of the national fishing industry.

The Organization could also be involved in matters of allocation. First of all, its functions concerning the formulation and application of principles regarding coastal State and distant water fishing State preferential rights would have direct implications concerning the allocation of the living resources of the sea. Essentially, the Organization would assist in defining the conditions under which allocation would discriminate in favour of coastal States or distant water fishing States. Secondly, the Organization would be responsible for elaborating and applying the levy system of common fisheries for fully exploited stocks. This system would implement a distinction between access to the fisheries for the living resources of the sea and access to the wealth of these resources. In this respect the participation of a global organization would be of crucial importance: it should not be left to fishing nations alone to decide to what extent non-fishing States would have access to the wealth of the sea's living resources.[67] A last allocation responsibility of the Organization would be more indirect: in formulating principles governing the closure of access to common fisheries for fully

[67]Neither should they be excluded from this decision.

exploited stocks, the Organization would assist in creating a framework conducive to an agreement on national quotas. However, working out such an agreement would not be the responsibility of the Organization, but of the States participating in the fisheries in question.

The World Marine Fisheries Organization would have substantial functions in respect of research. First of all, the aforementioned international group of neutral experts determining the condition of stocks would be part of the Organization's staff. Fishing nations would be obliged to submit to the Organization such information as these experts required. If a State lacked the capability of undertaking the necessary studies and if other international arrangements were unavailable,[68] the staff of the Organization could come to the assistance of the State in question. However, as a general rule, the research functions of the Organization would be concerned with the independent evaluation of data, rather than with their collection.[69] The main objective of these functions would be to enable the Organization to carry out its other functions, particularly those with respect to conservation. This does not imply that the Organization's research effort would consist exclusively of biological studies. As the formulation and administration of the levy system would require economic, social and legal information, the Organization's research work would also be directed at these aspects.

The World Marine Fisheries Organization could have several other responsibilities. It could, for example, have functions in respect of the enforcement of regulatory measures, which could even mean that the Organization would have at its disposal a team of neutral inspectors for supervising the inspection effort of fishing nations. As these international inspectors would be devoid of any national

[68]*E.g.*, regional fisheries organizations.
[69]*Supra* p. 71.

prejudices, such an enforcement system could enhance not only the effectiveness of enforcement arrangements, but also their non-discriminatory nature; this could make strict enforcement more acceptable to fishermen. A World Marine Fisheries Organization could also assist in avoiding intra-fisheries conflicts and in accommodating those inter-use conflicts that involve marine fisheries. In this regard the Organization could articulate the fisheries interests in the process by which the international law of the sea would assign priorities to the various uses of the sea.

Theoretically, the powers of the World Marine Fisheries Organization could range from binding decisions adopted by a majority vote to recommendations requiring the unanimous approval of all member States. The actual powers of the Organization would depend upon a variety of considerations, of which political acceptability would be the most important one. If the Organization were to function on the basis of binding decisions, many States would in all probability not become members or they would insist upon such decisions being taken by an unanimous vote only.[70] This could make the World Marine Fisheries Organization completely ineffectual: either its membership would be very limited or it would be incapable of reaching any decisions, except in entirely non-controversial matters. In addition, the achievement of the Organization's basic function – the formulation and administration of general world community principles – would be essentially a process in which political persuasion is the central element. Limiting its authority to recommendations only would not materially diminish the Organization's persuasive capacities.

A related and equally relevant consideration is that some of the responsibilities of the Organization would not require the power of binding decision. This would apply in particular

[70]None of the existing organizations has the power of binding decision.

to functions in respect of full utilization and economic efficiency. In these two areas there would be no inherent conflict between the interests of fishing nations and those of the world community as a whole: fishing nations would not gain at the expense of other nations if they decided not to utilize certain stocks fully or not to rationalize their fishing operations from an economic viewpoint.[71] However, this would not apply to conservation and allocation.[72] In these two areas the interests of fishing nations and the world community could collide: fishing nations could gain at the expense of the world community by overfishing certain stocks or by not allowing other States to share equitably in the wealth of the sea's living resources. This indicates that in these two areas decisions might be necessary in which the interests of the world community would prevail over the interests of nations participating in marine fisheries. Therefore, ultimately the Organization could need the power to take binding decisions on matters of conservation and allocation. This could, for example, include the authority to set catch quotas that would be binding on the States participating in the fisheries to which they would refer. However, considerations based upon political acceptability and upon the nature of its initial work suggest the advisability of not granting such forcible powers to the Organization in its formative period. The Organization could begin to operate on the basis of recommendations adopted by a majority vote. This would allow the World Marine Fisheries Organization to participate actively in the process of formulating general world community principles with respect to marine fisheries. If these general principles would have found some degree of acceptance, the Organization could then obtain more forcible powers in respect of conservation and allocation.

[71]*Supra* p. 44, p. 63.
[72]*Supra* p. 54, p. 69.

4.2.2 Structure

The structure of the World Marine Fisheries Organization would, first of all, consist of a plenary group in which all member States would be represented. It would meet once a year, but it could meet more frequently if necessary. This plenary group would be the centre of authority of the Organization and it would take all significant decisions. As a general rule, it would decide by a majority vote or, in order to enhance the political weight of a decision, by a two-thirds majority. The voting strength of a State could be proportionate to its share in the total world catch. However, this would give fishing nations a large degree of control over the decisions of the Organization, which could conflict with its basic objective of representing the general world community interests. Therefore, it would be preferable to make the voting strength of States proportionate to their population.[73] In addition to such a plenary group, the Organization would have a council composed of a number of States selected by the plenary group. The council's membership criteria could provide for periodic re-election and for equal representation of developing States, developed States, coastal States and distant water fishing States. The council's major responsibilities would be to prepare and implement the decisions of the plenary group and to oversee the activities of the Organization's staff. It would meet several times in the intervals between plenary meetings and decide on the basis of a majority vote. However, since its membership would rotate and since it would not be the Organization's centre of authority, it would be both impractical and unnecessary to base the council's decisions on weighted voting. One of the most important responsibilities of the council could be to endorse provisionally the determination of the staff that the exploitation of certain stocks had reached the level of the maximum sustainable yield.

[73]This would also reflect the fact that the exploitation of the living resources of the sea serves the needs of people, rather than of States.

The staff of the World Marine Fisheries Organization could be relatively small unless the Organization were to have substantial operational tasks, *e.g.*, with regard to fishery development projects in developing countries.[74] The essential responsibilities of the staff would be to enable the Organization to evaluate independently the regulatory measures adopted by fishing nations, and secondly, to decide when catches reach the maximum sustainable yield level.[75] As a general rule, the staff would not carry out the actual investigations; instead, the Organization would require fishing States to submit certain data in an agreed form to its staff. The staff would be headed by a director who would report to the council. As the research functions of the Organization would be concerned with all aspects of marine fishing operations, the staff would consist not only of marine biologists, but also of economists, lawyers and other social scientists.

The World Marine Fisheries Organization could be an independent international organization, although it could be part of an international organization concerned with all marine resources. Existing organizations already perform some of the Organization's functions, particularly the FAO and its Committee on Fisheries. However, bringing the Organization fully within the FAO structure could create a number of problems. First of all, there would be a possibility that in FAO the tasks outlined above would receive less special attention than if they were entrusted to an independent organization. Secondly, existing commissions have been rather reluctant to become part of FAO.[76] Thirdly, such action could result in very complex legal arrangements, which could impede the efficient functioning of the World

[74]But see *infra* p. 317.
[75]The implications of this decision have been discussed above, *supra* p. 300.
[76]*Supra* p. 152.

Marine Fisheries Organization.[77] Therefore, it seems preferable to give the Organization an independent status, *e.g.*, as a specialized agency of the United Nations. Problems of duplication of functions and activities could be easily avoided, especially since the functions of the World Marine Fisheries Organization as outlined above would be largely non-operational in scope. FAO could, for example, continue to administer and carry out fishery development projects in the developing countries, but the formulation of relevant principles and guidelines would be a responsibility of the Organization. Such a division of functions would have the additional advantage that the size of the Organization's staff could be kept relatively small. As this would minimize the costs of the Organization, it would also minimize the risk of financial considerations preventing a State from becoming a member. The costs of membership could be further reduced if the revenues from the levy system of common fisheries for fully exploited stocks were used for financing the staff.

4.3 Regional Fisheries Organizations[78]

4.3.1 Functions and Powers

Future regional fisheries organizations would not differ fundamentally from the existing fisheries commissions.[79] The most significant changes would originate in the future international law of marine fisheries itself, rather than in the law dealing with the structure, functions and powers of these future regional organizations. Of particular relevance would be the fact that the future international law of marine fisheries would close access to common fisheries for fully

[77]See *e.g.*, the problems of CARPAS in respect of membership, *supra* p. 111; in this respect it is of significance that the USSR is not a member of FAO.
[78]A draft Convention for the Establishment of a Regional Fisheries Commission is contained in Appendix II.
[79]See Chapter III and Chapter IV.

exploited stocks and would consider regional fisheries bodies as organizations of States that are agents of the world community.[80] However, like the existing commissions, future regional fisheries organizations would be responsible for the regulation of particular marine fisheries. This regulatory responsibility would usually refer to all stocks in a certain area, but in the case of a highly migratory species it could refer to all areas in which this species would be exploited.[81] Future arrangements would also ensure that a system of regional fisheries organizations would cover all high seas fisheries, be it common fisheries or preferential right fisheries.

In dealing with common fisheries, future regional organizations would be concerned with all problem areas of marine fisheries: full utilization, conservation, economic efficiency, allocation, research and intra-use and inter-use conflicts. In the case of common fisheries for under-exploited stocks, future regional organizations would be responsible for developing the fisheries for such stocks to the extent that such development would be biologically possible and economically attractive. They could also have direct functions with respect to fishery development projects in the developing countries. If a stock were exploited at its maximum sustainable yield level, future regional bodies would be responsible for taking effective action in respect of conservation. They would also act in order to prevent the overcapitalization of the fisheries and in order to reach agreement on the allocation of the catch. In contrast to the existing regional commissions, future regional organizations would deal with such problems of conservation, economic efficiency and allocation under conditions of closed access to the fisheries, which would greatly facilitate their work. With respect to over-exploited stocks, future regional fisheries organizations could be made

[80]*Supra* p. 299, p. 304.
[81]*Supra* p. 130.

318

responsible for rebuilding such stocks to a higher level of abundance and for regulating access to the fisheries if commercial exploitation could be resumed. Their research effort, not being restricted to biological studies alone, would enable future regional commissions to carry out the above functions. Finally, they would be responsible for minimizing conflicts between different types of marine fisheries and between marine fisheries and other ocean uses.[82]

Future regional fisheries organizations would regulate common fisheries under an implicit or explicit mandate from the world community.[83] This would be evident, first of all, from the fact that they would function within the terms of the general world community principles discussed above. It has been mentioned that the formulation of these principles would be the responsibility of all nations of the world and not of fishing nations alone.[84] However, this would not mean that future regional fisheries organizations could not make very important contributions in this area. They could even begin to implement these principles 'unilaterally'. For example, if certain fisheries reached the maximum sustainable yield level, a regional organization could impose a levy on these fisheries and make the revenues available for some generally acceptable purpose as long as no new States would enter the fisheries in question. This could give the members of the regional organization *de facto* exclusive access to these fisheries. If the levy system of common fisheries for fully exploited stocks were to find acceptance, future regional organizations could also have functions in respect of its administration. Another aspect of the world community mandate of future regional fisheries bodies would be their obligation to report periodically to the World Marine Fish-

[82]Essentially, these functions would be quite similar to the functions of existing organizations, see Chapter IV.
[83]This would be a major difference with existing organizations, particularly if the mandate were explicit.
[84]*Supra* p. 304.

eries Organization concerning the fisheries for which they would be responsible and concerning their regulatory actions. Such a procedure would expose their activities to the scrutiny of the world community.

Future regional fisheries organizations could have very substantial responsibilities *vis-à-vis* coastal State and distant water fishing State preferential rights.[85] First of all, they could be the arenas in which States would attempt to reach agreement with respect to these rights. These negotiations would take place on the basis of the general world community principles, but would at the same time contribute to their further development. If the negotiations within the framework of a regional fisheries organization failed, the States concerned or the regional organization itself could bring the matter to the attention of the World Marine Fisheries Organization, which could then examine the dispute and adopt appropriate recommendations. A failure to reach agreement on the continued validity of preferential rights could also be submitted to arbitration.[86] Future regional fisheries organizations could have functions regarding the administration of preferential rights as well. For example, the agreement granting preferential rights to a coastal State could require this State to report on its preferential right fisheries to a regional organization.[87] If in their turn future regional fisheries bodies would be required to report to the World Marine Fisheries Organization concerning the regulation of preferential right fisheries in their area of competence, this procedure would ensure that not only the regulation of common fisheries for high seas stocks, but also the regulation of preferential right fisheries for such stocks could be examined on a world community level.

[85]Existing organizations have generally only indirect functions in this respect.
[86]*Supra* p. 288.
[87]See note 24.

The powers of future regional fisheries organizations would depend upon the powers granted to the World Marine Fisheries Organization. If this Organization had the authority to make binding decisions concerning any question that would require this,[88] the problem of compelling certain fishing nations to respect the interests of other nations would have been transferred from a regional level to a global level. From a world community point of view it would have become rather irrelevant whether organizations of fishing States discharged their responsibilities on the basis of recommendations or through binding decisions. However, if the World Marine Fisheries Organization did not have such forcible powers, future regional fisheries bodies could need the authority of binding decision, particularly in respect of conservation. If future regional fisheries organizations could adopt binding conservation measures on the basis of a majority vote, it would have become quite difficult for a single State to frustrate the adoption of effective fishery regulations. Although such powers would not ensure that fishing nations *as a group* would not act to the detriment of the world community, they could assist in preventing *individual* fishing nations from so acting. In regard to allocation, future regional fisheries organizations could operate on the basis of recommendations. This would be largely a matter of political acceptability; allocation by binding decision appears to be politically very unrealistic. In addition, as long as fishing States would not exceed allowable *overall* catch limits and would respect the general principles applicable to the levy system, there is, from a world community viewpoint, no compelling reason for binding decisions in matters of allocation. The same would apply to questions of economic efficiency: regional bodies would be responsible for promoting economic rationalization, rather than for making it compulsory. Full utilization and research

[88] *Supra* pp. 313-314.

functions could also be implemented on the basis of recommendations, although in respect of research, it would become an obligation of fishing States to provide certain data.[89] Here again, the powers to be granted to regional organizations would depend upon the authority of the World Marine Fisheries Organization: if the Organization could compel States to make all necessary information available, there is less reason for vesting such powers in regional fisheries bodies. The above suggests that future regional organizations would to a large extent be capable of acting on the basis of recommendations, but that under certain conditions the power to take binding decisions could be necessary with respect to questions of conservation and research.

4.3.2 Structure

There is little need to describe in detail the structure of future regional fisheries organizations since it could be similar to the structure of the existing fisheries commissions, particularly if the improvements suggested in Chapter III were adopted. Essentially, future regional fisheries organizations could consist of: (1) a plenary group that would meet as often as necessary and which would decide by a majority vote; (2) several scientific and other advisory committees; and (3) a relatively small international research staff which would be responsible for the evaluation, rather than the collection, of data and which could be funded from levies imposed upon the fisheries.[90] However, there could be one fundamental difference with the existing commissions. It has been discussed that the future international law of marine fisheries would eliminate open access to common fisheries for fully exploited stocks by giving certain States an exclusive right of access to these fisheries. This additional right could be combined with an additional obligation: States with a

[89] *Supra* p. 312.
[90] *Supra* p. 301.

right of access to a common fishery for a fully exploited stock would be required to become members of the regional organization responsible for this stock or to establish such a regional organization, if none already existed.[91] The future international law of marine fisheries could prohibit a State from using its rights of access to common fisheries unless it were a member of the appropriate regional fisheries organization. Such an arrangement could prevent a fishing State from evading its responsibilities *vis-à-vis* other nations and the world community by not taking part in the international regulation of marine fisheries.

[91]Establishment of, and membership in, existing organizations is a completely voluntary matter, *supra* p. 124.

Final Remarks

1. LEGAL REFORM IN THE INTERNATIONAL COMMUNITY[1]

The nature of legal reform is intimately linked to the characteristics of the society in which it is to take place. Thus, the process of reforming the international law of marine fisheries and the law of international fisheries organizations will reflect the peculiarities of the international community.[2] This community is, compared with national societies, still in a primitive stage of development:[3] it has not yet fully succeeded in substituting the rule of law for the rule of force and States – the basic entities of the international community – are subject to a minimum of substantive norms of conduct, while individuals overwhelmingly accept the coercive powers of the national society in which they live. The primitive nature of the international community is also evident from the fact that legal reform is essentially a decentralized process of informal growth, rather than of formal decisions – a process dependent upon the voluntary cooperation of States.[4] However, this does not necessarily mean that only States participate in such reform or that their voluntary consent is a prerequisite for change under all conditions. Other entities that contribute to changes in

[1] C Y Black, *Challenges to an evolving legal order*, in *The future of the international legal order*, vol. 1, *Trends and patterns*, Princeton 1969, pp. 3–31. W Friedmann, *The changing structure of international law*, New York 1964. W Friedmann, *Law in a changing society*, Berkeley 1959.
[2] R A Falk, *Settling ocean fishing conflicts: the limits of 'law reform' in a horizontal legal order*, in *The status of law in international society*, vol. 1, *An orientation toward the political setting of the international legal order*, Princeton 1970, pp. 540–553. *Ibidem*, in *The future of the fishing industry of the United States*, Seattle 1969, pp. 326–333.
[3] Friedmann, *op. cit.*, note 1, 1964, pp. 118–120; the stage of development of the international community has even been compared with a 'jungle condition', G Schwarzenberger, *A manual of international law*, New York and Washington 1967, p. 380.
[4] Falk, *op. cit.*, note 2, 1970, p. 540.

international law range from international organizations to individuals; and voluntary cooperation of States becomes a relative concept in the face of often compelling circumstances.[5]

Apart from non-peaceful methods, there appear to be four major instruments for bringing about changes in the international law of marine fisheries and the law of international fisheries organizations: (1) international adjudication; (2) custom; (3) international agreements; and (4) the work of international organizations.[6] International courts have played an important role in the evolution of the international legal system.[7] Judicial decisions are an accepted source of international law and several of its rules owe their origin and their acceptance in the international community to such decisions. These decisions could also assist in bringing about desirable changes in the international law of marine fisheries and in the functions, powers and structure of international fisheries organizations.[8] However, the general reluctance of States to submit disputes to legal settlement and the reluctance of courts to exceed the limits of a particular case restrict the potentialities of this specific instrument for change. Custom, defined as a general practice accepted

[5]For a most comprehensive discussion of these questions, see M S McDougal, H D Lasswell and W M Reisman, *The world constitutive process of authoritative decision*, in *The future of the international legal order*, vol. 1, *Trends and patterns*, Princeton 1969, pp. 73–154.
[6]See Art. 38 Statute of the International Court of Justice.
[7]M Virally, *The sources of international law*, in *Manual of public international law*, M Sørensen ed., New York 1968, pp. 148–152. Friedmann, *op. cit.*, note 1, 1964, pp. 141–146. H Lauterpacht, *The development of international law by the International Court*, London 1958.
[8]In this connection it is of interest that the United Kingdom and the Federal Republic of Germany have instituted proceedings against Iceland before the International Court of Justice on 14 April 1972 concerning Iceland's decision to extend, as from September 1972, its exclusive fishery limits to a distance of 50 miles from its coast. The Court issued Interim Measures of Protection on 17 August 1972.

as law,[9] is another important source of international law.[10] An unilateral claim may constitute the first step towards the development of new customary international law, even though initially such a claim may conflict with an established rule. Customary rules can also emerge from other international practice, *e.g.*, international agreements, provided that such practice develops into a general custom which is considered by a *communis opinio*[11] among States as representing a rule of law. This process will certainly contribute to the creation of the future international law of marine fisheries, particularly since it can be initiated by unilateral action. On the other hand, the criteria defining a rule of customary international law are vague and make its acceptance conditional upon the passing of time. Thus, custom is a rather inaccurate and slow moving instrument for change. International agreements[12] do not have such problems; they result in more precise arrangements and they can respond rather quickly to new circumstances. However, an inherent characteristic of international agreements is that they require the consent of all parties. The more fundamental the scope of an agreement, the more difficult it will be to secure such consent. In addition, the legal arrangements of an agreement have effect between the parties only.[13] International agreements are also better instruments for solving than for preventing problems – if a problem has not yet become serious, States see little reason for signature or ratification. This

[9]Art. 38 Statute of the International Court of Justice.

[10]Virally, *op. cit.*, note 7, pp. 128–143. H W Briggs, *The International Law Commission*, Ithaca 1965. Friedmann, *op. cit.*, note 1, 1964, pp. 121–123.

[11]Which can be formed by explicit or tacit consent, see I C MacGibbon, *Customary international law and acquiescence*, in *British Yearbook of International Law* 1957, pp. 115–145.

[12]Virally, *op. cit.*, note 7, pp. 123–128. Friedmann, *op. cit.*, note 1, 1964, pp. 123–126. Lord McNair, *The law of treaties*, London 1961.

[13]Except for a few types of agreements which produce effects *erga omnes*, see H Kelsen, *Principles of international law*, New York 1956, p. 345.

difficulty is not necessarily a feature of the fourth instrument[14] for changing the international law of marine fisheries. International fisheries organizations could be capable of anticipating problems and of taking timely action. This makes the participation of the existing international fisheries organizations in the creation of the future international law of marine fisheries a matter of crucial importance. The continuity of their concern with the problems of marine fisheries could allow these organizations to initiate changes in existing legal arrangements before problems deteriorate to a point where irreparable harm has been inflicted upon the living resources of the seas.

These few remarks concerning the nature of legal change in the international community suggest that there is little profit in speculating on how the existing international law of marine fisheries will be transformed into the future international law of marine fisheries. First of all, the extreme complexity of the process of reforming existing legal arrangements makes any scenario a futile exercise. Secondly, as has been mentioned, the proposals made are in no way intended as a grand design to solve all the present and future problems of marine fisheries, but merely as one possible direction in which the international law of marine fisheries and international fisheries organizations could be developed by a process of informal growth. To specify an outline for their implementation would give the above proposals a finality that is not intended. However, there is no doubt that the future legal regime of marine fisheries will be the outcome of a difficult and time consuming process which will be marked not only by agreement and success, but by conflict and failure as well.

[14]Friedmann, *op. cit.*, note 1, 1964, pp. 135–141. C W Jenks, *The proper law of international institutions*, London 1962. A J P Tammes, *Decisions of international organs as a source of international law*, RdC 1958, vol. 94, pp. 265–364.

It is also possible to look upon changes in the international law of marine fisheries and the law of international fisheries organizations from a different perspective. Mankind's attitude towards the living resources of the sea has been that of the primitive hunter. The principle of the freedom of fishing on the high seas reflects this attitude; it gives those who wish to exploit the resources a right of capture free from any responsibilities. However, in exploiting the living resources of the seas the era of rights without responsibilities has long since passed. Therefore, the most fundamental aspect of reforming the existing international law of marine fisheries is that such reform must represent a change in mankind's attitude towards the living resources of the sea from that of the primitive hunter to that of the farmer who accepts responsibility for the resources he exploits.[15]

[15]G Hardin, *The tragedy of the commons*, *Science* 1968, pp. 1243–1248.

Appendix I

CONVENTION FOR THE ESTABLISHMENT OF A WORLD MARINE FISHERIES ORGANIZATION[1]

The States parties to this Convention:

– Recognizing that the living resources of the high seas are the common property of mankind;

– Recognizing that all nations must have access to the wealth of the living resources of the high seas;

– Recognizing that it is an obligation of all States to ensure the rational exploitation of the living resources of the high seas;

– Recognizing that these principles can only be implemented through international cooperation;

Have agreed as follows:

Article I – Establishment

1. The States parties to this Convention establish the World Marine Fisheries Organization (hereinafter referred to as 'the Organization') upon the terms and conditions hereinafter set forth.

Article II – Membership

1. The original members of the Organization shall be those States which have signed this Convention within ninety days after it was opened for signature and which have subsequently deposited an instrument of ratification.

2. After the entry into force of this Convention, States may become members of the Organization by a notification in writing to the Organization.

[1] This Draft Convention is intended as a model only; it does not take into account all variables discussed in the preceding Chapters.

3. At any time after the expiration of ten years from the entry into force of this Convention, States may withdraw from the Organization. Such withdrawal shall take effect ninety days after notification of the Organization.

Article III – Objectives

1. The objectives of the Organization shall be to ensure the rational exploitation of the living resources of the high seas and to bring about an equitable allocation of the wealth of these resources among the member States.

Article IV – Functions

1. The Organization shall assist in bringing about the fullest desirable use of the living resources of the high seas. To this end, it shall:

   (a) promote national and international fishery development programmes;

   (b) assist developing nations;

   (c) assist in expanding maricultural fisheries;

   (d) ensure that States with a right to exploit the living resources of the sea use such right to the fullest extent possible.

2. The Organization shall take action to ensure the conservation of the living resources of the high seas. To this end, it shall:

   (a) adopt rules and principles concerning the obligation of fishing States to prevent exploitation of stocks of fish beyond the level of their maximum sustainable yield;

   (b) adopt rules and principles concerning procedures for elaborating all necessary conservation measures;

(c) adopt rules and principles concerning the obligation of fishing States to rebuild to their former level of abundance stocks of fish which have been exploited beyond the level of their maximum sustainable yield, unless such over-exploitation is not deemed unacceptable by neutral experts;

(d) propose action against those States that persistently violate the above rules and principles;

(e) make such recommendations on matters of conservation as it deems necessary.

3. The Organization shall assist in bringing about an economically efficient exploitation of the living resources of the high seas. To this end, it shall:

(a) adopt rules and principles concerning the closure of access to common fisheries for stocks subject to exploitation at the maximum sustainable yield level;

(b) make such recommendations on matters of economic efficiency as it deems necessary.

4. The Organization shall take action to ensure an equitable allocation of the living resources of the high seas. To this end, it shall:

(a) adopt rules and principles establishing justification for coastal State or distant water State preferential rights;

(b) adopt rules and principles determining which States shall have access to common fisheries for stocks subject to exploitation at the maximum sustainable yield level;

(c) adopt rules and principles concerning the levies which shall be paid by States with a right of access to such common fisheries;

(d) adopt rules and principles concerning the redistribution of the revenues from such levies;

(e) make such recommendations on matters of allocation as it deems desirable, and particularly with respect to the practical implementation of the principles establishing justification for preferential rights.

5. The Organization shall assist in making available such scientific and other information as is required for a rational exploitation of the living resources of the high seas. To this end, it shall:

(a) adopt rules and principles concerning investigations to be carried out by fishing nations;

(b) adopt rules and principles concerning scientific and other information which shall be made available to the Organization;

(c) determine the maximum sustainable yield of stocks of fish and its relationship with the catches of such stocks.

6. The Organization shall perform such other functions as are necessary for achieving its objectives. To this end, it may, *inter alia*:

(a) make recommendations concerning the enforcement of conservation and other regulatory measures;

(b) make recommendations concerning intra-fisheries conflicts and inter-use conflicts involving marine fisheries.

Article V – Powers

1. The Organization shall implement its functions through recommendations to its member States, except that:

(a) after the expiration of three years from the entry into force of this Convention, the Organization shall implement its functions under Article IV, para. 2(a), para. 2(c), para. 5(b) and para. 5(c) by decisions which shall become binding upon member States one month after their adoption by the Organization, except for those member States which have lodged a formal objection;

(b) after the expiration of six years from the entry into force of this Convention, the Organization shall implement its functions under Article IV, para. 2(a), para. 2(c), para. 5(b) and para. 5(c) by decisions which shall be directly binding upon the member States, and its functions under Article IV, para. 1(d), para. 2(b), para. 2(d), para. 3(a), para. 4(a), para. 4(b), para. 4(c), para. 4(d) and para. 5(a) by decisions which shall become binding upon member States one month after their adoption by the Organization, except for those member States which have lodged a formal objection;

(c) after the expiration of nine years from the entry into force of this Convention, the Organization shall also implement its functions under Article IV, para. 1(d), para. 2(b), para. 4(c), para. 4(d) and para. 5(a) by decisions which shall be directly binding upon the member States.

Article VI – The General Conference

1. There shall be a General Conference consisting of one delegate from each member State who shall be a high ranking fishery official of such member State. He may be accompanied by experts and advisers who may participate in the meetings of the General Conference, but who shall have no vote.

2. The General Conference shall have a regular annual meeting and may have such extraordinary meetings as shall be convened by the Council or a majority of the member States. A majority of member States shall constitute a quorum.

335

3. The General Conference shall elect a Chairman and may establish such subsidiary bodies as may be required. It shall adopt its own rules of procedure. The Agenda of the meetings of the General Conference shall be drawn up by the Council in consultation with the member States.

4. The General Conference shall take all decisions necessary for the achievement of the Organization's objectives and for the implementation of the Organization's functions. The General Conference shall decide by a simple majority of those members voting, except that the directly binding decisions under Article V, para. 1(b) and (c) shall be taken by a majority of all member States. Each member of the General Conference shall have one vote for each million people, or part thereof, of its population.

Article VII – The Council

1. There shall be a Council consisting of thirteen member States and composed as follows:

(a) five shall be the States with the largest catches in marine fisheries;

(b) two shall be elected by the General Conference from among developed fishing States, not otherwise represented;

(c) two shall be elected by the General Conference from among developing fishing States, not otherwise represented;

(d) two shall be elected by the General Conference from among coastal States, not otherwise represented;

(e) two shall be elected by the General Conference from among distant water fishing States, not otherwise represented.

2. The Council shall meet as often as the business of the Organization may require. Seven member States constitute a quorum for the meetings of the Council. The Council shall select a Chairman and adopt its own rules of procedure.

3. The Council shall carry out the directives of the General Conference and discharge the following responsibilities:

   (a) draw up the Agenda for the meetings of the General Conference and prepare such preparatory documents as the General Conference or the Council may deem necessary;

   (b) prepare budget estimates and authorize the disbursement of funds;

   (c) appoint the Executive Director of the Organization subject to the approval of the General Conference;

   (d) report to the General Conference concerning the scientific findings of the staff of the Organization and particularly concerning the relationship between the catch of stocks of fish and their maximum sustainable yield.

4. The Council shall decide by a majority of the votes cast. Each member of the Council shall have one vote.

Article VIII – The Staff

1. The Organization shall have an administrative secretariat and a permanent internationally recruited research staff consisting of employees of the highest standards of efficiency, technical competence and integrity. The staff shall not seek or receive instructions from any member State. It shall be headed by an Executive Director.

337

2. The research staff shall conduct such scientific, technical, economic, social or legal research as may be required for the achievement of the Organization's functions. Its work shall be guided by the following principles:

(a) the primary responsibilities of the research staff of the Organization shall be to identify gaps in the existing knowledge of the sea's living resources and their exploitation, to keep itself informed of research in progress, to analyze and evaluate the results of such investigations and to assist in the exchange of the results;

(b) the member States shall give the Organization's research staff all assistance which the staff may need in carrying out its functions;

(c) if there are no other methods available for obtaining certain data, the Council may authorize the research staff to carry out the necessary investigations.

Article IX – Relations with other Organizations

1. The Organization shall be brought into relationship with the United Nations in accordance with Article 57 of the Charter of the United Nations as a specialized agency in the field of marine fisheries.

2. The Organization shall cooperate with other intergovernmental and non-governmental organizations whose interests and purposes are related to the objectives of the Organization. It may conclude such cooperative agreements as it deems necessary.

Article X – Finances

1. The finances of the Organization shall be administered by the Executive Director who shall be responsible to the Council.

2. The Council shall submit to each annual meeting of the General Conference estimates concerning the expenditures of the Organization and concerning the contributions of member States.

3. Contributions of member States shall be proportionate to their share in the total world catch.

Article XI – Legal Status

1. The Organization shall possess full legal personality and in particular the capacity to contract, to acquire and dispose of immovable and movable property and to institute legal proceedings.

2. The Organization and the persons serving on its staff shall enjoy in the territory of the member States such privileges and immunities as are necessary for the fulfilment of their functions.

Article XII – Amendments

1. Amendments to this Convention may be proposed by any member State and the Council. Amendments shall enter into force three months after having been approved by the General Conference with a two-thirds majority of all member States.

Article XIII – Entry into Force

1. This Convention shall enter into force when twenty five States have deposited their instruments of ratification with the Secretary-General of the United Nations, or when the share in the total world catch of the States which have deposited their instrument of ratification exceeds twenty per cent, whichever occurs first.

Appendix II

CONVENTION FOR THE ESTABLISHMENT OF A
REGIONAL FISHERIES COMMISSION FOR THE
SOUTH WEST PACIFIC OCEAN[1]

The States parties to this Convention:

– Desiring to ensure the rational exploitation of the stocks
of fish of the South West Pacific Ocean;

Have agreed as follows:

Article I – Establishment

1. The States parties to this Convention establish the
Regional Fisheries Commission for the South West
Pacific Ocean (hereinafter referred to as 'the Commission')
upon the terms and conditions hereinafter set forth.

Article II – Convention Area

1. This Convention shall apply to all waters of the South
West Pacific Ocean and adjacent seas south of 15° South
Latitude and west of 170° East Longitude, with the
exception of waters subject to the exclusive fishery
jurisdiction of coastal States.

2. The Commission may divide the Convention waters into
such sub-areas as it deems necessary.

Article III – Objectives

1. The objective of the Commission shall be to ensure the
rational exploitation of the stocks of fish in the Convention
area.

[1]The South West Pacific Ocean is used as an example only; the Draft
Convention does not specifically deal with the fishery problems of this
region, nor does it take into account all variables discussed in the preceding Chapters.

Article IV – Functions

1. The Commission shall assist in bringing about the fullest desirable use of the stocks of fish in the Convention area. To this end, it shall:

   (a) promote national and international fishery development programmes;

   (b) give financial support to such programmes from the income of levies on fisheries for fully exploited stocks;

   (c) assist States in developing maricultural fishcries;

   (d) ensure that States make the fullest possible use of their preferential rights or rights of access to common fisheries for fully exploited stocks.

2. The Commission shall take action to ensure the conservation of the stocks of fish in the Convention area. To this end, it shall:

   (a) adopt effective conservation measures;

   (b) base such conservation measures on scientific and other evidence;

   (c) rebuild to their former level of abundance stocks of fish which have been exploited beyond the level of their maximum sustainable yield, unless such over-exploitation is not deemed unacceptable by neutral experts;

   (d) recommend action against States which refuse to accept conservation measures;

   (e) make such recommendations on matters of conservation as it deems necessary.

3. The Commission shall assist in bringing about an economically efficient exploitation of the stocks of fish in the Convention area. To this end, it shall:

(a) subject to the provisions of para. 4 of this Article, make such recommendations on matters of economic efficiency as it deems necessary.

4. The Commission shall take action to ensure an equitable allocation of the stocks of fish in the Convention area. To this end, it shall:

(a) on the basis of rules and principles adopted by the World Marine Fisheries Organization, determine which member States shall have access to common fisheries for fully exploited stocks;

(b) on the basis of rules and principles adopted by the World Marine Fisheries Organization, determine the levies which shall be paid by member States with a right of access to common fisheries for fully exploited stocks, and establish procedures for the payment of such levies to the World Marine Fisheries Organization;

(c) on the basis of rules and principles adopted by the World Marine Fisheries Organization, establish procedures for negotiations concerning coastal State and distant water fishing State preferential rights;

(d) bring the failure of any negotiations on preferential rights to the attention of the World Marine Fisheries Organization, or take other appropriate action;

(e) make recommendations to States with a right of access to common fisheries for fully exploited stocks on the allocation of catches or fishing effort;

(f) make such other recommendations on matters of allocation as it deems desirable.

5. The Commission shall take action to ensure that such scientific and other information is available as is required for the achievement of its objectives. To this end, it shall:

(a) require member States to provide all necessary information concerning their fisheries and the stocks they exploit;

(b) establish procedures for the independent evaluation of such information;

(c) make such recommendations on matters of scientific and other research as it deems necessary.

6. The Commission shall perform such other functions as are necessary in order to achieve its objectives. To this end, it may, *inter alia:*

(a) make recommendations concerning the enforcement of conservation and other regulatory measures;

(b) make recommendations concerning intra-fisheries conflicts and inter-use conflicts involving marine fisheries.

Article V – Powers

1. The Commission shall implement its functions through recommendations to the member States, except that:

(a) decisions under Article IV, para. 2(a), para. 2(c), para. 4(a), para. 4(b) and para. 5(a) shall become binding upon member States one month after their adoption by the Commission, except for those States which have lodged a formal objection. If States lodge objections, the decision shall not become binding during an additional period of one month in which other States may lodge objections and in which the originally objecting States shall reaffirm their objection;

(b) after the expiration of five years from the entry into force of this Convention, decisions under Article IV, para. 2(a), para. 2(c), para. 4(a), para. 4(b) and para. 5(a) shall be binding upon member States after their

343

adoption by the Commission, unless the Commission by a two-thirds majority of all members decides to adhere to para. (a) of this Article.

Article VI – Organization

1. The Commission shall be composed of one national section for each member State. A national section shall consist of not more than three official delegates who may be accompanied by experts and advisers, and shall include representatives of the various national fishing interest groups of member States.

2. The Commission shall have a regular annual meeting and such extraordinary meetings as may be requested by a majority of the national sections.

3. The Commission shall elect a Chairman and may establish such subsidiary bodies as may be required for the achievement of its objectives. Subject to the provisions of this Convention, it shall adopt its own rules of procedure.

4. There shall be an Executive Committee consisting of the Chairman of the Commission and representatives of four member States selected by the Commission. It shall meet at least two times in the intervals between the regular annual meetings of the Commission and as often as the business of the Commission may require. It shall draw up the Agenda for the meetings of the Commission and prepare such preparatory documents as it deems necessary. It shall take all decisions required for carrying on the business of the Commission in the intervals between annual meetings.

5. Each national section shall have one vote. The Commission shall decide by a majority of the members voting, unless this Convention requires a two-thirds majority vote.

344

6. The Commission shall appoint an Executive Director who shall appoint the staff of the Commission. The staff shall not seek or receive instructions from member States. It shall carry out such scientific, technical, economic, social or legal research as may be required for the achievement of the Commission's objectives, and it shall objectively evaluate the research programmes of member States.

Article VII – Membership

1. All States substantially engaged in the fisheries for which the Commission is responsible shall be members of the Commission. If a State substantially engaged in the fisheries for which the Commission is responsible is not a member of the Commission, the Commission may recommend collective action against such a State.

Article VIII – Relations with other Organizations

1. The Commission shall cooperate with the agencies of the member States, with the fishing industry of member States, with non-governmental and intergovernmental international organizations and with all other organizations whose functions and objectives are related to the objectives of the Commission. The Commission may conclude cooperative agreements.

2. The Commission shall submit such reports to the World Marine Fisheries Organization as the Organization may require.

Article IX – Finances

1. Each member State shall pay the expenses of its representatives at the meetings of the Commission or its subsidiary bodies.

2. Joint expenses of the Commission shall be paid from the levies provided for in Article IV, para. 4(b).

Article X – Legal Status

1. The Commission shall possess full legal personality and in particular the capacity to contract, to acquire and dispose of movable and immovable property and to institute legal proceedings.

2. The Commission and the persons serving on its staff shall enjoy in the territory of the member States such privileges and immunities as are necessary for the fulfilment of their functions.

Article XI – Amendments

1. Amendments to this Convention may be proposed by any member State. Amendments shall enter into force three months after having been approved by a two-thirds majority of all member States.

Article XII – Entry into Force

1. This Convention shall enter into force when more than a majority of the signatory States have deposited their instrument of ratification with the Depository Government.

Bibliography

Accioly, H, *La liberté des mers et le droit de pêche en haute mer*, Revue
Générale de Droit International Public 1957, pp. 193–202.

Aglen, A J, *Problems of enforcement of fisheries regulations*, in *The future
of the sea's resources*, L M Alexander ed., Kingston, R I 1968, pp. 19–23.

Alexander, L M, *Offshore geography of Northwestern Europe: the political
and economic problems of delimitation and control*, Chicago 1963.

Alexander, L M, *Offshore claims and fisheries in North-West Europe*,
in *Yearbook of World Affairs* 1960, pp. 236–259.

Allen, E W, *Law, fish and policy*, International Lawyer 1971, pp. 621–636.

Allen, E W, *The freedom of the seas*, American Journal of International
Law 1964, pp. 984–985.

Allen, E W, *A new concept for fishery treaties*, American Journal of International Law 1952, pp. 319–323.

Allen, E W, *The fishery proclamation of 1945*, American Journal of
International Law 1951, pp. 177–178.

Alverson, D L, *Fishery resources in the Northeast Pacific Ocean*, in *The
future of the fishing industry of the United States*, Seattle 1968, pp.
86–102.

Arnold, V L and Bromley, D W, *Social goals, problem perception and
public intervention: the fishery*, San Diego Law Review 1970, pp.
469–488.

Azzam, I, *The dispute between France and Brazil over lobster fishing in
the Atlantic*, International and Comparative Law Quarterly 1964,
pp. 1453–1459.

Bardach, J E, *Aquaculture*, Science 1968, pp. 1098–1106.

Bardach, J E, *Harvest of the sea*, New York 1968.

Bayitch, S A, *Interamerican law of fisheries. An introduction with documents*, New York 1957.

Bayitch, S A, *International fishery problems in the Western Hemisphere*,
Miami Law Quarterly 1956, pp. 499–506.

Bell, F H, *Agreements, conventions and treaties between Canada and the
United States of America with respect to the Pacific halibut fishery*,
Report of the International Pacific Halibut Commission No. 50,
Seattle 1969.

Bell, F H, *The Pacific halibut*, in *The future of the fishing industry of
the United States*, Seattle 1968, pp. 272–274.

Bergmann, W, *Fischereirecht*, Cologne and Berlin 1966.

Bierzanek, R, *La nature juridique de la haute mer*, Revue Générale de Droit
International Public 1961, pp. 233–259.

Bingham, J W, *Report on the international law of Pacific coastal fisheries*,
Stanford 1938.

Bishop, W W, *The 1958 Geneva Convention on Fishing and Conservation
of the Living Resources of the High Seas*, Columbia Law Review 1962,
pp. 1206–1230.

Bishop, W W, *International Law Commission draft articles on fisheries*, American Journal of International Law 1956, pp. 627–636.

Bishop, W W, *The need for a Japanese fisheries agreement*, American Journal of International Law 1951, pp. 712–719.

Borgese, E M, *The ocean regime: a suggested statute for the peaceful uses of the high seas and the seabed beyond the limits of national jurisdiction*, Center for the Study of Democratic Institutions, Occasional Paper No. 1, Santa Barbara 1968.

Bos, M, *La liberté de la haute mer: quelques problèmes d'actualité*, Nederlands Tijdschrift voor Internationaal Recht 1965, pp. 337–364.

Bottemanne, C J, *Principles of fisheries development*, Amsterdam 1959.

Bouchez, L J, *The regime of bays in international law*, Leyden 1963.

Boyer, A, *La réglementation internationale des pêches maritimes*, Droit Maritime Français 1965, pp. 707–719.

Breucker, J de, *La Convention sur l'exercice de la pêche dans l'Atlantique Nord*, Revue Belge de Droit International 1970, pp. 165–202.

Breucker, J de, *La Convention de Londres sur la pêche du 9 Mars 1964*, Revue Belge de Droit International 1966, pp. 142–166.

Breucker, J de, *L'Extension des limites de pêche et le régime juridique de la pêche dans la Mer du Nord*, in Annales de Droit et de Sciences Politiques 1963, pp. 115–131.

Browning, D S, *Inter-American fisheries resources. A need for co-operation*, The Texas International Law Forum 1966, pp. 1–39.

Burke, W T, *Some thoughts on fisheries and a new conference on the law of the sea*, Law of the Sea Institute, University of Rhode Island, Occasional Paper No. 9, March 1971.

Burke, W T, *Contemporary legal problems in ocean development*, in Towards a better use of the ocean, Stockholm, New York and London 1969, pp. 15–114.

Burke, W T, *Aspects of internal decision-making processes in intergovernmental fishery commissions*, Washington Law Review 1967, pp. 115–178.

Burke, W T, *Law and the new technologies*, in Offshore boundaries and zones, L M Alexander ed., Columbus, Ohio 1967, pp. 204–225.

Carroz, J E, *National fishery bodies and the apportionment of the yield from the living resources of the sea*, paper at a Center for the Study of Democratic Institutions Preparatory Conference on the Legal Framework and the Continental Shelf, Kingston, R I 1970.

Carroz, J E, *Establishment, structure, functions and activities of international fisheries bodies – Regional Fisheries Advisory Commission for the South West Atlantic (CARPAS)*, FAO Fisheries Technical Paper No. 60, Rome 1966.

Carroz, J E, *Establishment, structure, functions and activities of international fisheries bodies – Indo-Pacific Fisheries Council (IPFC)*, FAO Fisheries Technical Paper No. 57, Rome 1965.

Carroz, J E, *Establishment, structure, functions and activities of international fisheries bodies – Inter-American Tropical Tuna Commission (IATTC)*, FAO Fisheries Technical Paper No. 58, Rome 1965.

Carroz, J E and Roche, A G, *The international policing of high sea fisheries*, in *Canadian Yearbook of International Law* 1968, pp. 61–90.

Carroz, J E and Roche, A G, *The proposed International Commission for the Conservation of Atlantic Tunas*, *American Journal of International Law* 1967, pp. 673–702.

Chapman, W M, *Some problems and prospects for the harvest of living marine resources to the year 2000*, paper at a meeting of experts at UNITAR, February 25–27, 1970.

Chapman, W M, *The theory and practice of international fishery development-management*, *San Diego Law Review* 1970, pp. 408–455.

Chapman, W M, *The United States fish industry and the 1958 and 1960 United Nations conferences on the law of the sea*, in *International rules and organization for the sea*, L M Alexander ed., Kingston, R I 1969, pp. 35–64.

Chapman, W M, *Governmental aspects of harvesting the living resources of the sea*, *Natural Resources Lawyer* 1968, pp. 119–129.

Chapman, W M, *Fishery resources in offshore waters*, in *Offshore boundaries and zones*, L M Alexander ed., Columbus, Ohio 1967, pp. 87–106.

Chapman, W M, *United States policy on high seas fisheries*, *Department of State Bulletin* 1949, vol. 20, pp. 67–71 and p. 80.

Christol, C Q, *The social complex of world fisheries: law in support of world needs*, in *The future of the fishing industry of the United States*, Seattle 1968, pp. 305–310.

Christy, F T, Jr., *Implications for fisheries of the US draft convention on the sea-bed*, paper at Marine Technology Society Symposium on the Law of the Sea: a Year of Crisis, February 1971.

Christy, F T, Jr., *Fisheries and the new conventions on the law of the sea*, *San Diego Law Review* 1970, pp. 455–469.

Christy, F T, Jr., *New dimensions for transnational marine resources*, *The American Economic Review* 1970, pp. 109–113.

Christy, F T, Jr., *Fisheries goals and the rights of property*, in *Transactions of the American Fisheries Society* 1969, pp. 369–378.

Christy, F T, Jr., in *The future development of world fisheries* (panel), in *The future of the sea's resources*, L M Alexander ed., Kingston, R I 1968, pp. 136–137.

Christy, F T, Jr., *The distribution of the sea's wealth in fisheries*, in *Offshore boundaries and zones*, L M Alexander ed., Columbus, Ohio 1967, pp. 106–122.

Christy, F T, Jr. and Brooks, D B, *Shared resources of the world community*, in Commission to Study the Organization of Peace, *New dimensions for the United Nations*, New York 1966, pp. 135–165.

Christy, F T, Jr. and Scott, A, *The common wealth in ocean fisheries. Some problems of growth and economic allocation*, Baltimore 1965.

Colombos, C J, *The international law of the sea*, 6th ed. London 1967.

Comitini, S, *Economic and legal aspects of Japanese fisheries regulation and control*, *Washington Law Review* 1967, pp. 179–196.

349

Commission to Study the Organization of Peace, *New dimensions for the United Nations: the problems of the next decade*, New York 1966.

Craig, J A and Hacker, R L, *The history and development of the fisheries of the Columbia River*, Washington 1940.

Crutchfield, J A, in *International fisheries regimes* (panel), in *National policy recommendations*, L M Alexander ed., Kingston, R I 1970, pp. 345–350.

Crutchfield, J A, *National quotas for the North Atlantic fisheries: an exercise in second best*, in *International rules and organization for the sea*, L M Alexander ed., Kingston, R I 1969, pp. 263–275.

Crutchfield, J A, *The Convention on Fishing and Living Resources of the High Seas*, Natural Resources Lawyer 1968, pp. 114–124.

Crutchfield, J A, *Overcapitalization of the fishing effort*, in *The future of the sea's resources*, L M Alexander ed., Kingston, R I 1968, pp. 23–29.

Crutchfield, J A, *Management of the North Pacific fisheries: economic objectives and issues*, Washington Law Review 1967, pp. 283–307.

Crutchfield, J A, *Economic objectives in fishery management*, in *The fisheries*, J A Crutchfield ed., Seattle 1965, pp. 43–65.

Crutchfield, J A and Pontecorvo, G, *The Pacific salmon fisheries. A study of irrational conservation*, Baltimore 1969.

Dagget, A P, *The regulation of maritime fisheries by treaty*, American Journal of International Law 1934, pp. 693–717.

Davis, M, *Iceland extends its fisheries limits: a political analysis*, Oslo 1963.

Dean, A H, *The second Geneva Conference on the Law of the Seas*, American Journal of International Law 1960, pp. 751–789.

Dean, A H, *The Geneva Conference on the Law of the Sea: what was accomplished*, American Journal of International Law 1958, pp. 607–628.

Dodyk, P M, *Comments on international law and fishery policy*, Clearinghouse for Federal Scientific and Technical Information, Doc. PB 179 427, Springfield, Va. 1968.

Dunlop, H A, *Management of the halibut fishery of the North-Eastern Pacific Ocean and Bering Sea*, in *Papers presented at the International Technical Conference on the Conservation of the Living Resources of the Sea*, Rome 1955, pp. 222–243.

Dykstra, J J, *Remarks*, in *The United Nations and ocean management*, L M Alexander ed., Kingston, R I 1971, pp. 49–52.

Dykstra, J J and Holmsen, A A, *Cost of fishing and foreign competition, New England*, in *The future of the fishing industry of the United States*, Seattle 1968, pp. 105–108.

Edwards, R L, *Fishery resources of the North Atlantic region*, in *The future of the fishing industry of the United States*, Seattle 1968, pp. 52–61.

Emery, K O, *Human food from ocean and land*, Science 1967, pp. 1279–1281.

Falk, R A, *Settling ocean fishing conflicts: the limits of 'law reform' in a horizontal legal order*, in *The status of law in international society*, vol. 1, *An orientation toward the political setting of the international legal order*, Princeton 1970, pp. 540–553.

Falk, R A, *Settling ocean fishing conflicts: the limits of 'law reform' in a horizontal legal order*, in *The future of the fishing industry of the United States*, Seattle 1968, pp. 326–333.

Ferron, O de, *Le droit international de la mer*, Geneva 1958 and 1960, 2 vols.

Food and Agriculture Organization, *Fishery country profiles*, FAO Fisheries Circular No. 140, Rome 1972.

Food and Agriculture Organization, *Report on regulatory fishery bodies*, FAO Fisheries Circular No. 138, Rome 1972.

Food and Agriculture Organization, *Limits and status of the territorial sea, exclusive fishing zones, fishery conservation zones and the continental shelf*, FAO Legislative Series No. 8, Rome 1969. A more recent version is: FAO Fisheries Circular No. 127, Rome 1971.

Food and Agriculture Organization, *The living resources of the seas: an illustrative atlas*, FAO Fisheries Circular No. 126, Rome 1971.

Food and Agriculture Organization, *Report of the consultation on the conservation of fishery resources and the control of fishing in Africa*, FAO Fisheries Reports No. 101, vol. 1, Rome 1971.

Food and Agriculture Organization, *Technical Conference on Marine Pollution and Its Effects on Living Resources and Fishing 1970. Conclusions and recommendations as approved*. Document FIR:MP/70/Rec., Rev. 1, Rome 1971.

Food and Agriculture Organization, *Yearbook of fishery statistics 1947–1970*, Rome 1948–1971.

Food and Agriculture Organization, *Final Act of the Conference of Plenipotentiaries on the Conservation of the Living Resources of the South-East Atlantic 1969*, Rome 1970.

Food and Agriculture Organization, *The prospects for world fishery development in 1975 and 1985*, FAO Fisheries Circular No. 118, Rome 1969.

Food and Agriculture Organization, *Reports of the sessions of the FAO Fishery Committee for the Eastern Central Atlantic (CECAF)*, FAO Fisheries Reports, Rome 1969–1971.

Food and Agriculture Organization, *Reports of the sessions of the Indian Ocean Fishery Commission*, FAO Fisheries Reports, Rome 1968–1971.

Food and Agriculture Organization, *The state of world fisheries*, World Food Problems No. 7, Rome 1968.

Food and Agriculture Organization, *Work of FAO and related organizations concerning marine science and its applications*, FAO Fisheries Technical Paper No. 74, Rome 1968.

Food and Agriculture Organization, *The management of fishery resources*, Rome 1967.

Food and Agriculture Organization, *International fisheries bodies*, FAO Fisheries Technical Paper No. 64, Rome 1966.

Food and Agriculture Organization, *Reports of the sessions of the Committee on Fisheries*, FAO Fisheries Reports, Rome 1966–1971.

Food and Agriculture Organization, *Convention, statutes and rules of procedure of the Commission for Fisheries Research in the Western Pacific*, FAO Fisheries Technical Paper No. 50, Rome 1965.

Food and Agriculture Organization, *Reports of the sessions of the Advisory Committee on Marine Resources Research*, FAO Fisheries Reports, Rome 1963–1969.

Friedmann, W, *The future of the oceans*, New York 1971.

Friedmann, W, *The changing structure of international law*, New York 1964.

Fullenbaum, R F, *A survey of maximum sustainable yield estimates on a world basis for selected fisheries*, Working Paper No. 43 United States Bureau of Commercial Fisheries, Washington 1970.

Fulton, T W, *The sovereignty of the sea*, Edinburgh and London 1911.

Garcia Amador, F V, *Latin America and the law of the sea*, Law of the Sea Institute, University of Rhode Island, Occasional Paper No. 14, July 1972.

Garcia Amador, F V, *The exploitation and conservation of the resources of the sea. A study of contemporary international law*, 2nd ed. 2nd enl. printing Leyden 1963.

Gidel, G, *Le droit international public de la mer*, Paris 1932–1934, 3 vols.

Girard, M J, *Note on the General Fisheries Council for the Mediterranean*, in *Papers presented at the International Technical Conference on the Conservation of the Living Resources of the Sea*, Rome 1955, pp. 262–266.

Goldie, L F E, *The oceans' resources and international law. Possible developments in regional fisheries management*, Columbia Journal of Transnational Law 1969, pp. 1–53.

Goldie, L F E, *Sedentary fisheries and Article 2(4) of the Convention on the Continental Shelf. A plea for a separate regime*, American Journal of International Law 1969, pp. 86–97.

Goldie, L F E, *Sedentary fisheries and the North Sea continental shelf cases*, American Journal of International Law 1969, pp. 536–544.

Gordon, H S, *The economic theory of a common property resource: the fishery*, Journal of Political Economy 1954, pp. 124–142.

Gottlieb, A E, *Canadian contribution to the concept of a fishing zone in international law*, in *Canadian Yearbook of International Law* 1964, pp. 55–77.

Graham, M, *Concepts of conservation*, in *Papers presented at the International Technical Conference on the Conservation of the Living Resources of the Sea*, Rome 1955, pp. 1–14.

Graham, M, *A first approximation to a modern theory of fishing*, in *Papers presented at the International Technical Conference on the Conservation of the Living Resources of the Sea*, Rome 1955, pp. 56–61.

Gregory, H E and Barnes, K, *North Pacific fisheries. With special references to Alaskan salmon*, New York 1939.

Gros, A, *La Convention sur la pêche et la conservation des ressources biologiques de la haute mer*, Receuil des Cours de l'Académie de Droit International 1959, vol. 97, pp. 1–88.

Gulland, J A, ed., *The fish resources of the ocean*, FAO Fisheries Technical Paper No. 97, Rome 1970.

Gulland, J A, *Fisheries management and the limitation of fishing*, FAO Fisheries Technical Paper No. 92, Rome 1969.

Gulland, J A, *The concept of the maximum sustainable yield and fishery management*, FAO Fisheries Technical Paper No. 70, Rome 1968.

Gullion, E A, ed., *Uses of the seas*, Englewood Cliffs 1968.

Hansen, P, *The importance of conservation of stocks of fish and sea mammals in Arctic waters*, in *Papers presented at the International Technical Conference on the Conservation of the Living Resources of the Sea*, Rome 1955, pp. 322–326.

Hardin, G, *The tragedy of the commons*, *Science* 1968, pp. 1243–1248.

Herrington, W C, *Operation of the Japanese fishery management system*, Law of the Sea Institute, University of Rhode Island, Occasional Paper No. 11, August 1971.

Herrington, W C, *Canadian license control for salmon*, Law of the Sea Institute, University of Rhode Island 1970.

Herrington, W C, *The future of the Geneva Convention on Fishing and the Conservation of the Living Resources of the Sea*, in *The future of the sea's resources*, L M Alexander ed., Kingston, R I 1968, pp. 62–65.

Herrington, W C, *The Convention on Fisheries and Conservation of Living Resources: accomplishments of the 1958 Geneva conference*, in *Offshore boundaries and zones*, L M Alexander ed., Columbus, Ohio 1967, pp. 26–36.

Herrington, W C, *International issues of Pacific fisheries*, Department of State Bulletin 1966, vol. 55, pp. 500–504.

Herrington, W C, *Comments on the principle of abstention*, in *Papers presented at the International Technical Conference on the Conservation of the Living Resources of the Sea*, Rome 1955, pp. 344–350.

Herrington, W C, *Problems affecting North Pacific fisheries*, Department of State Bulletin 1952, vol. 26, pp. 340–342.

Herrington, W C and Kask, J L, *International conservation problems, and solutions in existing conventions*, in *Papers presented at the International Technical Conference on the Conservation of the Living Resources of the Sea*, Rome 1955, pp. 145–167.

Inter-American Tropical Tuna Commission, *Annual Reports*, La Jolla 1953–1971.

International Commission for the Northwest Atlantic Fisheries, *Annual Proceedings*, Halifax 1953–1962, Dartmouth 1963–1972.

International Commission for the Northwest Atlantic Fisheries, *ICNAF handbook*, Dartmouth 1969.

International Commission for the Northwest Atlantic Fisheries, *Second annual report for the year 1951–1952*, St. Andrews 1952.

International Commission for the Northwest Atlantic Fisheries, *Report of the first annual meeting*, Washington, DC 1951.

International North Pacific Fisheries Commission, *Annual Reports*, Vancouver 1956–1972.

353

International North Pacific Fisheries Commission, *Report of the first annual meeting*, Vancouver 1955.

International Pacific Halibut Commission, *Annual Reports*, Seattle 1970–1972.

International Pacific Halibut Commission, *Regulation and investigation of the Pacific halibut fishery*, Seattle 1954–1969.

International Pacific Salmon Fisheries Commission, *Annual Reports*, New Westminster 1939–1972.

International Whaling Commission, *Reports of the Commission*, London 1950–1972.

Jackson, R I, *Current developments in international fishery arrangements*, in *The future of the fishing industry of the United States*, Seattle 1968, pp. 269–272.

Jackson, R I, *International fisheries and marine pollution*, FAO International Conference on Oil Pollution of the Sea 1968, paper No. 1, Rome 1968.

Jackson, R I, *Some observations on the future growth of world fisheries and the nature of the conservation problem*, in *The future of the sea's resources*, L M Alexander ed., Kingston, R I 1968, pp. 10–14.

Jessup, P C, *The Pacific coast fisheries*, American Journal of International Law 1939, pp. 129–138.

Jessup, P C, *The international protection of whales*, American Journal of International Law 1930, pp. 751–752.

Jessup, P C, *L'Exploitation des richesses de la mer*, Recueil des Cours de l'Académie de Droit International 1929, vol. 29, pp. 401–514.

Johnson, D H N, *Icelandic fishery limits*, International and Comparative Law Quarterly 1952, pp. 71–73 and pp. 350–354.

Johnson, R W, *The Japan-United States salmon conflict*, Washington Law Review 1967, pp. 1–43.

Johnson, R W, in *A symposium on the Geneva Conventions and the need for future modifications*, in *Offshore boundaries and zones*, L M Alexander ed., Columbus, Ohio 1967, pp. 270–273.

Johnson, R W, *State and federal laws which retard high seas fishing development*, in *Transactions of the Second Annual Marine Technology Society Conference and Exhibit* (supplement), June 27–29, 1966.

Johnson, R W, *Fishery developments in the Pacific*, in British Institute of International and Comparative Law, *Developments in the law of the sea 1958–1964*, London 1965, pp. 133–150.

Johnston, D M, *The legal theory of fishery organization*, in *International rules and organization for the sea*, L M Alexander ed., Kingston, R I 1969, pp. 431–438.

Johnston, D M, *New uses of international law in the North Pacific*, Washington Law Review 1967, pp. 77–114.

Johnston, D M, *The international law of marine fisheries. A framework for policy-oriented inquiries*, New Haven and London 1965.

Kamenaga, T, *The management of world fisheries*, in *The future of the sea's resources*, L M Alexander ed., Kingston, R I 1968, pp. 122–124.

Kane, T E, *Aquaculture and the law*, Sea Grant Bulletin No. 2, Miami 1970.

Kasahara, H, *International arrangements for fisheries*, in *The United Nations and ocean management*, L M Alexander ed., Kingston, R I 1971, pp. 38–43.

Kasahara, H, *Future regime for high seas fisheries*, in *The future of the sea's resources*, L M Alexander ed., Kingston, R I 1968, pp. 134–135.

Kasahara, H, *Food production from the ocean*, in *Conference on Law, Organization and Security in the Use of the Oceans*, Columbus, Ohio 1967.

Kask, J L, *Marine Science Commission recommendations on international fisheries organization*, in *National policy recommendations*, L M Alexander ed., Kingston, R I 1970, pp. 286–297.

Kask, J L, *Tuna – a world resource*, Law of the Sea Institute, University of Rhode Island, Occasional Paper No. 2, May 1969.

Kask, J L, *Present arrangements for fishery exploitation*, in *The future of the sea's resources*, L M Alexander ed., Kingston, R I 1968, pp. 56–62.

Kellogg, R, *The International Whaling Commission*, in *Papers presented at the International Technical Conference on the Conservation of the Living Resources of the Sea*, Rome 1955, pp. 243–256.

Koers, A W, *The enforcement of fisheries agreements on the high seas: a comparative analysis of international State practice*, Law of the Sea Institute, University of Rhode Island, Occasional Paper No. 6, June 1970.

Koers, A W, *The enforcement of international fisheries agreements*, in *Netherlands Yearbook of International Law* 1970, pp. 1–31.

Lador-Lederer, J J, *L'Evolution du droit international des pêcheries*, *Journal du Droit International* 1958, pp. 634–685.

Laing, A, in *International fisheries regimes* (panel), in *National policy recommendations*, L M Alexander ed., Kingston, R I 1970, pp. 324–326.

Larkin, P A, *Critique: fisheries management provisions in the Commission Report*, in *National policy recommendations*, L M Alexander ed., Kingston, R I 1970, pp. 297–305.

Leonard, L L, *International regulation of fisheries*, Washington 1944.

Leonard, L L, *Recent negotiations toward the international regulation of whaling*, *American Journal of International Law* 1941, pp. 90–113.

Lucas, C E, *International fishery bodies of the North Atlantic*, Law of the Sea Institute, University of Rhode Island, Occasional Paper No. 5, April 1970.

Lucas, C E, *Regulation of the North Sea fisheries under the Convention of 1946*, in *Papers presented at the International Technical Conference on the Conservation of the Living Resources of the Sea 1955*, Rome 1955, pp. 167–183.

Lynden, D W van, *The Convention on Conduct of Fishing Operations in the North Atlantic*, *Nederlands Tijdschrift voor Internationaal Recht* 1967, pp. 245–258.

355

McDougal, M S and Burke, W T, *The public order of the oceans. A contemporary international law of the sea*, New Haven and London 1962.

McHugh, J L, *Domestic wrangles and international tangles*, Woodrow Wilson International Center for Scholars, Washington 1971.

McHugh, J L, *Role and history of the International Whaling Commission*, Woodrow Wilson International Center for Scholars, Washington 1971.

McKernan, D L, *International fishery regimes – current and future*, in *National policy recommendations*, L M Alexander ed., Kingston, R I 1970, pp. 336–345.

McKernan, D L, *International fisheries arrangements beyond the twelve mile limit*, in *International rules and organization for the sea*, L M Alexander ed., Kingston, R I 1969, pp. 255–260.

McKernan, D L, *A developing policy for international fisheries*, in *The future of the sea's resources*, L M Alexander ed., Kingston, R I 1968, pp. 147–150.

McKernan D L, *International fishery policy and the US fishing industry*, in *The future of the fishing industry of the United States*, Seattle 1968, pp. 248–259.

Meyer, C B V, *The extent of jurisdiction in coastal waters*, Leyden 1937.

Mikhailov, V S, *On the comparative efficiency of production of some products of the land and sea*, Okeanologia 1962, pp. 385–392.

Mikhailov, V S, *International law and the regulation of fisheries and other maritime industries in the Pacific*, in *Soviet Yearbook of International Law* 1960, pp. 189–206.

Ministry for Foreign Affairs of Iceland, *Fisheries jurisdiction in Iceland*, Reykjavik 1972.

Moiseev, P, *Fluctuations in the commercial fish populations of the North-Western Pacific in relation to environmental and other factors*, in *Papers presented at the International Technical Conference on the Conservation of the Living Resources of the Sea*, Rome 1955, pp. 266–290.

Molen, G H J van der, *The principle of abstention and the freedom of the seas*, Nederlands Tijdschrift voor Internationaal Recht, Special Issue 1959, pp. 203–212.

Moore, G, *The control of marine pollution and the protection of living resources of the sea*, FAO Technical Conference on Marine Pollution and Its Effect on Living Resources and Fishing, Document FIR: MP/70/R–15, Rome 1970.

Morin, J Y, *La zone de pêche exclusive du Canada*, in *Canadian Yearbook of International Law* 1964, pp. 77–107.

Mouton, M W, *The establishment of rules of international law on a world basis or a regional basis, with particular reference to limits on fisheries*, in *Annuaire Européen* 1966, pp. 79–106.

Mouton, M W, *The continental shelf*, The Hague 1952.

Muller, S Fz, *Mare clausum. Bijdrage tot de geschiedenis der rivaliteit van Engeland en Nederland in de zeventiende eeuw*, Amsterdam 1872.

Murphy, G I, *Vital statistics of the Pacific sardine and the population consequences*, Ecology 1967, pp. 731–736.

356

Nagasaki, F, *Some Japanese far-sea fisheries*, Washington Law Review 1967, pp. 197-230.

Nakamura, K, *The Japan-United States negotiations concerning king crab fishery in the Eastern Bering Sea*, in *Japanese Annual of International Law* 1965, pp. 36-45.

Nguyen Quoc, D, *La revendication des droits préférentiels de pêche en haute mer*, in *Annuaire Français de Droit International* 1960, pp. 77-110.

North-East Atlantic Fisheries Commission, *Reports of the meetings*, London 1964-1972.

North Pacific Fur Seal Commission, *Proceedings of the annual meetings*, Washington, DC 1960-1972.

North Pacific Fur Seal Commission, *Annual Report for the fiscal year ending June 30, 1959*, Washington, DC 1960.

North Pacific Fur Seal Commission, *Report of the first meeting*, Washington, DC 1958.

O'Connell, D P, *Sedentary fisheries and the Australian continental shelf*, American Journal of International Law 1955, pp. 185-209.

Oda, S, *International law of the resources of the sea*, Recueil des Cours de l'Académie de Droit International 1969, vol. 127, pp. 355-484.

Oda, S, *Distribution of fish resources of the high seas: free competition or artificial quota ?*, in *The future of the sea's resources*, L M Alexander ed., Kingston, R I 1968, pp. 29-32.

Oda, S, *Japan and international conventions relating to North Pacific fisheries*, Washington Law Review 1967, pp. 63-75.

Oda, S, *Some observations on the law of the sea*, in *Japanese Annual of International Law* 1967, pp. 37-50.

Oda, S, *International control of sea resources*, Leyden 1963.

Oda, S, *Recent problems of international high sea fisheries: allocation of fishery resources*, Philippine International Law Journal 1962, pp. 510-519.

Oda, S, *The 1958 Geneva Convention on the fisheries: its immaturities*, Die Friedens-Warte 1960, pp. 317-339.

Oda, S, *Japan and the international fisheries*, in *Japanese Annual of International Law* 1960, pp. 50-62.

Oda, S, *New trends in the regime of the seas. A consideration of the problems of conservation and distribution of marine resources*, Zeitschrift für ausländisches öffentliches Recht und Völkerrecht 1957, pp. 61-102 and pp. 261-286.

Ohira, Z, *Fishery problems between Soviet Russia and Japan*, in *Japanese Annual of International Law* 1958, pp. 1-18.

Ohira, Z and Kuwahara, T, *Fishery problems between Japan and the People's Republic of China*, in *Japanese Annual of International Law* 1959, pp. 109-125.

Oliver, E J, *Wet war: North Pacific*, San Diego Law Review 1971, pp. 621-638.

Oudendijk, J K, *Status and extent of adjacent waters. A historical orientation*, Leyden 1970.

Our nation and the sea, Report of the Commission on Marine Science, Engineering and Resources, Washington 1969.

Oxman, B H, *The preparation of Article 1 of the Convention on the Continental Shelf,* Clearinghouse for Federal Scientific and Technical Information, Doc. PB 182 100, Springfield, Va. 1968.

Panel reports of the Commission on Marine Science, Engineering and Resources, vol. 2, *Industry and technology,* Washington 1969.

Panel reports of the Commission on Marine Science, Engineering and Resources, vol. 3, *Marine resources and legal-political arrangements for their development,* Washington 1969.

Panel reports of the Commission on Marine Science, Engineering and Resources, vol. 1, *Science and environment,* Washington 1969.

Papandreou, A, *La situation juridique des pêcheries sédentaires en haute mer,* Athens 1958.

Pontecorvo, G, *Critique on national quotas for the North Atlantic fisheries: an exercise in second best,* in *International rules and organization for the sea,* L M Alexander ed., Kingston, R I 1969, pp. 276–279.

Poulsen, E M, *Conservation problems in the North-Western Atlantic,* in *Papers presented at the International Technical Conference on the Conservation of the Living Resources of the Sea,* Rome 1955, pp. 183–194.

Raestad, A, *La chasse à la baleine en mer libre, Revue de Droit International* 1928, pp. 595–642.

Reiff, H, *The United States and the treaty law of the sea,* Minneapolis 1959.

Reintanz, G, *Internationale Rechtsgrundlagen der Hochseefischerei, Wissenschaftliche Zeitschrift der Martin-Luther Universität Halle-Wittenberg* 1962, pp. 1211–1242.

Report of the International Technical Conference on the Conservation of the Living Resources of the Sea 1955, New York 1955.

Riesenfeld, S A, *Protection of coastal fisheries under international law,* Washington 1942.

Royal, L A, *The international Fraser River sockeye salmon fishery,* in *Papers presented at the International Technical Conference on the Conservation of the Living Resources of the Sea,* Rome 1955, pp. 243–256.

Santa Pinter, J J, *Latin American countries facing the problem of territorial waters, San Diego Law Review* 1971, pp. 606–621.

Schaefer, M B, *Some recent developments concerning fishing and the conservation of the living resources of the high seas, San Diego Law Review* 1970, pp. 371–408.

Schaefer, M B, *Harvesting food from the sea,* in *Ocean Engineering, Proceedings of a 1968–69 Seminar Series,* University of Delaware.

Schaefer, M B, in *The future development of world fisheries* (panel), in *The future of the sea's resources,* L M Alexander ed., Kingston, R I 1968, pp. 127–128.

Schaefer, M B, *Methods of estimating effects of fishing on fish populations,* in *Transactions of the American Fisheries Society* 1968, pp. 231–241.

Schaefer, M B, *Biological and economic aspects of the management of commercial marine fisheries*, in *Transactions of the American Fisheries Society* 1959, pp. 100–104.

Schaefer, M B, *The scientific basis for a conservation programme*, in *Papers presented at the International Technical Conference on the Conservation of the Living Resources of the Sea*, Rome 1955, pp. 14–56.

Schaefer, M B, *Scientific investigation of the tropical tuna resources of the Eastern Pacific*, in *Papers presented at the International Technical Conference on the Conservation of the Living Resources of the Sea*, Rome 1955, pp. 194–222.

Schaefer, M B and Alverson, D L, *World fish potentials*, in *The future of the fishing industry of the United States*, Seattle 1968, pp. 81–86.

Scott, A, *The fishery: the objectives of sole ownership*, *Journal of Political Economy* 1955, pp. 116–124.

Selak, C B, *Fishing vessels and the principle of innocent passage*, *American Journal of International Law* 1954, pp. 627–635.

Selak, C B, *Proposed International Convention for the High Seas Fisheries of the North Pacific Ocean*, *American Journal of International Law* 1952, pp. 323–330.

Selak, C B, *Recent developments in high seas fisheries jurisdiction under the Presidential Proclamation of 1945*, *American Journal of International Law* 1950, pp. 670–681.

Shuman, S I, *Pacific fishery conservation conventions. A comparison of organizational structures*, *Sydney Law Review* 1958, pp. 436–459.

Smith, H A, *The law and custom of the sea*, 3rd ed. London 1959.

Southey, C, *The international fishery: a proposal based on the new welfare economics*, in *The United Nations and ocean management*, L M Alexander ed., Kingston, R I 1971, pp. 53–63.

Spiropoulos, J, *The contribution of the International Law Commission to the codification of the law on fishing and conservation of the living resources of the high seas*, *Nederlands Tijdschrift voor Internationaal Recht*, Special Issue, 1959, pp. 332–335.

Stroud, R H, *Sport fishery and recreation demands on the continental shelf*, in *International rules and organization for the sea*, L M Alexander ed., Kingston, R I 1969, pp. 239–246.

Sullivan, W I., *A warning: the decline of international fisheries management looking particularly at the North Atlantic Ocean*, in *The United Nations and ocean management*, L M Alexander ed., Kingston, R I 1971, pp. 43–49.

Surrency, E C, *International inspection in pelagic whaling*, *International and Comparative Law Quarterly* 1964, pp. 666–671.

Swygard, K R, *Implications for the future distribution of the sea's resources if present regimes continue in force*, in *The future of the sea's resources*, L M Alexander ed., Kingston, R I 1968, pp. 65–70.

Swygard, K R, *Politics of the North Pacific fisheries. With special reference to the twelve mile bill*, *Washington Law Review* 1967, pp. 269–282.

Teclaff, L A, *Jurisdiction over offshore fisheries. How far into the high seas?* *Fordham Law Review* 1966–1967, pp. 409–424.

Thibaut, F, *L'Amérique latine et l'évolution du droit international de la mer*, *Revue Générale de Droit International Public* 1971, pp. 742–758.

Thompson, W F, *Fishing treaties and salmon of the North Pacific*, *Science* 1965, pp. 1786–1789.

Tomasevich, J, *International agreements on conservation of marine resources with special reference to the North Pacific*, Stanford 1943.

Treaties and other international agreements on oceanographic resources, fisheries, and wildlife to which the United States is a party, by the Legislative Reference Service of the Library of Congress for the use of the Committee on Commerce of the United States Senate, Washington 1970.

Turvey, R, *Optimization and suboptimization in fishery regulation*, *The American Economic Review* 1964, pp. 64–76.

United Nations, *Feeding the expanding world population: international action to avert the impending protein crisis*, New York 1968.

United Nations Conference (second) on the Law of the Sea, *Official records and preparatory documents*, Geneva 1960.

United Nations Conference (first) on the Law of the Sea, *Official records and preparatory documents*, Geneva 1958, 6 vols.

United Nations Economic and Social Council, *The sea – exploitation and conservation of living marine resources*, UN Doc. E/4842, 12 May 1970.

United Nations Economic and Social Council, *Activities of the organizations of the United Nations system*, UN Doc. E/4487, annex XI, 24 April 1968.

United Nations Economic and Social Council, *Food resources of the sea beyond the continental shelf excluding fish*, UN Doc. E/4449/Add. 2, 7 February 1968.

United Nations Economic and Social Council, *Marine science and technology: survey and proposals*, UN Doc. E/4487, 24 April 1968.

United Nations Economic and Social Council, *Non-governmental organizations*, UN Doc. E/4487, annex X, 24 April 1968.

United Nations Economic and Social Council, *Non-United Nations intergovernmental organizations*, UN Doc. E/4487, annex XII, 24 April 1968.

United Nations Economic and Social Council, *Resources of the sea – Introduction and summary*, UN Doc. E/4449, 21 February 1968.

United Nations General Assembly, *Conservation problems with special reference to new technology*, UN Doc. A/AC. 138/65, 14 March 1972.

United Nations General Assembly, *Exploitation and conservation of living marine resources*, A/Res/2413 (XXIII), 17 December 1968.

United Nations legislative series, Laws and regulations on the régime of the territorial sea, New York 1956, (supplement 1960).

United Nations legislative series, Laws and regulations on the régime of the high seas, New York 1951–1952, 2 vols (supplement 1959).

Van Cleve, R and Johnson. R W, *Management of the high seas fisheries of the Northeastern Pacific*, Seattle 1963.

Verzijl, J H W, *The United Nations Conference on the Law of the Sea*,

Geneva, 1958, Nederlands Tijdschrift voor Internationaal Recht 1959, pp. 1–42 and pp. 115–139.

Vignes, D, *La Conférence européenne sur la pêche et le droit de la mer*, in *Annuaire Français de Droit International* 1964, pp. 670–689.

Visser 't Hooft, H Ph V, *Les Nations Unies et la conservation des ressources de la mer*, The Hague 1958.

Voelckel, M, *Aperçus sur l'application de la Convention européenne des pêches*, in *Annuaire Français de Droit International* 1969, pp. 761–773.

Voelckel, M, *La Convention du 1er Juin 1967 sur l'exercice de la pêche en Atlantique Nord*, in *Annuaire Français de Droit International* 1967, pp. 647–672.

Volkov, A A, *Contemporary principles of international regulation of open sea fishing*, in *Soviet Yearbook of International Law* 1966–1967, pp. 203–218.

Wakefield, L, *Fishing interests on the shelf*, in *International rules and organization for the sea*, L M Alexander ed., Kingston, R I 1969, pp. 230–234.

Wedin, J H, *Analysis of the needs of the United States fishermen*, in *The future of the fishing industry of the United States*, Seattle 1968, pp. 259–262.

Wedin, J H, *Impact of distant water on coastal fisheries*, in *The future of the sea's resources*, I M Alexander ed., Kingston, R I 1968, pp. 14–19.

Weissberg, G, *Fisheries, foreign assistance, custom and conventions*, *International and Comparative Law Quarterly* 1967, pp. 704–724.

Weissberg, G, *Recent developments in the law of the sea and the Japanese–Korean fishery dispute*, The Hague 1966.

Whiteman, M K, *Digest of international law*, Washington 1963–1969, 14 vols.

Wiegand, J S, *Seizures of United States fishing vessels. The status of the wet war*, San Diego Law Review 1969, pp. 428–446.

Windley, D W, *International practice regarding traditional fishing privileges of foreign fishermen in zones of extended maritime jurisdiction*, American Journal of International Law 1969, pp. 490–503.

Wolff, T, *Peruvian – United States relations over maritime fishing: 1945–1969*, Law of the Sea Institute, University of Rhode Island, Occasional Paper No. 4, March 1970.

Yamamoto, S, *The abstention principle and its relation to the evolving international law of the seas*, Washington Law Review 1967, pp. 45–62.

Young, R, *Sedentary fisheries and the Convention on the Continental Shelf*, American Journal of International Law 1961, pp. 359–373.

Zenny, F B, *Establishment, structure, functions and activities of international fisheries bodies – General Fisheries Council for the Mediterranean (GFCM)*, FAO Fisheries Technical Paper No. 78, Rome 1968.

Zenny, F B, *Establishment, structure, functions and activities of international fisheries bodies – Permanent Commission of the Conference on the Use and Conservation of the Marine Resources of the South Pacific*, FAO Fisheries Technical Paper No. 77, Rome 1968.

Index